SAILING ACRO[...]

Negley Farson was born in New Jersey in America in 1890, and inherited his unusual first name from his grandfather. He received the education of a young man from the American upper classes, but proved to be a rebellious youth and developed his keen interest in sailing as a teenager. This led to his own American dream: to sail across Europe in a ship. Farson always 'suffered' from wanderlust and in 1925 he made this dream a reality by embarking on the six-month voyage described in this book – which was first published as a graphic series of articles in *The Chicago Daily News*, where he became Foreign Correspondent.

His vessel was the *Flame*, a twenty-six foot yawl, which leaked like a sieve as a result of having spent the previous eighteen months on dry land. When one man and his girl (the 'Crew') take to sea in such a vessel and when – at one point – that man is an American sailing an English boat in a Dutch river with a German chart, inevitably it leads to complications and misunderstandings.

A born raconteur, with a ready wit, Negley Farson describes this once-in-a-lifetime voyage with great good humour, and *Sailing Across Europe* became the first of his many books. He died in England in 1960 aged seventy, by then an Anglo-American, and *The Chicago Daily News* carried the story under the heading 'A Chicago Legend Dies'.

This edition of *Sailing Across Europe* is introduced by Gordon Brook-Shepherd, well-known Foreign Correspondent, and currently Chief Assistant Editor of the *Sunday Telegraph*. Mr Brook-Shepherd has travelled extensively during the course of his career, and has published many books as the result of his experiences.

Also available in the Century Travellers series:

EOTHEN by A. W. Kinglake
SOUTHERN CROSS TO POLE STAR by A. F. Tschiffely
SOUTHERN GATES OF ARABIA by Freya Stark
THE VALLEYS OF THE ASSASSINS by Freya Stark
A TRAMP ABROAD by Mark Twain
HOLY RUSSIA by Fitzroy Maclean
A THOUSAND MILES UP THE NILE by Amelia B. Edwards
FORBIDDEN JOURNEY by Ella Maillart
FULL TILT by Dervla Murphy
A RIDE TO KHIVA by Fred Burnaby
GOLDEN CHERSONESE by Isabella Bird
THE TOMB OF TUTANKHAMEN by Howard Carter
VISITS TO MONASTRIES IN THE LEVANT
    by Robert Curzon
WHEN MEN AND MOUNTAINS MEET by John Keay
LORDS OF THE ATLAS by Gavin Maxwell
SOUTH by Ernest Shackleton
ONE MAN'S MEXICO by John Lincoln
OLD CALABRIA by Norman Douglas
ISABEL AND THE SEA by George Millar
A WINTER IN ARABIA by Freya Stark
SULTAN IN OMAN by James Morris
TRAVELLER'S PRELUDE by Freya Stark
BEYOND EUPHRATES by Freya Stark
WHERE THE INDUS IS YOUNG by Dervla Murphy
THE CRUISE OF THE NONA by Hilaire Belloc
GOOD MORNING AND GOOD NIGHT
    by The Ranee Margaret of Sarawak
IN MOROCCO by Edith Wharton
PERSEUS IN THE WIND by Freya Stark
A PERSON FROM ENGLAND by Fitzroy Maclean
THE STATION by Robert Byron
WANDERINGS IN SOUTH AMERICA by Charles Waterton
WILD WALES by George Borrow
IN ETHIOPIA WITH A MULE by Dervla Murphy
TRAVEL AND ADVENTURE IN SOUTH-EAST AFRICA
    by F. C. Selous
ALEXANDER'S PATH by Freya Stark
THE LEISURE OF AN EGYPTIAN OFFICIAL
    by Lord Edward Cecil
A YEAR AMONGST THE PERSIANS by Edward Browne
WHEN MISS EMMIE WAS IN RUSSIA by Harvey Pitcher
TWO MIDDLE-AGED LADIES IN ANDALUSIA
    by Penelope Chetwode
A PILGRIMAGE TO NEJD by Lady Anne Blunt
TRAVELS WITH A DONKEY by Robert Louis Stevenson
EIGHT FEET IN THE ANDES by Dervla Murphy

SAILING ACROSS EUROPE

NEGLEY FARSON

INTRODUCTION BY
Gordon Brook-Shepherd

CENTURY PUBLISHING
LONDON

LESTER & ORPEN DENNYS DENEAU
MARKETING SERVICES LTD
TORONTO

First published in Great Britain in 1926
by Hutchinson & Co. Ltd

This edition published in 1985 by
Century Publishing Co. Ltd,
Portland House, 12–13 Greek Street,
London W1V 5LE

Published in Canada by
Lester & Orpen Dennys Deneau Marketing Services Ltd,
78 Sullivan Street, Ontario, Canada

ISBN 0 7126 0802 8

The painting on the cover is 'A View of Koblenz' by James Webb

Reprinted in Great Britain by
Richard Clay (The Chaucer Press) Ltd
Bungay, Suffolk

TO

NANA

INTRODUCTION

The most magical of all the memorable moments which the Danube has given me over the years happened late one May afternoon in 1978, sitting on a gravel bank somewhere in that huge tangled web of lakes and waterways which forms its delta. I say 'somewhere' for the spot has no name and I could never find it again. Indeed, I only got there at all because a special pilot and a pencil-thin, six-passenger Soviet hydrofoil – which could penetrate the web away from the main channels – had been organised for the day. (I had gone to Bucharest for a ninety-minute interview with the Rumanian Communist leader, President Ceausescu, and after that Olympian event, any private request that the English visitor might make would be met.) Mine – apart from exploring the wonderful bird life of the delta outside the shipping lanes – was to be taken to a spot where I could actually feel a particular event happening. At last, after two hours of twisting and turning along the watery maze (the boat having to reverse-thrust its engine every mile or so to clear the weeds from the propellers) the hydrofoil had fulfilled my wish. I sat on a stone at the top of the bank with my hands outstretched, a yard apart, dipping in the one-mile-an-hour current below. The right hand, when I brought it to my mouth, still tasted fresh. The left was salt. I was at the precise point where the river, after its 1,725-mile journey down the valleys and plains of seven countries, was sliding into the Black Sea. To take part in this absolute transition from the European land mass to the ocean in such quietness and privacy was something which the author of *Sailing Across Europe* might himself have envied. The climax to *his* navigation of the Danube had to take place amid all the dirt, noise and bustle of the passenger vessels and black tramp-ships, which moved with him down the main Sulina channel. 'Suddenly' he writes, 'we felt the sea – a "lift" in our senses.' He adds, almost ruefully in

7

INTRODUCTION

view of the muffled significance of the moment: 'There
was nothing to mark it.'

But the whole point is that whereas I had been taken
in comfort on this particular journey (and over the years
on countless others by steamer or motor-boat along this
river's banks), Negley Farson had done it all himself. Or
rather, with a woman companion whose delightful personality shines out from the pages despite the fact that
she is only referred to throughout as 'Crew'.

Many of the best things we do are triggered by sudden impulse. This certainly applied to Farson's life
when, as a reporter for the *Chicago Daily News* he and
'Crew' (who was then his colleague and who eventually
became his wife) looked out in despair at their breathless, sticky American city 'with dust and newspapers
swirling down the streets', and just took down an office
atlas and decided then and there to sail across Europe. It
is this feeling of joyous release, of getting away from it
all, of actually living out a day-dream, that permeates
every page of his journal and carries us along with the
two of them in the tiny cabin of the twenty-six foot yawl
they bought in England for the journey. Of course, their
little boat, *Flame*, was not the first nor the last to make
the trip as a private venture. But surely, no journey
before or since has been blessed with a navigator who
handled a pen even better than his sails. The adventure
itself, and the constantly changing landscape it drew him
into, both get the language they deserve.

Thus the Bavarian summer countryside (he is still on
the Main, sailing south-east for his target): 'Rushy
lagoons flanking the rock-faced banks . . . sweeps of
brass-coloured wheat tufted with orchards of apricot . . .
saints, sword in hand, on stone bridges . . . a waving
sky-line of blue mountains . . .'

And the eagerly-awaited Danube itself, when the little
Flame is first shot into its ice-green flood above Ratisbon: 'At such gorges, it seems to dive into the very heart

8

of the mountains and disappear ... It might be the
Mississippi. And then, with the suddenness of a picture
found in a book, one shoots towards a little sugar-loaf
hill with a grey castle on top ...'

Then, having passed through Vienna (which the
Danube, far from blue, actually avoids) and Budapest,
which the river gloriously bisects, they glide along the
flat marshy expanses of Serbia where, at sunset, 'the
Flame seemed to be sailing into the heart of an opal'.

Both skipper and 'Crew' are as fascinated by the
people who inhabit the Danube Basin as by the great
river itself, and there are delightful vignettes of excur-
sions among the locals ashore. The grandest of these was
to take tea with Admiral Horthy, the 'Regent' of Hungary, ruling a country which by then had neither king
nor navy. The salons of the royal palace of Gödöllö
(one of several such former Habsburg residencies in
which the one-time imperial officer was now disporting
himself) formed an overpowering contrast to the
cramped cabin of the *Flame*, and there is just a hint here
that the author may have been taken in by this wily and
controversial ex-sea-dog, who cloaked all his personal
ambition in the mantle of Magyar nationalism. But once
away from palaces and politics, Farson and 'Crew' are
totally and happily in their element – whether eating
around camp fires with the cowherds of the Hungarian
'pusta'; dining with a Serbian priest in the Banat; fishing
for sterlet off Moldova island, or dancing the Bulgarian
'Horo' with the peasants of Sistov.

The timing of their journey, which lasted from 15
June to 10 December 1925, is of interest in itself. Only
seven summers before, most of this Danube Basin was
either ruled by, or dominated by, the eleven-nation empire of the Habsburg Monarchy. When the *Flame* sailed
down the river, that empire, defeated in the battle fronts
of World War One and splintered into fragments politi-
cally at home, had dissolved into a series of small bicker-

ing republics, including one in what was left of
'German-Austria' herself. Farson often comments in
amazement at the jumble of races which greeted him
almost every time he set foot ashore. Indeed, these
Danubian ethnic communities were living even more
divided under the banner of 'self-determination' than
they had been under the vanished double-headed eagles
of the Habsburgs.

Yet – and this is a point he does not choose to bring
out – the river went on uniting what the peace-makers of
Versailles had divided. It continues to defy the politicians. The Danube is more than a river. It is a common
cradle, older than mankind, for all who live on its banks.
If the *Flame* did that same journey again today, she
would have the Iron Curtain as well as the Iron Gates to
negotiate, for she would be sailing through a region
more starkly divided than ever before in its history. Yet
a pervading sense of community remains. As when
Farson stepped ashore fifty years ago, the road which
links the old sister-capitals of Vienna and Budapest is
still marked 'No. 1' on the motor maps of both Austria
and Hungary, though Communist watch-towers now
separate their borders.

Happily, politics was not Farson's concern on his
voyage. Indeed, whenever there was any danger of his
getting embroiled in them by being asked to state a pre-
ference as between Magyar or Rumanian, or between
Bulgar and Serb, he would either turn a deaf ear, or, if
relentlessly pressed, claim the non-involvement of the
non-European.

Yet, despite this effort at detachment there are times
when, precisely because his own powers of observation
are so acute, he strikes the centre of a political target
without even aiming at it. Thus, on his way down the
Rhine (a river whose banks I also came to know well, in
this case as a student at Bonn some ten years after the
Flame's journey) he has this to say about the vitality of

the German nation so soon after its total defeat in 1918:

'The spectacle of the mammoth Krupp works at Hochfeld, the almost feverish industrial activity from Emmerich to the Ruhr – these branded one's consciousness with the inevitable come-back of these people. Germany seemed a nation in training.'

And later, going ashore at Bamberg, he is shown in a barracks shed, ('We had a fine regiment of Uhlans here, before the war') the skeleton of a fourteen-metre glider being constructed between two wooden horses. The man in charge, a heel-clicking individual in a leather flying jacket, had brought down three English planes in the recent war and was determined, he announced, to help prepare German aviators properly for the next one. Farson's comment: 'I felt that this calm, blue-eyed man was the type to be feared.' One cannot help regretting that the tiny eight feet by six feet cabin of the *Flame* did not have room for a couple of those European statesmen, who were soon to embark on policies of disarmament and appeasement in the face of a mounting threat from more and more Germans donning leather jackets.

Yet these occasional sombre touches, though important to record, are really marginal to Farson's theme. The log-book of the *Flame* is the story of two human beings, happy with each other, and joyous over the adventure they had embarked on. Clearly, it had lived up to the wildest imaginings conceived over their atlas in that faraway Chicago newspaper office. The tingle of excited pleasure over a gamble that had come off so well can be felt in the pages today. The next best thing to having written *Sailing Across Europe* is to have the privilege of introducing it to another generation of readers.

GORDON BROOK-SHEPHERD
1985

CONTENTS

CONTENTS

SAILING ACROSS EUROPE

HOW IT HAPPENED

To sail across Europe had been a day-dream with me. But, somehow, it did not seem possible; not that it could not be done – two Englishmen did it in the early part of this century – but I had no money and had to stick to my job. I expect most of us are in that position. A little devil kept telling me to chuck my job and follow my bent. 'You're only going to live once!' said the devil.

'Hear! Hear!' said the Crew (she was not the Crew then), 'what's the use of having a good time when you're seventy?'

'But people don't do such things!'

'Some do,' said the Crew.

She hauled out the atlas again. 'Look! We start here in Holland . . . up the Rhine, Hungary, Serbia – and think of Bulgaria! Roumania . . . the Black Sea!'

I saw the Black Sea again, when we were flying high over the Russian fleet off Sebastopol. What wonderful days! I never can withstand an atlas. And Chicago that day was a blast furnace, breathless, sticky, with dust and newspapers swirling down the streets. . . .

'I wonder – ' I mused as the devil talked in my ear; 'of course we could buy a boat, a little cabin yawl or something like that. There would be no hotel bills to pay, and no railways. . . . How much have we got in the bank? Lord! is that all?'

But we had our good time instead of waiting till seventy.

CHAPTER ONE

'Double Dutch'

*

'MYNHEER SNOOK, you have failed me.'

'That is sorry,' said Mynheer Snook.

'Yes,' I insisted, 'you let me down. Just when I needed you most, you weren't there.'

Mynheer Snook was one of the amphibious Dutchmen who make their living on the waters of Rotterdam — that curious life, wherein land and water and their customs are inextricably mixed — where the calendars on shore show the time of the tide, and where every barge has its dog, its garden and the washing hung out. He held a lowly place in the marine aristocracy, being neither the possessor of a barge nor fine painted *boejer*, nor even the captain of one. He owned a dreary little boat, called *Emma* — a marine hack — in which I found him on the shady side of a leafy canal. We agreed he was to bring his marine *Dobbin* to meet the s.s. *Nyroca*, the British freighter that was bringing my yawl out from Southampton. He was to stand by while she was lowered into the water, give me a tow to Den Maas Yacht Club and lend me a hand with her rigging. All of which he had promised.

. . . . . .

'I will watch the little board by the fish market,' he told me, 'which says when a ship comes past the Hook. It is two hours from Hook of Holland to Rotterdam. When *Nyroca* comes — I'll be there.'

He seemed such a sensible person.

It was a very important arrangement — on my side, at least — as I had just bought the *Flame* and she was in a very unseaworthy condition. Eighteen months on dry land does

18

not do a little twenty-six-foot clinker-built boat any good. She still leaked like a sieve; her engine sometimes required five men to start it, and steering alterations made in Southampton in preparation for her cruise across Europe had turned out to be useless. When a man has to live, eat, sleep and wash for nearly a year on a boat, when he intends to take her into strange ports, up foreign rivers, over mountain canals and down such sluices as the Iron Gates of Roumania, it is essential that everything be just right. There are innumerable places between the North and Black Seas where a breakdown means disaster. I had shipped the *Flame* over, in fact, to have the work done in Holland. Quiet, peaceful Holland – where I could smoke a pipe and drink *Schiedam* with the honest old Dutchmen.

Perhaps it was the solidity of his wooden shoes that misled me, but I left Mynheer Snook serene in the belief that I had found a staunch friend in my need. And sitting on the dock, waiting for the overdue *Nyroca*, I revelled in this belief. Never had I seen such boatmen as the Dutch! They were superb. I have seen the oyster fleets in the Chesapeake, and working out of Bivalve, N.J.; I have seen them dock a sixty-foot 'bugeye' on the wind, without even scratching the paint – but here I saw casual Dutchmen, talking to their friends on the shore, take 2,000-ton lighters in and out of almost impossible traffic, with the ease of a nursemaid wheeling a pram through the park.

· · · · · · ·

Surely, I thought, this is the mariners' heaven. Streets lined with boats, floating cities. I saw families get up, light their stoves; I smelt bacon, and fragrant Dutch coffee; I saw sister Maetijlde feeding the dog; saw Papa taking a stroll on the deck with his youngest-born in his arms. I saw Mrs. Captain draw back the curtains in her spacious white cabin aft – saw her come on deck for a breath of moist, morning air – saw her smack sister Maetijlde for nibbling the gingerbread that was spread out for breakfast. I heard some one dust the keys of a piano. And I learned that there were two ends to each ship, socially speaking; and that while the crew might have his wife, and raise his babies in the foc's'le forward, he had no connection, other than business, with the proud, comfortable family of the white-painted, flowered domicile aft.

I sat there from seven o'clock until three, when the *Nyroca* having been fog-bound off the Hook, warped in, got her lines out, and made fast.

"'Ullo!' said her mate, 'and 'ow does Rotterdam hit you?'

I told him. 'Of course,' I said, 'it makes things difficult when you can't speak a word.'

'I never go ashore,' said the mate.

'Well,' I boasted, 'I've found a man who speaks English; Dutchman – coming here with his boat to tow me up to the yacht club.'

'You'll need him,' commented that cynic; 'the traffic here's worse than Piccadilly Circus.'

. . . .

By now the stevedores had the hatch covers off, the donkey engines were clanking, and the ordeal I went through watching the way they man-handled the *Flame* made me quite forget Mynheer Snook. It wasn't until she lay in the water, twenty feet below, beside a green, slippery wall, that I felt the blow of his absence.

'Have you seen my Dutchman?' I called up to the mate.

'No, what's he look like?'

'Short little man, blue cap, wooden shoes.'

20

'What? They all look like that.'

'Name's Snook.'

'Snook! 'Ullo Snook!' the mate bellowed along the length of the dock. His red face peered down at me over the rail. 'Sure that's his name?'

'Yes!' I screamed, clawing at the green wall with my finger nails. 'For Pete's sake, hurry up!'

'Right-o!' The mate disappeared and I heard him bellowing, 'Snook!'

When the mate returned I was no longer there. A 2,000-ton lighter had come in to deliver a tin of biscuits or something like that, shoving me out of the way. By now I was clinging to the bow of the *Jaribu*, fifty yards farther down.

'He ain't here,' called the mate.

'All right,' I howled. 'Get some one else. Get some one to give me a tow.'

'I've told you,' yelled back the mate, 'I don't know any more about this town than you do.'

'Well, get some one who does. What do you expect me to do?'

The mate told me.

.   .   .   .

Now, I know of no place more isolated, removed from communication, than the fore-foot of a steamship. Try and picture this scene; the little twenty-six-foot yawl, with her spars, masts and gear piled every way on her deck, bobbing up and down on a bouncing, mud-coloured sea at the bow of a filthy old Liverpool tramp. See the row of curious, placid faces staring down from the dock. See the fat, second stevedore – whom I had refused to tip because of his clumsiness – grinning and cracking jokes with his friends. See me, like a monkey on a stick, sliding up and down, clutching that rusty steel bow. And I couldn't speak Dutch!

A passing tug saved me, towed me up to the Royal Den Maas Yacht Club – which the hospitable Dutch had asked me to make use of – and left me there, snug in her haven, though feeling abashed on the crude little *Flame* in the midst of such beautiful yachts. Here Mynheer Snook found me.

'You are here,' he said, regarding me stolidly.

I went on with my work.

Mynheer Snook let his gaze wander along the tree-shaded stone walls of the haven, examine in turn each of the glistening white yachts and finally rest on the richly carved *boejer* beside me. 'I didn't come here for money,' he said, speaking slowly; 'I don't do thinga like that. I have a good name and I want to keep it. I don't like to see other people robbing the English, I – '

'I'm not English,' I burst out, 'I'm American. Clear out!'

.   .   .   .

The yellow hairs of Mynheer Snook's eyebrows all point upward, giving him the curious expression of having just been surprised. I saw pain in his blue Friesland eyes – these foreigners! Stepping out of his wooden shoes, he came into my boat. 'Sir,' he began, and in a manner tentative yet determined, he told the tale of his absence. He had calculated the time of *Nyroca's* arrival exactly – no mistake about that – but, having two hours to spare, he had gone off on another job in the meantime. 'Because,' he explained, 'I didn't want to charge you for the whole day.' The other job made him late.

'I'm disgusted,' I said. 'In England they told me I could depend on the Dutch. The English seldom speak that way

22

of anybody but themselves – they are careful whom they commend – so that was a very fine compliment.'

'*Ja!*' agreed Mynheer Snook, 'the Dutch do fine work. I am a captain.'

The explanation over, he was filling his pipe. Evading my glare, his eyes saw the steering-gear of Southampton. 'That is not right,' he said, using his pipe as a pointer, 'it should have a sleeve – so! That is dangerous.'

In an instant he had suggested the much-needed changes. He went over my boat like a doctor. I handed him tools. I saw the *Flame* under his skilled, battered hands becoming a crack little craft. And he, looking up, saw my smile of contentment.

'Double Dutch – eh? That's what they say in America. Double Dutch – but not dumb.'

I re-engaged him at once.

CHAPTER TWO

The Departure

*

'CHEERIO!'

The mate of the dirty old Liverpool freighter leaned over her rail, cupped his hands and called down with true British humour, 'You're going to have your blinkin' hands full, me lad – good luck!'

I waved my hand, clawed the wheel, and *Flame* shot out from the sheltering *haven* into the Meuse on the first leg of her 3,000-mile cruise across Europe. I was off! The heart- and purse-aches of fitting out in England and Holland were over; the miracle had arrived – I was off! Strange lands and strange people, strange –

'Toot! Toot-toot!' The ships of the world were rushing on me. Motor-boats, sailboats, steamboats, barges, tugs. Boats of every description and nation. Ocean liners. 'Toot-toot-toot-toot!' An outbound Frenchman bellowed furiously for me to get out of his way. A great steel ferry lurched out, changed her mind and spun around in the stream. As I rolled in their wash I remembered what an official had told me that morning – that Rotterdam, in May, had just passed Antwerp in tonnage, thus becoming temporarily the second seaport of Europe. At the time the statement had failed to impress me; now I got its full value. And if there is a port in this world with a water traffic thicker than Rotterdam's I have no wish to see it.

. . . .

I felt like a jay-walker at five o'clock in Fifth Avenue, like a green driver going down the wrong side of Regent Street. I would have appreciated some stop and go signals; some, even, abusive policemen. There were none. Just a welter of snorting, business-like tugs, tows half a mile long, of heaving, mud-coloured waters and black hulls lurching past. Traders for the Rhine, for the seven seas of the world! Barges for Dordrecht, for Haarlem and Delft; steamers for Batavia and the Plate! Belgians bringing coal from the Ruhr! And through it all the unconcerned, lumbering passage of red-sailed, broad-bosomed Dutch *boejers* and *schuits*.

My startled eyes met the amazing sky-line of Rotterdam – the sky-line that never stands still – that bewildering medley of painted funnels and flags, spars, masts, boat-decks, trees, windows, roof-tops and giant cranes, waving their steel arms, monster-like in the sky. The seven-arched spans of the great Willems bridge, dominating the background of the scene, seemed the only solid thing in it. I steered for the bridge.

An American, sailing an English boat, in a Dutch river, with a German chart, seems a confusing enough combination. Add to this the fact that the scale of the chart was in kilometres, not miles, that the buoys were not numbered, and you get some slight idea of my feelings. Realize also that while an island is an obvious thing on a chart – there it is, with the water all around it – it is a deceitful affair in real life. If it is big and lies close to shore you are not sure whether the water you see at its foot is the mouth of another river or not – it might not be an island. You cannot fly over to look, nor is it always possible to rush up to see if there is water at the other end of it. You have to chance it, trust your luck, and spurn all enticing water mouths until your instinct tells you that you have reached the one you are bound for. Canals every few hundred yards do not tend to simplify matters.

· · · · · · · ·

25

I was bound for the Lek, Lower Rhine, and it occurred
to me that I might read the names on the ships going up-
steam – as, driving in London, I would read the names on
the buses and trail the one bound for the same destination
that I was – but a study of the names shown on a passing
tug and five barges showed one Belgian, one German and
three Dutch hailing from widely divergent parts of the country. That alarmed me.

'*Den Lek?*' I called out, laying the yawl alongside one
of the Dutchmen.

'*Ja!*' Two men, standing in the water which lapped over
the barge side amidships, nodded, waved their arms and
pointed, each in a different direction.

I sheered off, tried again: '*Lek? Den Lek?*' I pronounced
it differently – perhaps that was the trouble.

The men looked perplexed, held a gesticulating argument with each other, scowled at me and walked off.

By now I had left the thick traffic. The stone walls,
docks and factory stacks of Rotterdam lay far behind, and
I felt sure that the curving, rush-lined river ahead was the
Lek. A brown-sailed barge went before me, wing-and-
wing, her main sheets almost sweeping the bank. A woman,
wrapped up against the chill, grey drizzle of rain, leaned
with her broad back against the tiller.

.   .   .   .

'*Den Lek?*' I called, and she nodded, regarding me curiously. Then she waved a brown hand straight ahead.

Ducks, alarmed by my voice, paddled out from the rushes,
headed into the wind and with a frantic splashing took the
air and shot past me. They circled and I watched them
come over, drop down close to the water and disappear
up the winding river ahead. I saw flat green country, with

26

the roads raised above, little tufts of green trees and beyond, around the curve of a bend, the red roofs of the village, its church steeple pointing finger-like in the sky – peaceful Holland.

At Lekkerkerk I put in for the Crew. She had gone to see a stained window in Gouda. A man on the road above me was skinning an eel; he waved it to me in welcome. I made fast to a barge, which was also tied to the road. Her two men took my lines, then rested their elbows on her rail and inspected me. An African water-bag perturbed them. With sign language I demonstrated its working, rapid evaporization of the water-sweat that oozed through. '*Ja, Ja!*' they nodded; that was a good thing on a boat. I stood there looking up at the roof tops and wondering what sort of village lay on the other side of the dike road. I heard cackles of laughter and saw a group of boys coming over the bank. One of them, a bright-looking youth, grinned and called down:

'Speak English?'

I told him I did, asked him where he had learned it, and the other boys shouted. The boy – he could not have been more than fifteen – removed his cigar and managed to ejaculate, 'School.' He thought hard for more words.

Two girls climbed up from the houses on the other side of the road and the poor lad tried to leave. I prevented it, explained in a combination of Dutch-English-sign language that a young lady was arriving at four-thirty on the bus coming from Gouda – would he tell her where I had the boat?

'Girl?' he repeated, smiling.

I nodded.

'My girl?'

'No,' I said, frowning; 'My girl. Go and meet her.' He went away with his gang.

27

They came back, the boy and the Crew, at the head of a cavalcade most of whom were carrying parcels. The Crew had been shopping.

'Lovely milk,' she said, 'and such cheeses!'

We started the motor, cast off. There was a friendly flutter of hands from the bank. At the bend we looked back. The man with the eel stood at the end of the long line of red roof-tops like a weather-vane – he waved its indecent carcass aloft in final farewell. We looked ahead. In the far blue distance, over a puff of green willows, the grey arms of a windmill caught the air, waved once, and then twice, like a welcome.

CHAPTER THREE

Up the Lek

*

IT is about 125 miles from Rotterdam to Emmerich on the German frontier. If you go by water there are two ways to get there – you can go by Dordrecht, up the Waal, or by that comparatively untravelled and beautiful waterway the Lek – lower Rhine. The Lek is off the main track. Steamers and that never-ending concourse of French, Belgian, German and Dutch barges use the Waal. Yachtsmen, when they know of it, take the Lek. Compared to that crowded marine highway, the Waal, it is like a quiet country lane.

There are few towns on its banks, and these are strangely unmodern, picturesque. At first you hardly see them – just the red roofs of their houses peeping over the dikes, coming more and more into view as you ascend the Lek, so that you see gables, the second-floor windows, and above Wyk actually meet the front door. Old-fashioned houses. You get the feeling of having rolled back a century. Above Lekker-kerk, which is less than twenty miles distant from Rotterdam, the churches dominate the quiet landscape. You can see their steeples for miles across the flat, open country, pointing pencil-like in the sky. There are few trees to obscure them – clipped willows, like green mushrooms, along the flat profile of the dike roads, an occasional parade of orderly poplars and, infrequently where the road dips down to a ferry, a few horse-chestnuts surrounding the resthouse.

. . . .

Ancient ferries, swung like a pendulum on a leash of four skiffs, steering from bank to bank by means of leeboards and rudders for the carved hay-wagons and two-wheeled country carts that await them. A trim, orderly country and – pro-

29

bably because the Dutch grow hay on their dikes and mow close – an apparently well-settled country. On hot, drowsy days one gets the impression of sailing along through the secluded corner of a well-kept country estate. Fat black and white cattle lie on the white river sands. Snipe feed at the water edge, ducks and cormorants. The scarlet roofs of the houses are dabs of colour on the level green ribbon of land.

But if the country is restful the river is not. The Lek has a swift current. Never more than two hundred yards wide, it sometimes narrows to fifty. Its surface is swirling. Always, on one side or the other, depending upon the sweep of the current, its banks are held by stone jetties. Always, at night as you drowse, you feel the thrum of the lower Rhine beneath your keel.

It is a fascinating country to cruise through, to see on a fresh, sparkling sunrise after rain. On windy days, when a sweater feels good, to win bend after bend, always with that pleasant expectation of seeing what lies beyond. Or to lie at night off a little village like Schoonhoven, with its high green wall and red arch through the dike, and hear – as you smoke your last cigarette – the tinkling church bells on shore playing little dance tunes, selections from opera, like an old music box. No wonder Dutchmen are placid.

.   .   .   .

The women are beautiful – some of them. One tires of hearing them spoken of always as ' broad-beamed,' ' broad-backed,' *à la percheron*; it shows but a superficial knowledge on the part of the author.

Opposite Rhenen my engine gave out and I had a nasty few minutes working *Flame* to the shore. I saw a Dutch clipper the *Twee Geber*, tied up to some pilings, and called out for some one to make fast my line. The painted doors of her deckhouse swung open, a blonde head appeared, its golden plaits piled high, like a crown. I had never seen such astonished blue eyes or such pretty ones; Ziegfeld would have crossed the ocean to get her. Yet she had my line in an instant and had swung a double hitch on the bitts, like the most salty jack tar. Then she stood there and smiled. Another girl came out to look at me, her shoulders wrapped in a towel. A fox-terrier puppy, which they had imprisoned by simply standing his kennel on end, got his elbows over his sky-pointed doorway and barked furiously. I lay there that night.

As it was a calm, cerise sunset I decided to cook in the cockpit, my stove on the engine box. The sight of the diminutive Primus amused them. With a critical eye they watched the way I boiled the eggs in my coffee. It displeased them; they, of course, being unaware of the artifice required to produce a meal on a one-burner stove. Their own, like all others on these spacious Dutch barges and ships, was of the ordinary kitchen variety. It had probably never occurred to them that a ship was not a much more comfortable place to live upon than the shore. Their cabin had two decks (floors?) and a drawing-room. I heard the whizz of a sewing-machine, and this probably accounted for the one girl's coming out always partly clad in that towel. Probably trying things on!

. . . . . .

The night came on thick and murky – just the night for those leering gargoyles of St. Cunera on shore. I was lying there, wondering what stupendous conceit could have imagined the creation of anything so massive in what must have been this village in 1492. What did it look like when fresh built? And what extraordinary mentality ever thought of a gargoyle? – their snarling, savage snouts smelling out

31

over Holland. That golden-haired girl and gargoyles and bow-men –

'Toot-toot!' I awoke with the blast of a horn in my ear, heard the heavy cough of a motor, lurched out of the cabin to see the black bulk of a motor-barge looming over me. Black silhouettes of men raced over her deck-load, waved their arms, shouted down. I gathered that I was occupying their berth. A rain had set in, a chill drizzle – it seemed to cut to the bone. In clinging pyjamas I cast off the stern line and hauled *Flame* alongside the *Twee Geber*. I climbed on her deck to let go the bow-line. The puppy dog recognized an intruder. He sprang to attack. Every time I leaned over to cast off I felt those sharp little teeth. I admired his courage, but –

'Agoost,' I said (I had heard them calling him that), 'if you don't leave me alone I am going to bite back.'

One of the girls, hearing his bark and my voice overhead, came on deck and retrieved him. The man of the *Twee Geber* came on deck. He wore a long, shroud-like nightgown. He rested his arms on the companion-way doors, sucked in a deep breath, and in a low, steady voice said things which I know would have burned the paper in print. He was marvellous.

The men on the barge stopped their shouting, answered in grunts. One figure moved silently aft, took down the running lights, hoisted a white light on the signal mast, entered the forecastle and slammed shut the door. The master of the *Twee Geber* withdrew.

I looked ashore. The lights of Rhenen were out. The black bulk of St. Cunera loomed alarmingly near and, on a white patch in the torn, streaky sky I saw one of those sneering gargoyles grinning down at us all.

CHAPTER FOUR

A Tow up the Rhine

*

BEING towed up the Rhine is not the placid, uneventful experience that one might imagine. The Rhine is one of the most congested marine highways in the world. From Emmerich on the German frontier, to Mainz, for 265 miles, one moves among a never-ending concourse of steamers and tugs with tows at least half a mile long.

From Emmerich to Duisberg and the region surrounding the mouth of the Ruhr the half-mile wide khaki flood is glutted with traffic. Above that point the traffic diminishes, but as the river narrows as well, the effect is almost the same. Off the big Krupp works at Hochfeld we saw more than a hundred barges lying in the stream. These barges were from 200 to 300 feet long, with capacities of from 2,000 to 3,000 tons. Six of them usually make up a tow. They have steel hulls, like steamers, are powerfully built and can do little harm to one another; but if an ordinary craft, such as a yacht, gets between them she is cracked like a nut. We know this because it happened to us, and had there been another way of getting *Flame* up to Mainz we should have taken it. However, there wasn't — not for a boat with a speed of only seven miles an hour — so at Emmerich we arranged for a tow.

The main street of Emmerich runs along the stone river-wall. It is flanked on the water side by a promenade of orderly lime trees, on the other by shipping offices and cafés. The tug captains gather there and drink beer while they wait for their charges to pass through the customs. Belgian, French, Dutch and German barges lie tugging fretfully at their anchors like some great international armada. Our captain, a ponderous man with a small eye like an elephant's, pointed to a tiny black tug, the *Harmonie*, and told us to lie alongside. He also intimated that he knew what to do with ten marks. That was at ten o'clock in the morning; at three o'clock we still lay alongside the *Harmonie* without having moved. A small boy who had come out from the shore in a skiff answered our anxiety concerning the whereabouts of the captain with the cryptic remark: 'Drinking beer.'

At three o'clock the captain's bulk was discernible in the stern sheets of a skiff. Two green-uniformed customs officials – not sprites themselves – held down the bow. A sad little man sat amidships, rowing furiously.

'*Jezt gehts los*,' said the captain. And after another hour, during which the customs officials visited the barges of pulp wood in our rear, we set off at a moderate walk up the Rhine.

We still lay alongside the tug, which shut off, half our view. But as the shores for the next fifty-five miles to above Duisberg were low, sandy, and littered with factories and steel works – exactly like South Chicago – we were content with our half. It had one advantage, this proximity to the tug – we could climb aboard to see what lay on the other side or talk to the captain.

We learned that the tug was a sort of family affair. The two boys – who did most of the work – were his sons. He had seven other sons as well and two tugs. These kept him quite comfortable. He did not like the war; it played the deuce with his food. And it was during one of these intimate conversations, with the fat captain leaning over his horizontal steering-wheel, explaining what a pity it was that the Kaiser had married so soon after the Kaiserin's death, how much it distressed loyal Germans, that our first accident happened.

We had accustomed ourselves not to feel apprehensive when swept within a few feet of towering black barges

The men leaning against the horizontal steering-wheels aft always sheered off. But this Belgian must have been sleepy –
'Hi! Captain!'

Even as I cried out the barge hit us. I heard the crunching of timbers, felt *Flame* trembling as she was slowly collapsing between the barge and the tug – then the splitting of wood. She's gone, I thought, expecting to come out of it on the end of our rope.

But the captain had suddenly galvanized into action; he spun the spokes of that wheel like a squirrel in a cage. The barge dropped astern. I leaned over the side, saw a hole the size of a finger where a rivet head had sheered through a frail strake.

'Wind,' the captain explained, 'blew me over. But that Belgian – !'

It was the only national animosity I witnessed in Germany.

With dusk the Rhine traffic stops. At eight o'clock the captain rang a bell over his head, the tug's engines slowed down and we saw men at the bows of the barges astern and heard the rattle of anchor chains. The captain put his hand to the side of his head, murmured 'Sleep,' and vanished below.

We went this way for three days, anchoring at night in the little places where the steamers never stop, starting off again at four in the morning. We towed astern now and in the morning went shopping, waved to the market boats which lie in midstream to provision the tugs and barges as they pass. They scuttled alongside and we took our pick of the piles of onions, turnips, butter, eggs and huge loaves of sour bread on their decks. They also sold a moderately good brand of beer. Their prices were reasonable – but the eggs were bad.

The Rhine towns turn their best faces toward the river. No advertisements mar the banks. Every town has its *Schwimmbads* – and it seemed as if all Germany was lying out in the sun convalescing; half naked men doing physical jerks; lying stark in green fields. This, the spectacle of the mammoth Krupp works at Hochfeld, the almost feverish industrial activity from Emmerich to the Ruhr – these branded one's consciousness with the inevitable comeback of these people. Germany seemed a nation in training.

Above Düsseldorf we came among the first of those formidable, two-stacked, paddle-wheel towing steamers. They made their own sea! The current was much swifter now. And for hours at the close of the third day we approached the peerless cathedral of Cologne, its twin spires looming purple-grey through the rain. We found the city in the whirl of its thousand-year celebration. Fifteen thousand singers – and I – lifted up our voices in praise.

Three days later we started off in tow of the tug *Paula*. Because of swift current – and what not – a hundred marks, this time, to Mainz. We were glad to get it, however, as many companies are now forbidden by their charters to tow yachts. To prevent argument, the genial Dutch captain towed us nearly a quarter of a mile astern. We passed under the beautiful bridge of Bonn – now undergoing repairs, with its gargoyles painted red – by the Drachenfels; past Coblenz – black French troops strutting under the lime trees! – and entered the Rhine gorge, the legendary Rhine. Promenades, *biergartens*, little vineyards – like shelves – and the famous ruined castles on their crags looking so neat that they might have been almost a stage setting.

Above the rocks of the Lorelei our dinghy heard the call of the sirens. We caught the last inch of its painter as it whisked past the transom. Here, in the Binger rapids, the cruise of *Flame* nearly ended. A pilot had been taken aboard each barge and the tug below the Lorelei, as the Rhine is treacherous there and less than fifty yards wide. The pilot on the barge before us evidently over-estimated our capacity. *Flame* was snatched through a permanent wave of white water and her bow bitts were completely torn out. Fortunately, the tow ropes were fastened to a second and stronger pair farther aft, which held fast. We passed the Mouse tower – now used with a white ball on a shaft to show when the rapids are clear – and entered smooth water.

Here we saw the last of those fishing-sloops that one sees all the way up the Rhine, and passed up with the flotilla of paddle-wheel tugs to Mainz. We had come out of the gorge into a broad Rhine again, a tranquil Rhine, running through a rolling farm land, its hills soft, hazy blue in the distance. But it is only a temporary easement of effort, for to-day we cross over and enter the Main and begin the 240-mile climb to Bamberg.

. . . .

With the purchase of a Stillson wrench at Mainz we began to feel that *Flame* was complete. The cruise up the Rhine had been as much a fitting-out period as those anxious days I had put in at Southampton. One thing which may not appear very important – the roof leaked! And after sleeping for a week with the frying-pan balanced over her ear the Crew decided that that was not good enough. Temporary repairs to the streaming seams in our cabin were made with adhesive tape. Towed alongside or in the wake of the *Paula* we could not get ashore – and the captain always picked a secluded spot to anchor for the night – so that while we found many quiet castles and vineyards we never reached any stores. In Mainz we bought brushes, paint, copper tacks, chocolates – and this famous Stillson wrench.

We also had a good lunch. Delicious little blue fish called *schleier*, which we had never met before – or since. Ask for them if you are ever in Mainz.

'Where is the Main?' we asked a German youth we found sitting on *Flame*.

'It's over there,' he said, pointing across the Rhine, 'and it looks exactly like coffee.'

With the Stillson wrench I beat our engine into activity. We crossed the Rhine and worked up along the tree-bordered banks, we saw the mouth of a black stream and dived into it – we came to canal locks!

'*Gruss Gott!*' exclaimed a man on the parapet, 'Praise God!'

'Exactly,' said we; 'please take our line.' And thus began our charming trip through Bavaria.

That night we lay off Floresheim, watched a stork balancing himself on one leg on his chimney top, and witnessed a pathetic substitute for the lost '*ofiziere*' – the Fire Brigade on parade.

The next night saw us walking under an incredibly full moon through the painted little Rapunzel Gasse of Frankfort –

Rapunzel, Rapunzel, let down your hair. . . .

CHAPTER FIVE

Checkmate in Bavaria

*

As I write this we are lying off the empty *schloss* of the mad king of Bavaria. And one might think that I were mad, too, for in a boat that leaks through the roof I am praying for rain.

We passed through here yesterday, gaily waved good-bye to the good people of Aschaffenburg who hung over the red limestone bridge to examine us, and entered the pleasant country beyond. Low, green farm land, rolling hills – very much like Dutch Pennsylvania – dotted with crooked little red-roofed half-timbered houses. We saw shepherds tending their flocks; little goose girls with long yellow plaits driving their hissing regiments to the stream. Conventional things which one had read about in *Grimms' Fairy Tales* as a baby – but never expected to see. Storks' nests on the chimney tops. And one black and white patriarch flapped by us, dangling his red legs as though broken, and dropped into a marshy field by the river-side. We saw fishermen, with their 'V' nets on long poles, poling along the edge of the rushes, the man at the stern thrashing about with his push-pole, scaring the little fish into the net. Yellow perch.

Except for the fishermen we were alone on the river. Too much alone; the solitude was quite sinister.

'Where are you going?' called out a fisherman.

'Wurzburg,' answered the Crew, adding modestly: 'but we shan't get there to-night.'

'That I can well believe,' said the fisherman.

We sailed gaily on.

Above Obernau we saw the cause of his humour. The Main here, although it looked as smooth as a mill pond, was pouring down with a speed of at least six miles an hour. Hugging the banks, sneaking up in the backwaters, *Flame* barely moved.

'At this rate,' said the Crew, 'we may reach Bamberg by Christmas.'

Although it was a disheartening thing to do, we put about and started back for Aschaffenburg. What a difference! The unusual speed was refreshing, cooled us while we unburdened ourselves of our feelings connected with those puerile officials in Frankfort. They had told us that the current above Aschaffenburg was negligible, and, should we care for a tow we would find many a kindly old Bavarian captain only too glad to assist us. What a joke!

At Aschaffenburg we were referred to the *Kette-Boot*. This rusty, black, convex-decked barge (I know no other way to describe it!) pulls itself up against the fierce current of the Main on a continuous chain 190 miles long to Bamberg. Surely a unique performance.

'Everything goes up on the *Kette-Boot*,' said the harbour-master.

We stared at the monster, looking like a cross between a machine shop and a broken-backed minelayer. There were four in the harbour. They did not look attractive.

'When does one start?' asked the Crew.

The harbour-master elevated his shoulder: 'I don't know. To-morrow – Thursday – Friday – when we make up a tow.'

'How long does it take?'

'I don't know. Five – six – eight days.'

We swallowed these disappointments, but were quite crushed by the next.

'*Nur bis Wurzburg.*'

40

'Only to Wurzburg?'

The harbour-master explained that a severe drought had dried up the streams in upper Bavaria; there was not enough water for the *Kette-Boot* to go farther than Kitzingen. Kitzingen is seventy miles from Bamberg!

'Quite impossible,' he said, 'to get up to Bamberg.'

'Not quite,' muttered the inmates of *Flame*; 'there are horses.'

And this is the position of affairs at the moment. Unless rains swell the Main the *Kette-Boot* gets no farther than Kitzingen, and *Flame* will have to be hauled by horses seventy tortuous miles to the high city of Bamberg. And the Crew and I have just finished on shore a comforting dinner of roast wild boar and Rhine wine.

'Think of Columbus,' suggests the Crew.

'And Cortez – crossing the isthmus.'

'Of course!' says the Crew, brightening. 'And Hannibal took elephants over the Alps.'

So, you see, we aren't done yet.

CHAPTER SIX

Climbing into Bavaria

*

RUSHY lagoons flanking the rock-faced banks of the Main; sweeps of brass-coloured wheat tufted with orchards of apricots, cherries and peaches, rising to the black depths of pine forests; walled cities; monasteries crowning each hilltop; saints, swords in hand, on stone bridges; a waving sky-line of blue mountains; an old mellow country – Bavaria.

The Main is a river of many surprises. Even on its banks it seems shrouded in mystery. In the first place it is not exactly a river. From its mouth on the Rhine, opposite Mainz, to Aschaffenburg, one climbs through twelve red sandstone locks, mounting 150 feet in fifty-four miles. It might be a canal – yet it has a swift current. So swift that above Aschaffenburg it is impossible to proceed without being hauled up by the *Kette-Boot*.

The *Kette-Boot* itself is one of the most surprising contraptions imaginable. Looking like a marine architect's nightmare, it performs the remarkable feat of pulling itself, on a continuous chain, 190 miles into the Bavarian mountains to Bamberg. The lock-keeper at Kostheim did not know how many locks there were up to Frankfort; shippers at Frankfort had never heard of the *Kette-Boot*. And the *Kette-Boot*, discovered in its lair in Aschaffenburg, did not know when, if ever, it could start up the Main.

Bamberg and the Ludwig's Canal seemed to assume a mirage-like elusiveness. Ever before us. Unattainable. A black doubt began to form in our minds.

'Surely,' we argued, 'you must know when a *Kette-Boot* starts for Bamberg?'

'Sixty centimetres,' gave out the harbour-master, 'is not

enough water.' He explained that rash *Kette-Boots* sometimes did not come back. 'We must have rain.'

'Rain! It has rained steadily for ten days on the
Rhine.'

'The Rhine,' said the patriotic Bavarian, 'is not the Main
above Aschaffenburg.'

Then it rained. It came down in drops the size of a shil-
ling. It came down for two days. The red *schloss* of Mad
Ludwig seemed to soften like gingerbread. Red rust spouted
out of the mountain of chain beside the hut of the harbour-
master. He thrust his head out one evening, walrus-like,
through the downpour:

'Eighty centimetres! The water is rising.'

'Hurrah! More rain!'

He squelched over that night, cried out in the dark across
the harbour:

'To-morrow a *Kette-Boot* starts for Bamberg!'

'Hurrah for the *Kette-Boot*! What time?'

'Six o'clock – do not oversleep.'

Sleep! At six o'clock when the *Kette-Boot* came clanking
past, we grappled with her, made fast with the grim determination of pirates on the old Spanish Main. But the *Kette-
Boot* was no fair galleon. Her decks were rusty and wet; a
horrible crunching came from her vitals as she digested the
beginning of her 190 miles of steel chain. A bleary, tousled
old skipper peered down through the rain. Fair, greasy
faces appeared at the portholes surmounted by an array of
strange hats – war hats; round sailor hats. One bald-headed
man evidently thought that the round wart on the top of his
skull was headgear enough.

'So,' he asked, 'you go with us?'

'Yes – to Bamberg.'

43

'Bamberg! It is most unlikely that we shall get up to Bamberg!'

The trouble had started again! The captain referred to shook his head, grinned at our dismay, told us that in his twenty-five years with the *Kette-Boot* he had known periods of three months to pass before it could get up to Wurzburg. The engineer, nursing his 120 horse-power motors, explained the intricacies of machinery, but, when asked about the chance of arriving at Bamberg with the *Kette-Boot*, shrugged his shoulders. The stoker hung his cap over the pressure gauge to indicate that if a high head of steam could do it it would be done. Meanwhile, with eight barges in tow and *Flame* lashed alongside, the *Kette-Boot* clanked up the Main.

That night we anchored off Dorfprozelten. Running from six in the morning until 8 p.m. we had covered thirty-three miles. Such was the speed of the *Kette-Boot*. It never stopped. When it wanted to deposit a barge, its steel arm, which guides the chain over the bow, was hauled to one side like a rudder; the captain slowed down the engines, rang a bell – and the barge cast off, using its headway to make shore and anchor. We were continually dropping and picking up barges in this fashion. It was a tedious but almost inevitable progression. When anyone wished to go ashore – and people did so quite frequently – they merely stepped into one of the skiffs towed alongside, paid out a long length of line and used the sheer of the current to shoot them to land. There they shopped, drank beer, chatted and finally ran on ahead to rejoin the *Kette-Boot*. If they wanted to stay ashore a long time they took a bicycle with them. Two girls came out from the shore for a visit. . . .

We were surprised, therefore, Sunday morning to find the *Kette-Boot* stopping. We lay off a little grey-walled town into

44

whose houses we could have tossed a biscuit. The engineer pointed to the captain, at that moment entering its church. Twice that day did we stop for the captain to make his peace. The last time he brought back three bottles.

We thought him rather sodden, a bit pompous for the skipper of a boat tied to a chain – but above Wurzburg our admiration developed. We had left the forest lands, the little villages with their ancient stone walls still intact (walls along which I used to trot in the mornings to buy butter for breakfast), and entered a country of vineyards – rambling grey limestone hills through which the Main raced like a sluice. A boathook jabbed down four feet hit a hard rocky bottom. There were places where we could reach out and touch the stone banks, places where the Main was so shallow that we felt *Flame* suck down and her keel hit the rocks. Our rudder jumped out. White waves tried to crawl over our transom. Barges astern went aground. Twice the *Kette-Boot* broke its chain. Wild racing aft to catch the last links slipping overboard; champing of the ratchet lock biting into the forward links; hammering as the sweating crew of the *Kette-Boot* riveted in a new link. And through it all, serene and sardonic, the grey-bearded captain, his back against the steering-wheel, issuing caustic commands! Captain Kettle could not have done better.

On the fifth evening we saw, gold in the sunset, the twin towers guarding the weir of the Rhine-Danube canal. They looked like the portals of heaven. *Flame* had scraped bottom the last few yards to the Regnitz. A close shave indeed! The *Kette-Boot* shed her chain, proceeded under water turbine into the massive stone locks – one fifth of a mile long – and we anchored that night for the first time in still water.

Dusk, and the captain leaning over the *Kette-Boot's* rail.

Yes, for twenty-five years he had been doing just this. He had seen the chain grow, year by year – Wurzburg, Kitzingen, Schweinfurt, Bamberg. He had seen the tow horses receding before it, seen the locks supplant it between Mainz and Aschaffenburg, and now here was the new Rhine-Danube canal which would turn the entire Main into one huge canal. It was the passing of the chain – and his life. He spoke of his family. His eldest daughter was a seamstress, the next worked in a chemical factory, the boy would soon be a mechanic – there were three others, quite young. He spoke of days in the war when he felt ashamed to come home with no food. The *Kette-Boot* towed hospital ships.

He talked there until he was just a voice in the darkness. He told us how he had bought a small house, mortgaged it in the period of inflation – and now the people wanted him to pay in state marks. He never could do it. He pounded the rail of the *Kette-Boot*. This, at least, in a world turned all topsy-turvy, was real.

'But, Captain,' I asked, through the darkness, 'when the Rhine-Danube canal does away with the *Kette-Boot*?'

'That,' came the old voice, with almost a grim satisfaction, 'will never come in my time.'

CHAPTER SEVEN

The Lost Waterway

*

FOUR miles longer than Suez, twice as long as the Panama, the only freshwater link across Europe connecting the North and Black Seas – the Ludwig's Canal! Probably the most unknown and least-used waterway in the world. The German Consulate in London had never heard of it. We traced its course on an atlas – from Bamberg to Kelheim, in Bavaria – explained how it crossed the Frankischer Jura mountains in a series of steps – climbed through the clouds – to let one down into Austria. The Germans produced a gazetteer. Yes, there it was! One hundred and one locks in 107 miles! It had been begun by Charlemagne! Twelve hundred years ago! *Himmel!* It must be like an old book – laid away and forgotten.

This obscurity perturbed us. We asked questions in Holland. What if the canal had disappeared? One of the most anxious half-hours of our lives was spent awaiting a long-distance telephone call into Germany.

'Yes,' came a faint voice over hundreds of miles of thin wire, 'the canal still exists for small boats.'

We asked about draught, beam and length, and were told that a boat that did not draw over three feet could get through. She must not exceed twelve feet in breadth. The voice died away, calling 'Good-bye.'

A vague affirmation. We tried to make certain, asking questions all the way up the Rhine, up the Main. Some had heard of it, but most had not. Some said there never had been such a canal. One sailor assured us that the Germans had sent two steamers through it, loaded with ammunition, during the war. Contradictions, misstatements!

47

Then one foggy morning *Flame* nosed her way into Bamberg. This was mysterious, too, this little age-old city, ghost-like through the mist. Around us we heard the ceaseless roar of swift waters, caught little glimpses of white, tumbling foam. Feeling our way along a row of fourteenth-century dwellings, we passed under a low stone bridge, made out the charming inscription, 'Renovated 1568,' and tied up to a glistening wet wall. The sun came up and, with it, a fat little man in a grey alpaca coat.

'Ha, ha!' he grinned down at us. 'You wish to go through the Ludwig's Canal?'

We replied that we did – answered with joy. The Ludwig's Canal was a fact.

'It will cost you much money,' he chortled, with an obscene delight. 'One hundred and fifty marks – at the least. And then there are taxes.'

He led us through a deserted courtyard, into a dark little room whose only window was obscured by three enormous fuchsias in pots. He pulled up the green jalousie and indicated two chairs.

'There will have to be measurements,' he explained, 'and we shall now have to write to Nurnburg for the permission. Are you on pleasure or business?'

'Which will be cheapest?'

'They are both the same; but we must know – it is the regulations.'

'Pleasure – have you had many such boats?'

'Ha, ha! You are not the first! There was a boat came through here in – let me see – in 1905. And another only a few years ago. Yes, but they were both fine, large boats – not like yours. One,' he said, looking over the useless spectacles on the end of his nose, 'had music.'

'Did he also have to pay 150 marks?'

The guardian of the Ludwig's Canal eyed me severely and explained that the musical sailor-man had come through before the new regulation. He brought out an old form, printed about the time Richmond capitulated, and showed me where, in a neat copperplate hand, he had inscribed the new regulations. There they were – 150 marks, at the least.

'In the inflation!' He patted lovingly a small ledger. 'You have no idea of the sums I had to add up – the accounts!' And there, in that one thin folder, he showed us the ships that had passed through the Ludwig's during almost the last twenty years. He sighed, showing us the empty years. 'Once we had many ships, but now they are all fading away.'

We waited two days in Bamberg, a city whose past still mocks the present. A city of crucifixes and saints, of smiling Madonnas, painted walls and old castles! A city of twisting streets, splendid squares and tumbling white rivers that dive under and swirl around time-worn grey walls. Bamberg is lethargic and drowsy. It gives one the feeling of a hot afternoon in midsummer, of hearing the bees hum in the flower-beds when you lie in a hammock, too lazy to read, and your book falls from your hand. Bamberg tried street-cars and gave them up.

The permission came. 'Ten marks extra,' smiled the round little man, 'for the motor; and three marks also because you are foreigners.' We paid.

'And you must have a pilot,' he added.

'A pilot! In a canal!'

'It is the regulations.'

We swore. In the languages at our command we told the little gadfly what we thought of regulations which required a pilot to take us through a canal. We said other things.

49

'Then,' he declared, 'I shall run alongside for the first few locks to see that you get through all right. You know that you have to throw out a line?'

A large part of the population of Bamberg ran along with him. The lock-keeper, hearing the toot of our horn, hurried to put on his blue cap — with the crown and gold anchor — strained his muscles against the old wooden gates. *Flame* chugged up a placid green strip of water and slid between dripping stone walls into an ancient lock less than one hundred feet long and fifteen wide. The gates closed behind us. The lock-keeper ran forward and opened the sluice. The water bubbled, swirled and poured white. We rose fifteen feet and met the smiling faces of Bambergers. Children and old men dressed in flannels helped the lock-keeper open the gates. Much puffing and straining of muscles. Shrieks of joy from the women and girls. We started the motor, cast off. 'Goodbye.' 'Good-bye, a pleasant voyage!'

Flame pushed, wonderingly, out into a smooth lane of green water, brushed aside the protesting lily pads and settled down to her work.

A loud cheer from the bank. 'Rah! Waving of hats! An event had transpired in Bamberg. Another ship had entered the Ludwig's Canal!

CHAPTER EIGHT

In the Ludwig's Canal

*

'MANY men and women sleep in these woods at nights.'

We were tied up to the bank of the Ludwig's Canal in the pine forest beyond Nurnburg and, as always, a group of pedestrians had settled down to watch us cook and eat our dinner. The towpath of the Ludwig's is an open road across Bavaria. The wanderer's highway. Even then, a group of *wandervogel* came swinging past, the lilt of their guitars dying away under the stars.

'But they are not bad men and womens,' came the voice; 'they are the–how you say?–the homeless. They can't find any work.'

A guttural murmur of resentment came from the vague forms above us. Why speak of such things? There must be plenty of work in the country? One hastened to tell us that next year things would be better; Krupp's would open a big works in Nurnburg that would employ 30,000. Besides, these people weren't all Nurnburgers; the police had surrounded the woods and arrested forty-one only that morning. Five they had imprisoned – they were criminals.

An argument started; the group aligned itself against the youth who spoke English. What did he know of work – or an empty stomach? One bitter voice announced that its owner had waded knee deep through the snows of Bavaria all the previous winter.

Sudden silence!

Two figures had moved into the glow of our riding-light. Gaunt men with tight lips. Unshaved. They stood there grimly silent, and examined us. A sinister scrutiny. No one spoke. Then they turned, slid down off the towpath and disappeared in the woods.

We slept fitfully that night, troubled with imaginings of pity and fear, of those furtive figures moving about in the woods. At daybreak I awoke, heard voices and, looking out, saw a man washing his face in the canal. He was old with grey hair. He washed himself very carefully. A woman stood above him doing her hair. She, too, was old; but the mass of her hair was still gold. I lay there, holding my breath, and, lying so, fell asleep.

The voices woke me again. The man and the woman stood on the canal bank above us. They were quite dressed. He wore a light grey business suit, clean collar and cuffs. Even as I looked he cocked his hat, jauntily. They talked in low tones to each other, looking down at our boat. Never have I seen such envy, regret, and such bitter knowledge as in those two gentle faces.

Afterwards I entered the woods. Most German forests are picked clean, like a lawn; the faggot gatherers collecting even small twigs. These woods were on low land, like swamp, carpeted with little tussocks of grass. I could see, around me, where people had slept – little moulds in the grass, like the lay of a deer. I pictured the raid of the previous morning; the sun glinting through the trees, the tired sleepers, the crawling cordon of police, the wild plunging alarm – the man hunt.

Germany is troubled with people tramping the country for work. Most of the small peasant colonies are self-sufficient. Families have tilled the same land for centuries and have no place for a stranger. The factories are in towns that have their own unemployed, and the foremen prefer to give the vacant jobs to the sons and daughters of farmers who live near by, and thus get a free supply of milk, butter and eggs. The trampers are lured on by the promise of 'over the hill.'

There are many, also, like the Hamburg Zimmerman, who

combine walking with work. They work steadily at ship-building in Hamburg in winter; in summer they stroll through the country collecting to build houses where wanted. Theirs is an age-old order. Their costumes, rather Mexican, with black, bell-like trousers, short jacket and wide black sombrero, are handed down from their fathers. We saw them in Düsseldorf, Cologne, Frankfort, Bamberg, Nurnburg — the length of our passage through Germany.

There are some who belong to no such definite clan, who are impelled to move on when the grass grows green under blue skies and hot sun — possessors of the 'restless foot.' Four of these, in barnacle fashion, attached themselves to the *Flame*. They found us going through a lock one rainy morning and asked if they could ride along as far as the next lock. On board they asked how far we were going. We, foolishly, said Vienna. So were they. They said they were in no hurry. They stayed with us four days.

They were *Spielers* giving musical concerts to get their food and lodging *en route*. One played the guitar, one the violin, and one a curious instrument like a potato, which emitted horrible grunts imitative of a saxophone. The fourth was a mousey, pale-faced little lad who did nothing — but eat.

The first glimpse of sun found them sitting on the cabin of *Flame* giving a full and perfectly maddening performance. Good souls; they thought they were paying their way! An ideal picture; *Flame* chugging along one of the few weedless stretches of the Ludwig's; towns in the green valleys lying below us; waving rushes — and music. They slept ashore, under logs, trees, in a *Gasthaus*, anywhere. Sometimes they wandered off and did not rejoin *Flame* until late in the day. Once the violinist went away with the mousey-faced lad. He rejoined us at nightfall — alone. Mousey-face, he explained, had been removed by the police. He was a runaway, under eighteen, without any papers. His parents had got him again.

We had a picture of ourselves, arriving with our own — though unwanted — orchestra in Vienna! But the weeds of the Ludwig's freed us from them. Long, back-breaking pulls through breathless, hot cuts, wading knee-deep through wet grass in a downpour — these convinced them that, perhaps, walking was better. And at sunset, near a lonely monastery in the mountains, we bade them good-bye.

There are other strollers whose life is that of romance. These are the *Wandervogel* — young girls and boys who live on the highways of Germany. Many of them are mere students, who will abandon the life after a time. Others are more intent on their purpose, if one may say that of so evasive a pilgrimage. They are walking with a set goal in their minds, yet they have no place to get to; they are getting away; escaping — they think — from the harsh industrialism which they are afraid will entrap them and sadden their lives. They play, and dance, the old folk-songs. A beautiful though pathetic attempt to regain a certain lost content and simplicity. They try to walk out of this age.

On star-dusted nights, with cold peaks above, their music will come faintly through the sighing of some pine-clad gorge. We have heard it so, gay and clear. Then their voices, the thrum of the strings — and in a sharp little march they come swinging past.

Sometimes violins and guitars were laid aside on the grass, and the *Wandervogel*, arms around their knees, told of little villages high up in the mountains, what the wind was like last night in the hills.

They were quite near their goal on the old towpath of the Ludwig's.

CHAPTER NINE

The Great Purpose

*

'We have lost so much because of the war that we try to make it up in other things.'

This from a young German writer in Bamberg to whom I had expressed my surprise at the athletic activity I had witnessed in Germany – the swimmers, sports, hikers and rowing-shells I had seen the entire length of the Rhine and Main districts. I had expected to find a people rather fatigued and despondent.

He smiled. 'Would you like to see our airplane factory?'

We were having dinner in the Theatre Café, and although it was not yet ten o'clock, the streets of Bamberg were dark. We walked down toward the canal and at an iron gate before some vast gloomy buildings he asked me to wait. He returned in a few minutes and told me that I could go in.

'These were barracks,' he said. 'We had a fine regiment of Uhlans here before the war.'

We crossed a grassy, wet square and entered a shed. The skeleton of a fuselage, mounted on wooden horses, took up the major part of a very small room. On one side earnest young men were rigging a wing. A blond, rather stout young man, wearing a leather coat and visored cap, came forward to greet us. He clicked his heels together as he bowed, eyeing me curiously.

'Herr Muller,' said the writer, introducing us and, aside to me, *sotto voce*, 'He brought down three English - in the war.'

Herr Muller took me over the plane. It was a beautiful thing, cobweb in its fine tracery of reinforcements and sections. The wings were flexible. It had a fourteen-metre wing spread. The *Harth* – a famous glider.

The workers were volunteers, students, enthusiasts, who found the time after hours. Three of them were girls. For their work they received instruction in aeronautics and flying. They were full of enthusiasm for the big gliding tests in the Rhone valley. One was a dentist.

'We are curtailed,' said Herr Muller. 'They will not let us build bigger planes. But we learn a great deal from such work as this. We have found that we can do almost as much with a twenty horse-power motor as we could with a hundred and twenty-motor during the war. And, of course,' he added, 'for the big work – we do that in Japan.'

The trained fingers of Herr Muller touched the controls, his mild eyes, looking through thick glasses, met mine, as with a perfect dignity and reserve he assured me that the Germans would be quite well advanced in aeronautics at the advent of the next war. I felt that this calm, blue-eyed man was the type to be feared.

Farther along in the canal my engine broke down. A man on the bank said there was an engineer in the town – a very good engineer. He came back with a lanky, curly-headed young German who worked miracles with my motor. Bashing our fingers together, trying to take apart rusted junctions, engendered a certain feeling of comradeship. It came out that he was a flyer, a member of Baron Richthofen's squadron – the dreaded red circus. He had been wounded three times, the last machine-gun bullet creasing his forehead and damaging his eyesight. Otherwise, he added, he would now be flying with the Riffs in Morocco. Most of his friends had gone there.

He came into our cabin after dinner for coffee and *Schnapps*, and talked till midnight – without restraint. He began with the French, execrated them, said that all the German children

56

were being taught what the French were doing in the Ruhr --
a familiar statement to me. All the sport carnivals, he said,
had one great purpose – to fit German manhood for war.
He was intense in his hate – fanatical. German youth, he
said, had one dream.

There would soon be another war – between Japan and
America, Japan, of course, would win. England would
make a vain effort to help us. That would leave Germany
free on the Continent. She would then subjugate France.
Japan, flushed with victory, would overrun China and
Siberia. Germany, master in Europe, would absorb European Russia. Then the great stage would be set. The war!
A Germanized Europe against a Japanese East. The only
war of real importance.

That would be something to live for.

'Well, well!' we said, and put the cork in the bottle of
Schnapps.

CHAPTER TEN

The Frankischer Jura

*

I HAD been staring at it some time before I became aware of its strangeness; I was looking down on the roofs of a town – through the porthole of a boat! They lay below in the valley glinting under the moonlight. Sharp, high roofs, capping low, white walls criss-crossed with beams. Through my round sea-glass they presented an unreal fairy picture, like an old kaleidoscope. I wondered if there was another place in the world where one could look out from a ship and see houses, and roads, and rivers winding below?

We had climbed from the high plateau of Bamberg into rocky, blue mountains. We had spanned gorges, had seen little rivers flowing below and had crossed ridges. We had seen locks lying behind us, locks lying ahead–like steps. There was one stretch beyond Nurnburg where there were forty-one locks in fourteen climbing miles. Now the long climb was over.

'Over the hump of Europe,' I announced to the Crew; 'we shall now slide down into Austria.'

But, as usual, the next day found me out on the towpath at the end of a rope. Most days found me like that, and I can say, without much exaggeration, that I pulled *Flame* over the Frankischer Jura. In some places the weeds were so thick that the surface of the canal looked like dry land. They fouled the propeller like rope. In the old days the weeds were cut, and one can still see the scows. But now the Ludwig's Canal is almost deserted. A veritable inland Sargasso Sea – and will soon pass into history.

The towpath is a highway over the Frankischer Jura. On it one meets all manner of men – peasants walking from village to village, *Wandervogel*, and rovers and tramps. It is

58

lined with fruit trees in a very uniform, even-distanced parade. Sometimes the path runs through deep cuts, sometimes along the crest of high ridges, where the cherry and peach tree wave against an open blue sky.

There are 101 locks in the 107 miles of the Ludwig's. And we had 101 conversations. Lock-keepers, like barbers, are talkers by trade.

In the lonely locks the talks were quite intimate. Babies were brought out and inspected. One bronzed, smiling keeper produced three boys dressed in bed-ticking, their little bullet heads bristly with stiff hair – like a toothbrush. He stood them in line like three lean pillows, and told us their names – War, Revolution, and Peace. He added that he had obtained leave three times in the war. We gave the triumvirate a ride – father pedalling the hundred yards to the next lock on his bicycle.

In the mountains, where they lie one after the other, three or four locks were tended by one keeper. The conversations, therefore, were progressive.

'As I was saying,' said one keeper as he strained at the gate bar, 'no one won anything in this war. I myself did not get out of France until 1920. They were not happy there.'

At the next lock: 'Before the war the company paid me 135 marks a month wages and gave me my house. Now I only get 125 marks and I have to pay them ten marks every month for the house.' He shook his head sadly: 'Then I had only one lock to tend – now I have five!'

At the last lock: 'And ten per cent. of my income goes to those French!'

Each lock-keeper has his house and enough land for a garden. Some keep bees. In the pine woods their clearings are like little plantations. One rainy night I entered a lock-keeper's lodge to buy milk and eggs for our breakfast. I saw in the big comfortable room, a Mannlicher rifle, a shotgun, a stuffed pheasant and black cock, and the heads of twenty small deer. The lock-keeper smiled broadly and waved his hand out toward the drenched depths of the forest.

'All this belongs to the count. I am not supposed to shoot, but I have opportunities.'

A few days later I also had 'opportunities.' We had passed out of the canal proper and into the Altmuhl, that beautiful river which was to lead us into the Danube. Passing one jagged ruin, I heard shots, and at the next lock asked the keeper if the hunting-season was on. I was astonished to find that the deer season was open.

We put *Flame* about, and at the little village below the ruin where I had first heard the shots the *Burgomeister* declared that he would be only too delighted to go out after deer. He took down an old shotgun from the wall, shouldered his rucksack and, evading the angry glare of his wife, who made it plain that he was deserting the store, he motioned me to follow him up into the woods.

We climbed until I thought my heart would break, and at last stood on the old battlements, where the wind blew strong and clear. With his hunting-stick the *Burgomeister* pointed out and named the towns lying below. Then we entered the forest. A long tramp brought nothing more substantial than fresh tracks.

'I will drive them,' said the *Burgomeister*.

He pointed down the sheer side of the mountain and told me to descend 200 metres. My foot slipped and I slid madly down the slope. When I thought I had done 200 metres I reached out and caught hold of a tree. I brushed the pine needles from my eyes and looked up. The *Burgomeister* nodded seriously to show that I had reached the right spot.

60

I sat there holding my breath for the next forty minutes. Two hares came toward me and I let them eat unmolested. A yellow fox came slinking past. Then the *Burgomeister*.

Next morning at daybreak we tried it again, on the other side of the valley this time.

'Full of deer,' said the *Burgomeister*. I saw a beautiful sunrise over the winding strip of the Altmuhl. The *Burgomeister* sat on his hunting-stick, removed a little section of reed from his cigarette case and on it made plaintive little mewing noises.

'The buck,' he said, 'he thinks it is a deer.'

I do not think that I would have had the heart to shoot an animal that came with any such pathetic pleading as that. However, none felt so inclined. At last the *Burgomeister* said he would try driving again. I lay down among the wet pine needles and leaves at the base of a great natural arch through grey rocks. Through a cleft in the trees I could see a castle miles away across the open valley. Suddenly, utterly silent, a little red doe ran toward me. I could have hit her with an apple. Another nerve-twitching wait and then – thud – thud – thud!

Ninety yards below a magnificent stag buck crashed through the brush.

I raised the gun, realized that it was a shotgun, a 16, loaded only with buckshot – and held fire. It was like a piece of tapestry, that picture; the plunging buck against the background of trees and the little grey castle on the blue hills beyond. Beautiful, but a poor consolation.

'Ah,' said the *Burgomeister*. 'July and August are not the good months for deer. You should have been here in June or September. The woods are full of deer then. Understand?'

I told him I did. It was an international excuse.

CHAPTER ELEVEN

Shooting the Danube

*

THE Danube is motion personified. It is almost alarming, after the drowsy repose of the Ludwig's Canal and Altmuhl, to face this icy-grey flood rushing out from the gorge above Kelheim. It was a moment we had planned for for years; yet we had no map, pilot, or chart, charts of the Danube being, apparently, non-existent. We would have to 'go it blind,' like the first savage going down on a log – or the Crusaders, who swept past Ratisbon with 400 row-boats in the eleventh century. With 'here goes' sort of zest we sent *Flame* out of the Altmuhl and were whirled away like a leaf.

Three hundred miles below lay Vienna. Industrious questioning had brought out the fact that this was to be an obstacle race. The first hurdle was the stone bridge of Ratisbon, built in A.D. 1300. Most of its arches are now choked up with sandbars and rocks, and the entire flood of the Danube literally squirts through two that still remain open. Only one of these ways is negotiable.

This is barely twenty feet wide, and there are pilots in Ratisbon to take people through it. Craft coming up-river are hauled through on a chain; Ratisbon was twenty miles off.

We seemed to get there like a flash. *Flame* bowled along the empty strip of the Danube, past a few straggling villages where one felt the first breath of the east in the black, radish-shaped church domes and entered a red-rocked and gloomily forested water-gap. We sped on, rounded a bend, and there, like an old colour-print, lay the red roofs, yellow walls and the towering twin spires of the cathedral of Ratisbon. The Danube broadens here, bends and then quickly contracts.

We saw, rushing toward us, the irregular, sloping stone bridge.

The pilot? The deuce with a pilot! Anyway, we didn't have time to stop.

The open arch is by the stone river-wall, which bends out into the stream just above it, shutting off half the view. This makes it difficult, when carried along by the swift current, to straighten out in time to hit the hole of the arch. I got a fleeting glance of Ratisboners hanging over the bridge with their mouths open; decided to scrape the stone wall, if necessary, as *Flame* was slow on her rudder and the arch opened its black mouth before us. We felt *Flame* rise on the compressed flow of water and, still working to keep her stern from crashing into the wall, I felt myself bouncing about and the hot sun on my neck.

We had shot the stone bridge of Ratisbon.

The exhilaration was a great deal like strong drink, and as treacherous, for, after that thrill, we decided to try for Vienna without taking a pilot. *Flame* had been insured against total loss from Southampton to Constantinople. Quaintly enough the policy also covered one against piracy.

Ratisbon, the old Ratisbona of the Romans, is the head of Danube navigation. There is a large harbour on the right bank of the river below the city, and entering this we saw, rusting at anchor, several Bulgarian steamers which, we were told, now belong to the French. These steamers give one a tremendous impression of power. They are paddle wheelers, nearly as broad as they are long, with, usually, two stacks. They are black, bullet-nosed, with convex decks. The Donau-Dampfschiffarts-Gesellschaft—a company now owned largely by the British—operates a fleet of these over the 1,500 miles between Ratisbon and Sulina on the Black

Sea. One of the captains very kindly offered us a tow to Vienna, which we, perhaps unwisely, refused.

'As you wish,' he said, shrugging his shoulders. 'I, myself, take a pilot.'

However, we had heard so much talk about *strubels*, whirlpools and rapids that we decided to get some kind of chart. A hunt through the shipping offices and shops of Ratisbon resulted in our finding a kilometre chart which showed the locations of towns and the distances between them, and a canoe map.

The last looked useful. It had all the whirlpools marked with little red curlicues, like bottled anchovies, and a red line traced to show where it was safe for a canoe to proceed. It also gave such warnings as 'Do not meet a steamer in these rapids!'

(This map only started with Passau, so we had to do the first — and worst — eighty miles of the Danube without any chart whatsoever.)

We were to find out, to our dismay, that it was distinctly worse than no chart at all; as, following the red line, we several times piled *Flame* on the rocks.

German canoes and *falt* boats can traverse morning dew! We were also to discover that the alleged buoying of the Danube is a myth, and that the worst obstacles are not the rocks and white rapids — which one could usually see to avoid — but the wide stretches of comparatively fair-running river where one went slap on a gravel bar in midstream. We learnt, oddly enough, that it was very often safer to run the white water than take the comparatively smooth water beside.

In many reaches, with its wild and densely forested hills and green water running over shallow beds of grey rock, the

Danube is exactly like a New England river – only on a large scale. It is a mountain river. And at such gorges as Schlogen it seems to dive into the very heart of the mountains and disappear. At other times the mountains recede, fall away, and one sees them in the far distance, rising tier upon tier, until their upper ridges are lost in the clouds. There are stretches where it broadens out and flows between willow-clumped islands, where yellow sand bars glare in the sun and blue herons flap overhead. It might be the Mississippi. And then, with the suddenness of a picture found in a book, one shoots towards a little sugar-loaf hill with a grey castle on top – an Arthur Rackham sort of mountain.

Romans, Huns, Goths, Longobards, Avars, and Crusaders; waves of savages and civilizations have swept down the Danube. They have all left their mark. And to-day shooting down through some blue defile, thinking how much it resembles the Fraser, west of the Rockies, one suddenly sees a grey ruin like Haichenbach. And robber knights leap into one's mind to drive out the reveries of Siwash and salmon.

CHAPTER TWELVE

Racing into Austria

*

As *Flame* is somewhat 'blind' because of the masts and gear lashed fore and aft over her cabin, I steer with my feet — standing up. And driving this way before a blue-black lightning storm, we came down from Ratisbon. *Walhalla* — that stray bit of Greece — loomed ghostly and unreal against the tempestuous sky. We swung into a black gorge, smoking with mist, raced along swirling, wind-twisted pines and shot into the open country beyond. There we got our first real taste of the Danube — the experience that was to warn us and let us know, once and for all, that this was no Mississippi, or Hudson, or Thames — but a fierce, impatient and unkindly flood that seems to feel it has a long way to go — and a short time to get there.

Night had drawn over like a thick blanket, and we decided to give up the attempt to reach Straubing. We could still see the shores, and the vague shape of a stone jetty held out the promise of a still-water anchorage. I put *Flame* about to head into it. She was swept downstream with the current. We nosed in toward the black water near shore, and Crew, in the bow, shouted soundings:

'No bottom. Yes — five feet. Four feet. Three —'

Crash! Still some forty yards out, *Flame* had hit bottom. The crash, which nearly threw the Crew overboard, was when — her headway lost — the current had whirled *Flame* around against a rock which we had already passed safely. The yawl lay on her side, heaving and straining, with a white wave on her upriver side. Industrious work with a boat-hook got us off.

We descried the lightish bulk of a barge along-shore and made for it.

A cadaverous giant, wearing nothing but a pair of old trousers, stood on its side with a light. He made fast our line, stared at us curiously:

'Where do you come from?'

We told him that we had just come down from Ratisbon.

'Ratisbon – that boat?' He shook his head, puzzled; that boat was never built in Ratisbon.

'Praise God!' he exclaimed, when we explained to him that we had started from Holland.

'And what for?'

'Pleasure,' we said, at the same time wondering how silly it sounded.

He shook his head silently, thrust a rod down between the side rails of the barge and *Flame*, and, going into a hut-like contraption on her deck, closed the door.

Crew already had the two little stoves going. I smelt coffee and bacon and eggs, and stepped down out of the black night into the cosy, well-lighted cabin of *Flame*.

The next day we made sixty miles and reached Passau. The last fifteen miles was a swift descent down a fast-narrowing strip of water torn with rocks. We could almost see the slant of the water and had the peculiar experience of sliding down a series of water-steps, which, when we jabbed down with a boat-hook showed deep water beneath. In one swift ravine we passed our first passenger steamer, and there must have been some Americans among the crowd which rushed to her rail, for we saw arms waving and pointing down to our flag, and our wave in return was greeted with a salvo of cheers. Approaching Passau at sunset we passed through a maze of raw workings, puffing donkeys and derricks, which mark the eastern lock of the great Rhine-Donau Canal, which some day will connect these

67

two great rivers of Europe. We swung about and, straining up against the current, made fast to the grey wall of the customs-house.

'Austria!'

Regardless of the crowd which was massing up at the iron barrier of the customs, oblivious of the army of green-uniformed astonished officials, I saw Crew, balanced on the top of our gear, pointing down river – a Cortez-like attitude. I felt a queer heave inside me as I saw the bright green wall of smooth mountain side below the iron bridge, and knew that next day would find us in a new country.

> It's like a book, I think, this blooming world,
> Which you can read and care for just so long.

German customs officials are a much-maligned service. They did not even enter our cabin, handed us out a free transit with a flourish, and the bottle of *Schnapps*, which I had opened to lubricate proceedings, was eventually drunk by myself. The Austrians made us feel persons of importance.

'You are Mr. Farson,' said the Herr Direktor. 'You are ten days late.'

I admitted it, blushing. Bavaria had been too beautiful.

'His Excellency, in London,' he said, 'has written us to expect you.' He bowed and handed me a paper: 'This will carry you through Austria.'

'Pay – pay – pay ! That's what you had to do in Germany?' whispered a minor official. 'Now you are safe.'

We hoped he was right, but added the mental reservation that if his countrymen were on a par with the Germans, they would be quite good enough.

The Austrian Herr Direktor evidently felt the same way, for he looked at the German *Plombs*, sealing our engine and

68

boat, and laughed genially. 'Let them stay. We will use the same ones.'

A horrified chorus: 'But what a small boat!'

Next nightfall found us tied up above the great bridge at Linz while a coloured searchlight played red, blue and green on the white church of Urfahr on the opposite hill. Passau, although it had no tramways or taxis, was a town of plenty and peace. Linz was sad and shabby, and in the pale spindley-legged children who stared, so curiously silent, at our boat, we saw the blow which the hand of war had dealt Austria. We received a strange warning:

'Don't leave your boat,' said an onlooker; 'there are many desperate men on the river-front. They might cut it adrift – and rob it below – on the islands.'

Next day we shot the Struden below Grein – a real whirl-pool – and in a blinding white cloud-burst, ran on the rock bar off the robber castle of Aggstein. We passed the massive Benedictine Abbey of Melk, the Medelite of the Nibe-lungen, which in A.D. 1089 had been reared on its mighty rock to bring civilization to the wild eastern marches – and entered the beautiful Wachau.

We steered now always for the rough water. Many rivers had poured into the Danube – at Passau the Ilz and Inns; the last ice-grey flood being twice the width of the Danube – and, instead of decreasing in speed, the murky torrent grew swifter. After trying to make several towns, we fetched up that sunset beside the wet rocks of Spitz.

The Wachau is a valley of vineyards and castles. And here, on a bold crag, lie the ruins of Durnstein, where Richard the Lion-hearted lay prisoner.

At three the next afternoon we saw, dark blue through the rain, the bridges and low sky-line of Vienna. We shot out of the river proper into the swift canal strip above Nussdorf, saw houses and smokestacks and factories around us – entered the heart of the city, where taxis, trams and fine motors whizzed over the numerous bridges – and came to rest on the Schottenring.

A frantic packing of bags; guns, cameras, sunshades, walking-sticks, thrown into a taxi. *Flame* locked up, to go to the ship-yard for repairs on the morrow. 'Meissl und Schaden,' we exult to the taxi. And in that old-fashioned hotel, in a room with flower-boxes at the windows – and courteous servants – we heard the hot water splashing into a luxurious bath.

'Half-way across Europe!' I call out to the Crew. 'Vienna – the city of pleasure. Shall we eat at the Opera Café or Sacher's to-night?'

'I don't care,' came a soft, drowsy voice; 'I don't think I shall ever get out of this bath.'

CHAPTER THIRTEEN

No Man's River

*

WE were warned, not infrequently, in Vienna that below there we should find the Danube very precarious. Not so much the river itself, but the people on its banks would make trouble for us. Customs posts, for instance, had a nasty habit of shooting if one didn't stop. The river ran between hostile nations like a line drawn between fighters. If one side was kind to us the other would make it tough as a result. One could never tell just what the Czechs would do; when they were nice they were very, very nice; and when they were not they were – simply God-awful! We left Vienna late one afternoon feeling that anything and everything might happen to us in the next forty-eight hours.

The first foray was Hainburg, which we reached about noon. For some reason, which I can never make out, they always seem to place the customs posts in the swiftest and narrowest bits of the river – ancient bridge-heads, I suppose. Hainburg, on the Austrian frontier, is an ancient town strung out at the foot of a sheer rocky hill on the outer curve of a sharp bend in the Danube. Two towing-steamers, coming in opposite directions, engulfed me before Hainburg. I saw a group of khaki-clad customs officials leaping up and down on the bank, signalling for me to come in and be 'passed.' Although we pointed up-stream, the current swept us steadily by them. Their shouts and gestures grew violent. I told the Crew that we should probably have to omit the formality of passing through the Austrian customs – and pass by them.

'Then get on the other side of the river,' she said, 'and zigzag a little.'

71

Thus we passed out of Austria. As if it had rushed to help us get past them, the Danube suddenly slowed down after Hainburg. We swept around the big bend at Deveny, the old castle, destroyed by the French, grim and grey on its peak, and entered a broad stretch of green water. There we saw the first of those buoys – sticks stuck in the river with branches on top – which are supposed to mark the ship's channel.

Following this simple device we were pitched suddenly into our cockpit and found ourselves hard aground in the very middle of a wide stretch of river. I jumped overboard, my mind full of misgivings. Were we to stay there for ever?

'You do look funny,' said the Crew, producing our camera; 'now stand like that – with the boat-hook. Better take the passport, too,' she advised, 'in case you're swept down the river.'

About two o'clock that afternoon we saw a high, gaunt ruin on the top of a hill, a town lying below it, and a bridge. This we knew was Bratislava – the home of the Czechs.

We slid past the old ruin of Maria Theresa's palace, under the bridge, and came up alongside a barge. The current was still quite swift, and several men ran to help us. Among them I saw three soldiers in uniform. Gosh!

When we were fast, one of the soldiers came to the barge side and smiled down at us; he saluted. I saluted. He said several things in Czech. I saluted – said several things in English. A draw. Another soldier came up. The Crew took him on – in German. No result. Then I saw something on his breast that reminded me of an odd bit of history; the trek of the Czech *légionnaires* into Russia – the St. George's cross.

72

'*Govoritie po Russkie?*' I asked.

'*Da! Govoritie?*'

It was like rubbing the lamp. The first soldier burst into Russian – the Czech tongue is very similar to Russian in spots – and other Czech soldiers galloped over the barge decks.

'You're going to stop, of course,' they chorused, 'and see Bratislava? We have a parade here to-morrow, the Legii.'

'Won't I have a great deal of trouble?'

'Of course not – this is Bratislava.'

This was our entry into old Presburg-Pozsony-Bratislava – the three-name town, where all the signs in the streets, all the menus, are in three tongues: Czech, German and Magyar. The police told me it was the deuce of a job having to be such linguists as at least before you threw a man into jail you ought to tell him why you are doing it.

Cafés have regular placards on their doorways. On one side a painted bunch of grapes, with under it the names *Vino-Wein-Bor*; on the other side a painted glass of beer and *Pivo-Bier-Sor*. Roast veal in the restaurant is *Tefacia-Pecienka*, *Kalbsbraten*, or *Borjusult*, depending upon whether Czech, German or Magyar blood flows in your veins. This old town, nearly half of whose inhabitants were German, was once the Hungarian capital, where the Hapsburgs were crowned. Among other things, this coveted bit of the little Carpathians was taken away from Hungary and given to the Czechs by the wise men at Paris.

Next day we passed down through a broad, tranquil river that seemed almost deserted. For forty miles we did not see a house, but a close inspection of the thick beech forest on the banks showed soldiers every now and then peering at us from the bushes. We knew that some place we had passed the Hungarian frontier on the right bank of the river and that for some distance farther on we should still flank Czechoslovakia on our left. But where and when and how far were questions unanswered.

Travellers have described this part of the Danube as being uninteresting and monotonous. Perhaps, from a steamer's deck, it might seem so. One misses a lot in such fashion. And I suppose that travellers, satiated with pine forests and mountains – which seems to be the only ' scenery' in Europe that is ever visited – would feel a little depressed by this stretch of deep beech forest criss-crossed with waterways. From close at hand, on the *Flame*, we could see the thousands of little waterfalls where the Danube plashed over its stone banks; the black cormorants fishing, and the motionless herons in the green bayous beyond. If we had had a canoe – and the Danube is a canoeist's paradise – we should have explored some of these fascinating waterways.

Occasionally we caught glimpses of the white walls of villages on the high ground farther inland. Little bulging black church domes. And at sunset that day we made out the bulk of a barge at the foot of a quiet run of water. We passed by three water-mills – those queer Noah's arks that lie out in midstream to let the swift water grind the wheat the peasants bring out in skiffs – and entered a smooth strip of fast-reddening water. We ran *Flame* on to a flat shore of mud, and saw over a sort of dike the grey thatched roofs of a village. Three soldiers ran towards us.

'Hungarians?' asked the Crew.

I saw the old St. George crosses of Russia again – we were still in Czechoslovakia. Great excitement! Our flag? Americans! A crowd of black booted peasant men, and bare-legged girls and women – looking like lamp shades in

74

the spread of their seventeen petticoats – trotted along with us and the commander of the port through the fields of sunflowers and corn to the village. A wide, dusty street flanked by acacias and little low, white, mud buildings.

In the inn we saw a group playing ninepins – bowling wooden balls down a dirt lane and betting furiously. The proprietor, flasks of gold-coloured wine clutched in his fat, hairy fingers, bade us sit under a big horse-chestnut, while the commander telephoned back to Bratislava to find out if we were what we said we were.

I heard the conversation, one end of it, at least, and from it gathered that the official in Bratislava was much disturbed over being interrupted at dinner. Meanwhile, the Crew had been deep in sign-talk with an old peasant woman, and I saw them go into the cornfield, the Crew snatching off the fat ears.

The next day at sunset we saw, like some strange mirage, the towering dome of the great Basilica of Esztergom – iridescent, and unreal against the bronze Hungarian mountains. We cast anchor off the palace of the primate of Hungary, and saw as we turned in to sleep that night a lonely sentinel on the crumbling red wall of the old fort once held by the Turks. There was barbed wire at the bridge-head leading into Czechoslovakia, the gleam of a bayoneted sailor on guard. The commander of the port, bidding us good night, pointed with his cigarette to the town on the other side of the Danube.

'I used to live over there, but now I can never go home.'

CHAPTER FOURTEEN

From Vienna to Budapest

★

IN Vienna there is a sidewalk café where news-gatherers from all the world meet; spies, agitators, revolutionists – and mere journalists. The London *Times* man chats with a swarthy Bulgarian, asking circuitous questions in an innocent manner. The Bulgar, knowing that the foppish young man behind them is an emissary of Moscow, answers accordingly. The Hungarian gives one reply to the Czech and its opposite to the *Daily News* correspondent. Information and misinformation are passed back and forth, bartered for and exchanged. Then each man goes out, weighs the mass in his judgment, sorts out the truth from the propaganda he has heard and sends a wire off to some place. The papers publish it that day or the next.

They said to me there, 'You are on the edge of civilization now – in Vienna.'

Sitting down here in Budapest, hearing the laughter and life of the gay evening parade on the Corso and seeing across the clean, tree-shaded Danube the stupendous grey pile of the royal palace, I am wondering on which edge they meant. Surely the savants of Vienna knew what they were talking about – this part of the world is their playground. Yet this city is infinitely more beautiful than Vienna, refreshingly cleaner, and gives one a feeling of security, contentment and well-being almost unknown in the Austrian capital.

A writer has to watch his superlatives when describing this pearl of the Danube, for Budapest seems the most adorable, bewitching and intoxicating city in Europe. It is all that Vienna might have been – and isn't.

FROM VIENNA TO BUDAPEST

Fine buildings, I know, do not denote stability. The violent upheavals of Russia usually explode before the yellow Virgin of Kazan cathedral. Lenin dropped his poison into the Russian mind from the beautiful balcony of the dancer Shizinskayia. Bela Kun slept in the ornate rooms of the very hotel in which I now write. And, if Vienna does impress one as being somewhat out-at-the-elbows, it is only to be expected when one realizes how atrociously Austria suffered from the war, and thereafter at the hands of the peace conference.

That is no gauge. Austria has stabilized her currency with the *schilling*; in Hungary one still goes about with a pocketful of thousand and million kronen notes. Cigarettes cost 25,000 per packet. That seems a gauge. Things cost more in Budapest. Yet there is a certain aimlessness in the atmosphere of Vienna, a sinister indifference, that makes one feel apprehensive. As if – 'To-morrow? Why, to-morrow I, myself, may be' – whirled around in another social explosion. There is a 'feel,' a quality to the atmosphere of all situations very often more veracious than their tangible substance.

I have two processions in mind as an instance.

In Vienna I went to the funeral of Mohaple. I went there quite prepared to hear shots – and run. For hours I watched a silent, dogged procession file past – some say the biggest funeral ever held in Vienna – and I heard almost no sound but the measured thud-thud of thousands of feet. People about me conversed in whispers. When the banners of the 'Hooked Cross' came past they fell utterly silent, seeming to be holding their breath. Then came the black-gaitered horsemen escorting the silver-decked hearse: Mohaple, the innocent victim of an hysterical mob, passed silently to his rest.

77

'What did you think of it?' I asked an observer afterwards.

'I think it marks the turn against Socialism. Did you see
the parade of street-car employees – the ones in blue with
red facings? There's a protest! The street-cars are run by
the city; the city is Socialist. Those men took an awful
chance with their jobs.' My friend shuddered as if a chill
had passed down his spine: 'But didn't that silence get on
your nerves?'

It had. That suspension of the expression of thought had
been as pregnant with trouble as an uplifted sword. The
local newspapers duly reported that the funeral of Mohaple
'went off quietly.'

Here in Budapest I went to see the procession of St.
Stephen. The procession from the Coronation Church of
high clergy, Government officials and nobles, bearing the
thousand-year-old mummified hand of St. Stephen, the
first king of Hungary. Between dense lanes of talkative
Hungarians, held back by police on prancing black horses,
approached one of the most solemn and picturesque processions in Europe. The churchmen, with bowed heads,
swept past in splendour of surplice, hats, crimsons, scarlets
and magentas. A flower-bed of young peasant girls. The
slow, challenging stride of companies of infantry – they
march, slapping down the entire sole of the foot, bending
the knees backward – a militant step. Hussars, in cream
coloured scarlet-lined cloaks thrown over their shoulders.
Nobles and aristocrats in a mosaic of gold, jewelled spurs,
feathered turbans, furs and black leather. Rising out of
their midst, scintillating in the vivid white sunlight, the
crystal casket containing the little blue, shrivelled hand.
Admiral Horthy, regent of the kingdom of Hungary, came

along with the rising cheer of the populace, wearing a wide emerald-green ribbon across his blue sailor breast.

I followed into the chapel, and with the long line passed by the spears of the four motionless guards clad in green and scarlet, before the priest, who wiped the kiss prints from the glass covering the sacred hand of St. Stephen.

'It is the last mediæval pageant in Europe,' said a friend to me afterward; 'a gorgeous spectacle. They have one every year.'

But it was much more than that. The defiant step of the soldiery, the determined look on the faces of the old nobles and aristocrats, the jewelled spurs, swords, feathers, the snapping, sharp step of the haughty, flashing hussars – these all had their voice – made it plain that:

'This is the old order of things. This is country and kingship and glory. We are the Magyars!'

Here are two processions, one a funeral that seeped through the silent streets of Vienna like the discharge from an old septic sore – the very symbol of a nation's disease. The other, a religious ceremony that, with its steel and pomp, spoke of a nation sound at heart, plagued by none save one burning thought – to regain its past glory.

As I write this the lilt of a haunting, melancholic refrain runs through my head. It is from the Hungarian operetta, *The Singing Captain* – about lost Transylvania:

'I have crossed the Kirielyholgo,
I have lost my hussar shako.
My God in Heaven! I swear that I shall find it,
I shall search it, I shall find it,
My dear old hussar shako.'

CHAPTER FIFTEEN

Admiral Horthy, Governor of the Kingdom of Hungary

*

PERHAPS no present ruler in Europe has been more consistently misrepresented and is less clearly defined in the public eye than Admiral Horthy, Governor of the Kingdom of Hungary. Regent of an empty throne, guardian of the possessions and lands of the crown of St. Stephen – and elected to this office, some say for life – he is called 'Your Serene Highness.' Yet he refuses to wear any other than the blue and gold uniform of an admiral – in the navy which no longer exists.

Driving along the twenty-five miles of jolty road to the summer palace of Godollo, I wondered what sort of man we would meet. I had heard him discussed in Chicago, London – and only a fortnight before in Vienna – as a Dictator.

The dirt and stone road went through flat, open country; except for the little white, thatched-roofed villages and long-horned Hungarian cattle, might have been Illinois. Yellow melons ripened in waving fields of corn. We mounted a rising hillside of scrub oak, went through thick woods, and I saw a khaki-clad guard standing before a yellow picket fence. His bayoneted rifle flung over his back projected above the bushy cock feathers in his curly-brimmed black felt hat. Still looking through the grove of oak and horse-chestnut to catch a first glimpse of the old hunting-lodge of the Hapsburgs, we were whirled into a driveway and brought up before a low, buff-coloured stone and plaster building. A captain of the guard, hand on sword hilt, clicked his smart boots and bowed sharply.

We were led through an archway, up a curved flight of

80

stone steps to a landing bright with many flowers in pots and fairly bristling with the antlers of deer, across the empty parquet floor of a ball-room. Then with an almost disconcerting suddenness we found ourselves in a pleasant, homely drawing-room, filled with books and flowers, where three men and a very beautiful woman were having tea.

'Your Serene Highness.'

Admiral Horthy was shaking my hand with a grip that cut short my bow.

'This is an old friend of ours,' said Madame Horthy, turning to a magnificent old man, dressed in the braided black coat and top boots of old Hungary, 'Baron Pronay.' Smiling, brown-haired Istvan Horthy came forward and was introduced as 'my son.' We sat down around the little tea-table. . . .

There is a certain, almost super-abundant, physical and mental vitality about Admiral Horthy that is infectious. Born in 1868, he gives one the impression of being hardly a day over forty. His brown eyes are sparkling and his black hair has the sheen of great health. He has a clean-cut, square face, with a nut-cracker chin, that is singularly merry. The Admiral loses himself completely in his subject while talking, sits on the edge of his chair and grips one with his eyes. There is a crispness about the smart set of his blue and gold uniform, a restless activity of his spare, well-knit figure, which reeks of the quarter-deck.

I asked if he did not yearn to get back to blue water again.

'I would walk,' he said, smiling tragically, making a gesture of helplessness with his hands.

'But only a bird can get out of this country!' he protested. Hungary to-day is completely cut off from the sea by a ring of not too friendly states. Again the same vivid gesture – the mounting flight of a bird.

He laughed ruefully: 'Our ancestors did not pick the right place for a kingdom – the best place for a kingdom is an island. Look at England ! Our Parliament is just six years younger than England's, and at that time, in the beginning, we were the same in number of people. To-day, Hungary has only 8,000,000, and the British must have 35,000,000 at least!'

He spoke with a passionate admiration of his beloved Magyar race, told of the days following the Bela Kun orgy.

'We had nothing. Our country had been sacked – we could not pay for anything. Even the soldiers.'

Here I got a sharp touch of reality that even an avenging army is paid.

'But,' – the Governor clenched his fine hand – 'we had loyalty' – a coin, evidently, that always rates at par value in hot-blooded Hungary.

And it was easy to understand the successful leadership of this admiral through such troubled times, for Governor Horthy is the type of man that has the power of arousing tremendous personal devotion. He has the divine fire. In the furious naval battle he fought in the Straits of Otranto his ship received eighty-six direct hits; he was wounded three times, and, on a cot, brought his battered flagship into port.

Putting down my teacup, I met the deep-seated stare of Baron Pronay – like an old eagle. 'A friend of mine,' he said suddenly, 'told me that he lived for three months in New York, and saw only one horse!'

I mentioned that I was going down to see the Hungarian stud farms at Mezohegyes. The old nobleman smiled.

'Excellent! But Mezohegyes is modern – the Hungary of to-day; you should also go to the Hortobagy, there you will see the Hungary of 300 years ago. . . .'

At this instant a servant came in to announce that the four-in-hand of Baron Pronay was waiting. The old gentleman stood up to go; Admiral Horthy rose to accompany him, smiling aside the graceful protestations of the old nobleman and went with him through the door. . . .

'Hungary of 300 years ago!' smiled Madame Horthy. 'That is also Baron Pronay. He is the last of the old Hungarians. He still dresses as they did; his life in his castle is almost mediæval.'

Madame Horthy related, how, in the Bela Kun terror, the Bolsheviks had occupied his castle. But, when they had attempted also to imprison the old aristocrat, not only the peasantry of his estate, but the village as well, marched in a body to the gates, declaring: 'No, this we will not suffer – that you should take our baron!' And the Reds, not knowing quite what would come of it, left him in peace.

Admiral Horthy returned, still smiling from saying goodbye to his guest. 'He will never use a motor,' he said, shaking his head. 'He is charming.' The Admiral spoke lovingly of the fine age which Baron Pronay represented.

'Ha!' he exclaimed suddenly, shrugging his shoulders, 'I have had no leave for six years.' He pointed to the cigarettes, lighted one for himself: 'How did you bring your boat across Europe?'

We told him of our beloved *Flame*. His eyes smiled.

'How many men have you?' asked Madame Horthy.

I indicated the Crew – and they laughed. 'Think, Nicholas,' exclaimed Madame Horthy, 'they do everything for themselves!'

83

'Fine!' said the Admiral. 'Well, my dear, that's what we used to do – when we went sailing.'

The conversation drifted naturally to the things he loved best. He spoke of early days on the sea, his two trips round the world – of tiger-shooting in Poona.

'The only time,' he said, laughing suddenly, 'when I was tempted to skip ship.'

He explained how an urgent summons had recalled him and his brother-officers on the eve of a big tiger-shoot arranged for them by the Maharajah of Cooch Behar. He spoke of polo in Constantinople, of Egypt before the English were there, of the British aptitude for tolerant colonization. He admires them.

'It was not pleasant,' he said, 'to fight such fine people.' He spoke of shooting geese on the Hortobagy; how, with sixteen geese in his skiff, his dog had clambered aboard and capsized them.

'Think!' he exclaimed, laughing heartily, 'after a life at sea – I had to come to the Hortobagy to get wrecked!' He spoke of the long flights of geese dropping down from the sky, of red sunsets, with all the poetry and emotion of the inveterate hunter. He raised his sunburned hands, pointed as though holding a shotgun.

Chatting there in that cosy room, with the rain driving outside, about the pleasant life of sport and adventure, one forgot the life this man was leading – the ministers, who would motor out to Godollo on the morrow – the routine of state.

'I shall be happy,' said Madame Horthy, 'when we can get back to our own estate in Central Hungary. Perhaps next year it will be ready for us; my garden is there. This is not ours.'

'All this,' said the Admiral, suddenly solemn, – he pointed to the carpet, the chairs, waved a hand toward the drenched trees of Hungary. – 'belongs to the crown of St. Stephen.'

The crown of St. Stephen! There, in his unswerving loyalty to this ancient crown, one finds the key to the character and actions of Admiral Horthy. One can see him, torn between allegiance to country and king, pleading with his sovereign not to imperil all that the crown of St. Stephen entailed. One can picture him, reasoning it out for himself – just what the crown of St. Stephen denoted. Many a man with fewer opportunities would have made himself king. Yet this man, whose whole natural bent is for the sea and sport and outdoor things, has sacrificed them all to shoulder the burden of a crown that he will never wear, and that, but for him, might have passed out of existence six years ago.

'There may be many kings for this country – but never this country for a king!'

To Admiral Horthy the crown of St. Stephen is Hungary. Who will one day wear that crown is a question that only the future can decide. Meanwhile it has a staunch watch-dog.

.   .   .   .

A few days later we found a note at our hotel from this most courteous of Governments saying that the City of Debrezcen had invited us to be its guests on the Great Hungarian Plain. The Government also gave us M. Andor Sentmiklosi, of the Foreign Office, as charming a companion as one could wish. And Andor Sentmiklosi brought his collapsible bath-tub.

CHAPTER SIXTEEN

The Inn on the Puszta

★

THE veterinary had come down to the station. He rasped to the professor:

'I am looking for some one to drink with me to-night.'

The *csikos*, cowboy, on the buckboard made not the least effort to help us. Although he had been impressed into service as driver, he was still a *csikos* of the Hortobagy – a free man. He smoked contemptuously, his cigarette dangling over his stubbly rough jaw and chin-strap. One leg hung listlessly over the other. I could see, between his black boots and divided blue skirts, his bare knees glistening white in the moonlight. His whole bearing expressed the creed of his cast:

'God in His heaven is certainly a great God – but neither am I a dog.'

Sentmiklosi, the professor and I struggled out with our bags, the professor still wiping some *Schnapps* from his lips. 'The veterinary,' he said, and added explainingly: 'Only the oxen drink alone on the Hortobagy.' The *csikos* spoke to his horses.

There is a path of rough stones from the station to the inn on the Puszta, but only a tyro would use it. The *csikos* took the edge of the ditch. We pitched along, one wheel whirling in space. The acacia-trees vanished, left us alone on the Puszta, facing a bleak horizon, barren, and desolate, as if drawn with a ruler. Then straining my eyes in the moonlight I saw, like a gibbet, the black balance-arm of a well.

There is a picture, by Verestchagin, of a wild, lonely steppe, utterly desolate and implacable, empty, except for a pile of human skulls on the top of which sits a crow – that is the Puszta, the great Hungarian plain.

The innkeeper strolled out and shook hands all around. He rearranged his moustachios. A little girl shot out like a rabbit, seized and kissed the Crew's hand, and walked off with our camera. The *csikos* lighted a fresh cigarette.

In the last clump of acacias, chalky white in the moonlight, stood the low, mud-walled inn, cavernous shadows under its porticoes – strangely Mexican. We lugged our bags past the horse-racks and dumped them on the red tiles of the veranda.

'I suppose,' said Sentmiklosi, 'we shall now have to drink.'

The professor, however, had not left the horse-racks. He was leaning, lost in reverie, drinking in the fresh, cold wind of his adored Puszta. His shaved head gleamed like a fresh skull. He turned, speaking for my understanding, in German:

'*Der Hortobage – Der Hortobage.*'

He is a fine fellow, the professor. The Hortobagy is his passion. He roams its wild plain, sleeping under the stars and watching the red fire of its sunrise. In his veins still flows the blood of countless generations of nomads. Even teaching geography to pasty-faced students in winter fails to make him forget the smoke of old camp-fires. He walked towards us slowly. As to the question of rooms, he did not seem to care, but followed us about moodily, stopping to gaze out of the porticoes. But then he had been to the inn on the Puszta.

The inn is divided into two sections. One belongs to the city of Debrezcen, the other is for those who pass by. The rooms are on the side of the quadrangle that faces the Puszta;

they are low, square, with windows that pierce walls two feet in thickness. Each room has two windows, one facing the archway under the portico, the other the patio. They are double windows, with heavy iron-bar grills between the small panes. They remind one of the days, not so long ago, when life was a tricky thing on the Puzsta, and of the song:

'God has made the Robber Fellow,
And has rewarded all the Rich Men with him.

For if the Robber Fellow would not be,
The Rich Men would never pray to God.'

The inn smelt of sour milk, puppy dogs, and the spilt wine of a hundred years.

'Has this sheet been changed since the last man slept in this bed?' asked Sentmiklosi, holding up an amber-coloured clot that was securely attached to the comforter by buttons.

'No,' said the innkeeper.

'Could I have a fresh one?'

The innkeeper, looking at him wonderingly, said, 'Yes, perhaps it might be arranged.'

Our room had green chalked walls and a conventional design on the slope toward the ceiling, overhung by a magnificent shooting-scene. Nine wild geese, almost life size, honked over our heads from one corner. In the rushes of the opposite side a huntsman pointed a smooth-bore fowling-piece. Five geese swam, unperturbed in the corner alongside him; three rose into the air from the diagonal corner — and one goose fell dying. A certain amount of red wine — and I saw those geese falling by hundreds.

The Crew dipped her face in the small basin of water already poured out. I followed after. There was neither light nor a looking-glass. Rosza, the little bare-footed girl with the handkerchief tied over her head, darted in, always without knocking, and, apparently, without reason. She just darted in – and then out.

People kept arriving at the inn on the Puszta in a most unexplainable fashion. They seemed suddenly to come into being from no place. A stunning-looking, black-eye-browed Hungarian girl came along under the porticoes, vividly black in her white riding-coat and tam-o'-shanter.

Sentmiklosi explained that this was Sunday night, therefore there would be a big company for dinner – the captain of the Hortobagy, his two ex-hussar sons, relations and friends, also sweethearts. 'He is here,' said Sentmiklosi.

I saw, talking with the professor, a perfect centaur of a man. He was the horseman personified. I had never seen such a fine figure of a man, one so born to the horse, the free life of the plain. He was small, like our American plainsmen, what one would call a 'tight' figure – inexpressibly dapper and neat. Like all old Hungarians, he wore tight-fitting, stiff, sharp-toed black boots. They reached the top of his thin calves. His slightly bowed legs were encased in slim, rather tight-fitting trousers.

Like all Hungarians, he wore a second coat, draped over his shoulders – they never seem to use the sleeves of their great-coats in Hungary except to sew them up and carry things in them. He was puffing a priceless, long meerschaum pipe, puffing complacently – occasionally. His trim moustachios pointed, dagger-like, to very deep-set wind-shaded eyes. He bowed with the grace of an ancestry to which the bow was an art. Then – Why attempt to describe the wisdom and perfect flow of welcome I saw in those expressive brown eyes?

'We must leave them alone,' said Sentmiklosi. 'Many litres of red wine will have to be drunk before they decide on the programme of to-morrow. Will it be the chestnut as the off horse, or the black one? Shall we take two buck-boards, or will the captain ride on his horse? This is the Hortobagy.'

Thirty people gathered in a room less than twenty feet square, and prepared to eat dinner and make a night of it.

'The veterinary,' said Sentmiklosi, 'has company. How he loves it!'

I saw the horse-doctor, or part of him, behind a huge *stein* of beer. Between gulps he was talking to a laughing, grey-haired old lady. 'The wife of the – how you call it? He is a professor who studies locusts and butterflies and insects. He is here for research.'

'Bug man,' I said.

'Yes,' said Sentmiklosi, 'that is it. She is the husband of the bug man.'

When I saw the little entomologist I realized that Sentmiklosi's mistake of the relationship had been in truth very accurate.

We sat on a bench with our backs to the wall. The inn-keeper, always smoking a cigarette, shuffled in with sandalled feet, usually with flasks of wine between hairy fingers; but the first dish was soup. This was red, and in this gory hot pool I fished out a ladle of chicken's feet, blind-eyed herds – and more chicken's feet. Also unmentionable inte-riors. The professor opened his mouth.

He had an odd way of eating, rather scientific, in fact, based on the principle of the thrashing-machine. The edible parts went down his throat, while simultaneously a steady stream of bones, beaks, and claws was ejected sideways past his jaw to the floor. The captain had a flare for the eyes, gouging them out of the chicken heads with his fork, and by a process of suction obtained all that lurked within the skull. Very deft! I saw him remove the covering of a chicken-foot as if popping a grape.

As no one but the oxen ever drink alone on the Hortobagy, it was necessary, when anyone felt thirsty, to propose a toast all around. This required a stiff head – and much ingenuity. We toasted, internationally, in German, out of courtesy to the Crew and myself. I used my available vocabulary, and then thought up a most useful sort of standard kind of toast:

'*Auf uns!*' I toasted, raising my glass.

'*Auf uns!*' gaily roared out the professor, the veterinary, the station-master, the bug man, the two ex-hussar sons, five pretty girls, and a cadet from the army. The innkeeper rushed for another supply of red wine.

The next course was pig. And I can't see why Americans do not adopt some of these simple fashions of preparing food. For instance, with the pig – woolly Mongolica – all that is necessary, after scalding him to remove his thick coat of grey hair, is to lay him on a board, take an axe, and simply chop him into sections. He is then thrown in a pot with two or three handfuls of paprika, and boiled.

'*Auf uns!*' gurgled the professor, caught midway between a Mongolica ear and the toast of the captain.

'*Auf*–' said the Crew. She could no longer say '*uns.*'

The night wore on but not out. Blue smoke lay in heavy layers about the oil-lamp on the ceiling. The dashing ex-hussar sons changed their places frequently, leaning facing the backs of their chairs, in deep conversation with their lady friends. The veterinary, whose voice boomed through the laughter and chat like a bull-frog's, waved his arms, let his lower lip droop and stared with lowered head at whoever addressed him. The bug man danced the *csadas*. People went out and came in; they went out without hats and came back with them. The girl with the white 'tam' put on her gauntlets, looked at them, cocking her little finger admiringly — drank more wine. Laughter, laughter, laughter!

Lacsi, the young ex-hussar, stood before me. Even in the Norfolk shooting jacket — he had shoulder-straps on it — he still looked the cavalryman. His smart brown boots glistened in the dim lamplight.

'I will sing you,' he said, 'the songs of the Hortobagy!'

In a voice that seemed to smell of old camp-fires, rich, full-throated, and wild, he roared out the old lays of the *csikos*:

'For I am a *csikos* on the Puszta, and not a *gulyas*,
I will wind my lasso on my shoulder,
I will saddle my white-footed horse,
And I will pull down the brilliant stars of heaven.'

He poured out two tumblers of wine, and gave me one, and we drained them. Bang! Lacsi put down his glass.

I staggered out into the moonlight. In the pale, flawless sky there was only the moon and one star. The trees by the inn standing motionless, the dead white walls under the moon. Horses moving.

I came back. Sang Lacsi:

'Innkeeper, innkeeper, make me a fish-dish,
And give me a good sealed wine.
And your servant keep as guard outside the door
To warn if the camp guard should come.'

'Wonderful!' I said, staring up into the flashing black eyes of Lacsi. Suddenly he pulled me over and kissed me. 'You should be a Magyar!'

I would like to be, but I don't think my physique would stand it. I left them — a small and rather determined party of veterans by now — and went in to undress under the flying wild geese. Suddenly I heard singing quite close at hand. I stopped, in the act of blowing out the small candle. I turned around. There they were in the patios, Lacsi and the army cadet, each with an arm around the other's shoulders, serenading me:

> '. . . saddle my white-footed horse,
> And I will pull down the brilliant stars of heaven.'

I climbed on a chair, thrust my arm out through the grating, a cold wind, almost of dawn, whistled through my pyjamas, but the warm grip of Lacsi held on to my hand.

'Magyars!' I saluted, and fell back into bed.

CHAPTER SEVENTEEN

Cowboys of Hungary

★

'The wild geese and the herons cry,
"Good man, you will remain alone, alone on the Puszta.
For here no one has a winter refuge,
Every bird hastens to his quarter." '

THE long north wind was piling up the white clouds on the Puszta like a sea. It whirled the scattered, flat plaques of water, sent the wild duck skirling aloft, whistling down the wild lonely plain. The *menes*, the horse herd, fed uneasily, flitching the short, ankle-deep grass. Crack! Crack-crack! A *csikos* galloped after some stragglers, drove them before him, his quirt snapping like pistol-shots in the air. He dropped off his little black mare, lifted off her the scant saddle like a cloth – the *csikos* saddle has no girth or cinch-strap – and slung it over his shoulder. He strode toward me.

Whether it is part of their arrogance or because of the chin-strap, the *csikos* seldom remove their flat-crowned, black hats. The professor bared his bald head, offered the *csikos* his tobacco pouch, and cracked a joke with him in Magyar. The *csikos* accepted some – kindly.

'It will be cold to-night,' said the professor.

The *csikos'* thin lips curled slightly; he shrugged his shoulders under the gorgeous embroidered cloak of white felt. What was cold to a *csikos*!

It was strange to stand there on this wild plain in far-eastern Hungary and see cowboys, and lassos, and quirts – to see the long line of cattle, white dots on the sky-line. Stranger still to see three black and white storks wading through a vivid patch of yellow daisies and sea lavender – the low mound of a pagan tomb far beyond them.

94

COWBOYS OF HUNGARY

Huns, Avars, Tartars, Magyars – the great Mongol hordes have swept over the Puszta, built their camp-fires, watered their horses, fought and slain one another – and passed into history. But the Puszta remains defiant of time – as it was in the days of Atilla. The very dogs that came with Yenghis Khan, nearly 800 years ago, are still there, white and woolly, guarding the sheep. The Turks came, swept the plains, offered shelter in the city of Debrezcen – and death to all who stayed outside its gates. For 150 years the Ismanlis held the Puszta. And through it all, fighting, hacking, their swords red with blood, the Magyars held fast. Something in these wild, desolate steppes held the blood of their hearts, blood they spilled freely to hold. To-day the *csikos* of the Puszta are Magyars. There are four classes of men on the Puszta – *csikos*, the horsemen (cowboys); *gulyas*, the cattlemen; *guhasz*, the shepherds ; *kondas*, the swine-herds.

The *csikos* are the aristocrats, but the *guhasz* are the cleverest. They are the philosophers of the Puszta. Perhaps because in the long, drowsy days they lie on their backs and ask questions of the sun and the blue skies; perhaps because of the close touch they acquire with the fundamentals of life when their charges are lambing. They are thrifty, and as each *guhasz* gets anywhere from ten to fifty per cent. of the new-born as part payment, depending upon his skill as a midwife, some of them are quite rich.

The *csikos* are spendthrifts, great drinkers, but must keep a certain amount of money to hand, as it is one of the rules applying to all the men on the Puszta that each is responsible, in cash, for any loss of his charges. Also, each *csikos* must own three horses.

All classes are only engaged by the year; and there is a

great 'market' in Debrezcen on the seventh day of each January, where their services are bargained for. For each horse under his charge the head *csikos* gets for a season ten kilos of wheat and a sum of money equal to four shillings. He has to pay his assistant *csikos* from this. The *csikos* are out on the Puszta from April 1st to November 1st without leaving it. Half of the Puszta is owned by the city of Debrezcen; the other half belongs to 4,000 or more private owners.

The *menes* (horse herds) are divided into two classes; the 'fancy drove,' for breeding purposes only; and the 'lazy drove,' the horses the city of Debrezcen sends out to recuperate for the summer. A nice thought, that – horses sent out on their summer vacation. It is quite typical of the kindly Hungarian – the kindest race I have met.

Foals came and nuzzled me as I talked to the *csikos*. Their mothers thrust searching, sniffing noses into my pockets. The chestnut herd surged around me, all over me, pushed and jostled – "Let me have a sniff.' One of them, very courteously, licked the side of my face. The *csikos* walked into the herd, flapped his saddle on to his mare, and was away on the instant. Crack! Crack! Crack! He galloped towards the blue sky-line.

They are hard men, these *csikos*, wonderful riders, though not in the same class with the Americans with the lariat, which they throw from on foot. Their saddle is merely an apology, or something to protect their blue divided skirts – or trousers? – from wear. They sleep out, wrapped in their thick white felt cloaks, and live almost exclusively on bacon – thick slabs of fat Mongolica – which they cook on sharp sticks over dung fires, and a paste, made from flour, which they half fry with chunks of bacon in an iron pot and then add water to taste. It is usually almost a mucilaginous soup.

Their faces around the glowing camp-fire glisten with grease. An angled stick thrust in a wooden cup in the ground serves as a crane from which they suspend the pot. Their cooking-places are usually the little horseshoe-shaped windbrakes made of rushes, that stand up, like Kanaka girdles, on the flat, open plain.

We sat one night, the professor, Sentmiklosi, the Crew and I, in one of these windbrakes, toasted sour bread with the *csikos*, and then drenched it in the fat which dripped from the thick slabs of white bacon we turned on sticks over the acrid, burning cow-dung. Above the waving rush-tops we could see the smoke snatched by the wind and pulled off down sky. We blinked, closed our eyes – and bit. We had not trusted the professor's recommendations, but discovered, on trying, a queer pungent taste to the greasy hot toast that was rather enticing.

One very old *csikos*, whose moustache drooped like a Chinaman's, withdrew from beneath this barrier a mangled piece of greasy toast his toothless old gums were having a hard time to masticate. He pressed it upon me, in friendship – and, in friendship, I ate it.

'That old *csikos*,' said the professor, 'should be a *gulyas* – he is starting now to fall off his horse. When a *csikos* starts to fall off his horse he always turns *gulyas*.'

I looked at the greasy, very Mongolian face, the black eyes sunk deep beneath a low sloping forehead. In the red light it did not need a great stretch of fancy to think that I was facing one of the nomadic horsemen of the great Mongol drive. The intricate designs, worked in many-coloured wool on his heavy white felt cloak, were the same as those I had seen in the Esterhazy collection in Budapest – centuries old.

It is said that, until the war, money was an almost negligible thing on the Puszta. The plainsmen were paid in wheat, pigs, and tobacco, and lived on a barter system entirely. If a shepherd wanted more wheat he took a sheepskin to a *csikos*. The *csikos* made it into a jacket. The man who had worn out his boots cut off the feet, nailed some wooden pegs into a round disk in their bottoms, and traded them to other plainsmen, who used them as salt sacks. The cattlemen made spoons and countless useful articles from the long horns of dead steers. The salt-cellar is always a horn-tip. He worked intricate knife-cases in leather – tobacco pouches from the bulls.

But the war did not change things greatly; some of the returning *csikos*, perhaps, felt a yearning to eat the fat things of the towns. It was, in fact, more the reverse; the *csikos* very nearly broke the hearts of the Austrian cavalry. The Austrians ride with their toes turned in slightly; the *csikos* hold them out. He held them out in spite of Austrian riding masters. Such is the way of the *csikos*.

The *gulyas* and *guhasz*, so often mocked in the songs of the arrogant *csikos*, have, oddly enough, the best of it on the Puszta. It is their huts one sees among the acacias that stand like islands on the flat, lonely plain. I went with a crippled shepherd one day. His little hut, made of rushes, plastered with mud on the inside, was immaculately clean. In a space not ten feet square he lived with his wife, young son, and a baby that snored in its crib.

There was a great, almost Biblical simplicity in that simple hut. The wind howled across the lonely Puszta outside; inside there was shelter. The rush wall of his home was carried out, extended, in a curved hook, like the letter 'J' to shelter his door. Like the windbrakes in the open, it had the hooked arm of wood stuck in the ground whereon the family did all the cooking. Three cats snuggled down in the still warm ashes of the small cow-dung fire. The rear of his hut held a rush lean-to in which snored two woolly Mongolicas. There he was – complete.

It was obvious that there was soon going to be another child in that crib. One wondered at the birth of man in that desolate world. Doctors, hospitals, schools, have no part in the life of the Puszta. Doubtless the new-comer would be born like the foals and young lambs.

A cruel life, perhaps, and yet – I heard the professor outside deep in talk with the old crippled *gulyas*:

'Only four years old,' exclaimed the old shepherd, looking admiringly down at his son. 'And how he can ride! He will one day be a *csikos*!'

The professor leaned over and patted the boy's bristly head. 'That's right, that's fine. Grow up and be a peasant like your father. My father also was a peasant; but I went to school and studied, and became a professor, and – I was wrong.'

Walking back, the professor told me to look at the sky-line. I didn't see it at first; then I saw the shimmering blue line of trees, floating gauze-like in the air – the Delibab! The Fata Morgana of the Puszta. Beautiful, alluring – and false.

'I have followed something like that in my life,' sighed the professor. 'I would have been better off as a *csikos*.'

CHAPTER EIGHTEEN

The Hunting Owl and a Royal Shoot

★

I HAVE shot snipe over stools in New Jersey, ducks over both live and wooden decoys in British Columbia, and I have had a peasant come down all the way from Archangel, in Russia, to try to 'sell' me a bear. But I had to come to Hungary to try shooting over an owl.

We were at Mezohegyes, on the Roumanian border, and a day after partridges had not brought us much luck. The director of forests was rather upset about things.

'Would you like to shoot this afternoon with the owl?'

'Shoot with the owl?'

'Yes,' he said, 'an *uhu*.'

I told him to bring the *uhu* along.

The *uhu* was a Transylvanian owl, about two feet high, with horns like a steer's. His name was Pista. He was put in his travelling-crate, and we drove across country.

'Here,' said the director of forests, 'we will try Pista.' He forthwith pulled Pista out of his crate — tied by the leg with a long leather strap — and thrust his perch in the soft earth at the edge of deep woods. 'Now,' said the director of forests, 'if we will go down inside.'

'You see,' said the director of forests, after we had descended into the rush-covered hole in the earth, 'all the enemies of the owl come to attack him in daylight. They know that he can't see.'

I looked out through the hole, about a foot square, that let us face Pista about twenty feet away. He was gazing into the sky, his enormous amber eyes wide open, hissing and snapping his cruel beak like a succession of mouse-traps going off. He was very nervous — swallowing hard. And as

I looked, curving with great swing-curves, came a hawk. It hung, fluttering, over the short-sighted Pista.

Bang!

I was so afraid of injuring Pista that I missed altogether. The hawk merely lifted in the air and dropped back. I saw two more swing down. *Bang!*

This time I hit, and the marauder came down.

It was one of the strangest experiences of my life – sitting in that hole at the edge of the forest and watching that ferocious picture. The enemies of the owl!

Poor old Pista had been shot over before, but I suppose he was always afraid that some one would miss and a big hawk would get him. He stared anxiously down into our hole, as if to say: 'Now keep on your toes down there, here comes a hawk!'

Occasionally, as if he feared from our silence that we had gone to sleep, he would spread his great yellow wings and drop into the grass. Then he flattened out. Perhaps he thought himself less conspicuous down there. At such times the director of forests went out, wheedled him, and finally got him to flap back to his perch. I tried it once, but the snap of those jaws put me off. 'Nice Pista,' I coaxed. 'Snap! Snap!' answered the *uhu*.

'You talk to him,' I implored the director of forests, 'I can't speak Magyar.'

The director of forests went out and patted Pista's head.

It was an extraordinary display of the savagery of the animal world. Every creature seemed to know that Pista was helpless. Hawks seemed to drop down through the miles from blue heaven. With sunset the crows came along, went into a perfect spasm of joy to see an owl out in daylight, flew back and forth, wheeled over him in armies, cursing,

calling him every name they could think of. A flight of
night-crakes croaked out what they thought about things.
Bang! Bang! Bang! answered the guns as the last word
from Pista.

'Attaboy!' said Pista, and I swear that he smiled. Potting
hawks over an owl is possibly an interesting, but not a very
glorious, performance. There was a smack of murder about
it. But then, as the director of forests said, there are too
many hawks in the world.

. . . .

A few days later I was fortunate enough to receive from
Admiral Horthy an invitation to a partridge shoot.

I presented myself at Godollo, the old hunting-lodge of
the Hapsburgs, and the Admiral took me into a big-win-
dowed room, where several friends of his, mostly admirals,
were still eating breakfast. It was raining hard. But the
Admiral, to my great pleasure, said that he did not believe
in changing plans once laid down – we would shoot.

'It was just the same on the sea,' he explained, his driver
sending the sixty horse-power car like a bullet over the wet
dirt roads, 'if you change, change; then no one is ever certain of things. The best thing is to make a plan – and go
straight ahead.'

When the car stuck in the mud, the Admiral got out and
pushed. We reached a wet field of corn, where there were
three huntsmen in grey and green, and a lined-up string of
boys. The Admiral's gun-bearer put together his pair of
16's. One member of the Admiral's party, the captain of
the shooting, gave us our stands on the edge of the field.
The boys made a wide circle and beat down through the
corn. . . .

Whirrr-whirrr! We could see the coveys get up. *Bang!*

Bang! The guns spoke on my right. Then, what seemed like five black bullets shot over my head. I shot about ten yards behind them.

The Admiral's 16 barked out, and – most beautiful sight in the world – a bird, killed in the air, came whirling down. A rocketer.

I was kind to the next birds I shot at also. I could have eaten my gun from sheer humiliation. But afterwards I was glad that I had shot so badly, as it gave me an opportunity to see how very kindly Hungarians and Austrians can be. I heard one gun say to another: 'The birds are fast to-day, aren't they?' 'Yes – frightfully. I fired four times at the air.' 'Takes a lot of practice to keep one's hand in at this.' All of this comforting conversation between two Hungarians being in English!

To my delight, Admiral Horthy announced, when we came to a large stand of corn, that we would shoot through this one in line. This was better than trying to hit sky-rockets coming over.

Whirrr-whirrr! The birds shot out of the wet corn. I shot before I even knew that I intended to shoot. The first brought a rolling ball of feathers into the corn. *'Kilo! Kilo!'* yelled a beater beside me, dashing after the bird. *Bang! Bang-bang!* The guns smashed out down the line. I saw Admiral Horthy's flip up. A miss – and a high bird, full hit, whirling down. My heart began to hammer at my ribs. This was a shoot! Lady came coursing past me, traversing for the Admiral's bird. Whirr! A bird came out from almost under my feet. *Bang!*

I then distinguished myself by potting a young pheasant almost over the Admiral's head. His gun-bearer stuck his head up among the tufts of the corn, told me of the crime

I had done. 'It doesn't matter,' called the Admiral, 'it was a very little one. Have you enough shells?'

He never heard my answer, as a whirr over his head sent him whirling around.

At the end of the corn-rows the partridges were banked up, and came out like little swarms of huge bees. Some, which had gone out into the field, came back over our heads – sky high. I saw the Admiral's son, Istvan Horthy, pull down two of those. We, in the middle of the line, had the luck of it, as most birds seemed to have bunched up just there. And I saw some very neat shooting from the Admiral and the two guns on either side. One of these, an old admiral, who, I understand, was somewhat of a war-dog, was very nonchalant about things. Through the open field I had seen him plodding along with his gun, hung by its strap round his neck. He removed it once, in a determined manner, to knock over a galloping hare. In the corn, I saw him lazily, but very accurately, picking birds out of the brown – and getting them more often than not. It made my toes curl to watch the way he let his bird get a lead. He had side whiskers like the old Emperor Franz Josef's.

We shot through a stand of young scrub oak in which there were wild boar, although we didn't see any, and got quite a number of hares. The boar are thick and in good condition this year, owing to the fine acorn crop. I was told that sometimes they make pilgrimages, crossing Hungary to the High Tatra. They were probably on one that day.

Here, on the edge of the road, the cars met us – they had been trailing us around all the day – and the birds were laid out and counted. Every tenth bird is pulled aside from the line. And every man who looked at them, enjoying his first post-shoot cigarette, suddenly realized that he was hungry.

I looked at these men, chatting so vivaciously before the fire after lunch. Every one of them had had a fine career – and lost it. Even Admiral Horthy – because his love is the sea. That rugged, rather high-cheeked old gentleman, talking about shooting moose in Canada, had commanded the *Helgoland* in the desperate battle in the Straits of Otranto. He told me how Admiral Horthy's ship disabled, signalling that she could steam only for ten minutes; he manœuvred across to draw fire.

Unconscious of the tremendous drama of the picture, he described seeing the high waves at the bows of the charging allies' cruisers and destroyers – how they turned broadside in line. 'I said to myself, "Now, this is it."' He described how he and the captain of one of the British cruisers had exchanged letters about it, after the war. One of those freaks of fate which occurred now and then during the war. The allies' forces had not pressed their advantage. 'We've nearly all the sailors here,' he said philosophically, and added, smiling, 'and no ships.'

CHAPTER NINETEEN

Life on the *Flame*

★

NOT long ago we lived for two years in a houseboat in British Columbia. We had two rooms – a kitchen-sitting and a bedroom, about twelve feet square. I shot and fished for most of our food; we cut our own wood, did our own cooking. We used to think we were roughing it. We used to brag about the way we made use of space, the chest of drawers I had made from old coal-oil cases, and the way we had our library under the bed.

To-day, when I look back on it, that houseboat seems a palace. I wonder, sometimes, what we could have found to put in all that space. Our abode to-day measures eight feet by six, we have to stoop to get into it – and stay stooped inside. This is the cabin of the *Flame*.

Ahead of this is the forepeak, like the toe of a boot, in which we crawl to get fresh changes of clothes, books, medicines, and our reserve of tinned provisions. In the extreme bow are jammed two suit-cases, and two duffel bags – our entire luggage for probably a year – on top of which sometimes reposes sixty fathoms of chain. If there is a square foot of this boat that is not put to some use it has not yet been discovered. I have climbed into a dinner-jacket in this cabin, lying on my back with my feet in the air, taking extraordinary care as I came upright not to put a crease in my shirt. Only a pygmy could stand upright in this cabin.

And yet that forepeak, somehow, spells romance. I have crawled in there to get a pair of dry shoes, and have sat there listening to the rattle of rain on the deck and the lap-lap of the Danube against our bow. There is a spare anchor in there – a whale of a mudhook – which I hope we shall never be called on to use. It is a tight, cosy little forepeak.

There is a bunk on each side of the cabin about eighteen inches wide, covered with waterproof green canvas cushions. By pulling these out at nights we gain another three inches, and thus make a bed. A wise designer saw that these bunks sloped inward, so that by rolling up in a cocoon of blankets we can wedge ourselves between them and the deck of the ship. Sleeping in such fashion it takes a very heavy wash from a steamer to roll us out on the floor.

There is a centre-board well, running down the middle of this cabin. Each side of it supports half a table. Opened up, this gives us a very comfortable varnished teak dining-table, about four feet by three. The cushioned bunks are our seats.

We do all our cooking on this with two small stoves that burn kerosene. Miracles are performed on this table each night. Breakfast, of course, is no trouble at all. We merely drop the eggs in the coffee and let it come to a boil. But dinner, our only other hot meal, is more elaborate. Here we let ourselves go. Dinner is the reward of the day.

We were a little rusty at first. The bacon would be cold before the eggs were half done; potatoes would appear a soft soggy mass. The coffee would be ready about the time we were yawning with sleep. No three things were ever served simultaneously. Then the old art came back, and to-night we had hot soup, veal steak with fresh beans, sliced tomatoes, cake, and fresh pears. Coffee. Things arrived in their appointed time, were ladled out from the pan to plates waiting for them. We heated the water for washing while we were eating our dinner. We are boat-broken again.

Yet it is extraordinary how slight changes can upset this

routine, and great accidents, even, fail to affect it. We gave two young Englishmen a lift down from Vienna. This necessitated cooking eight eggs. We never could cook those eight eggs! No amount of ingenuity on the part of the Crew could ever coax those eggs into a presentable, even eatable, shape. Scrambled was the closest we came to it. And these two young Cambridge undergraduates made more mess in our cabin than an army of chickens. Whenever they moved they knocked something over; they bumped their heads till they bled. We said good-bye to them in Budapest.

We started off feeling free people again. The first night we anchored, purposely, miles from a town — in a wide lonely stretch of the river. Life on the *Flame* was its old self again. While I put up the riding-light — so that some tug captain should not tow his charges into us — the Crew started dinner. Automatically each of us fell into step with his duties. It is my business to see that we find a safe anchorage, some spot in the river where we can turn in and sleep without being run down by a steamer. Sometimes ship's channel is on the fringe of the banks. On this hard gravel bottom I have to pay out a long length of cable. I have to be sure that *Flame* is strategically right for the night. In the dark, with this current, a man is distinctly out of luck if his anchor drags. I usually test it before turning in — pay out a few fathoms more cable. I sleep with one ear open.

The Crew sleeps like a log. Anchors, riding-lights, engine, and sails — these are not the concern of the Crew. By day she is on deck, does her trick at the wheel, steers *Flame* against the current until over the spot picked to anchor. But once the anchor is down the Crew's mind is free — free except for the important question of dinner.

Crew does the shopping. There are no tradesmen here to

come around for orders. Crew prowls through the markets, invents sign language in countries where she does not know the language. On the Rhine we used to take on our supplies of bread, eggs, and vegetables without ever going ashore — shop from the market boats that lie out in the stream. In Bavaria — land of milk and honey — shopping was no problem. Every little village had its market stalls in the square. Once, in the mountains, Crew knocked at the door of a convent and asked for some help — where could she find a market?

'Wait,' said the nun. She disappeared, and came back with a great sack of green beans. 'I have no weights, but I think this is a pound.' It certainly was.

The lock-keepers' wives miraculously produced honey, fresh milk and eggs. 'Run, Heini, and see how many there are.' And Heini would come back with a hatful of eggs that were still warm.

There is a melon-market in Bratislava that might be old Virginia. Water-melons, cantaloupes, and little yellow melons — like oranges — in great, sweet-smelling heaps. Milk is a mystery — and usually goat's. In Hungary goose-liver paste — almost *pâte* — is cheaper than butter. Partridges and venison cost less than ordinary meat. Corn — they call it *kuckruts* — is almost given away. White bread is hard to get, almost unknown, in the small peasant villages. We buy great slabs of sour grey stuff, hold it against our chests and draw the knife towards us. In 1,500 miles of travelling by water we have not bought one fish.

We have a 'frost-box' made of clay, which, when it is soaked, keeps butter quite hard. There is a tank under the deck aft holding ten gallons of fresh water. This we use for our cooking. An African water-bottle holding three gallons gives us cold drinking-water.

SAILING ACROSS EUROPE

A ship, no matter how small, is a little world in itself. Aboard one is quite independent. And it is a very nice world — or otherwise — depending upon how well you run it. A bit of carelessness — such as running short of matches — will mean that we will have no dinner, no riding-light, and a very mean night as a consequence. On the other hand, we can lie in this cosy cabin on a raw, rainy night, read until drowsy, and fall comfortably to sleep with the most seductive song in the world in our ears — the croon of swift-running water.

CHAPTER TWENTY

From Hungary to Jugoslavia

★

'BELOW Budapest the Danube traverses the vast Hungarian plain. Scenery monotonous, banks thinly populated, towns insignificant.'

Thus the guide-book man dismisses this part of the Danube.

I wonder what makes him write that way. Has he seen it? Or is it that nothing beneath the rank of a mountain or a thirteenth-century cathedral is worth mentioning? What if the banks are thinly populated? Is it not interesting to see long, lonely stretches of this river, untouched, unspoilt, looking just the same as they did when the Danube was the eastern frontier of Rome against the Mongols?

To-day we came down through a wilderness of willows where the Danube wandered between low, sandy islands, where it broadened, seemed to halt in half-mile-wide, satin-green pools, like a lake. We saw thousands of ducks, little rafts of them on the water; long strings on the sky-line, climbing in beating flight to the clouds. Not knowing whether we were in the right channel or not, we passed stretches of shore like the forest primeval, tangled thickets, light grey puff-balls of willows, trees standing in water – like a mirage. We passed little villages of white mud-houses, with old women washing clothes in the river, beating them on little boards set on four sticks. The red and pink garments drying on the green bank behind them looked like rows of hollyhocks.

We passed scores of water-mills, those ancient-looking Noah's-ark contraptions that are permanently moored in the stream to grind the wheat of the Alfold. By rights painted giraffes should have stuck their heads out of the windows, but dusty millers looked out, craning their necks. Off Paks there is a perfect flotilla of these mills, anchored exactly in the middle of nearly a half-mile-wide stretch of river. We saw the peasants row out to them in their low black skiffs, loaded with great sacks of wheat – and come back with flour.

These mills are a blessing. They give one a safe place to anchor. Steamers may go on either side of them, but each mill has a regular old-fashioned street-lamp on its bow to warn all travellers to steer clear at night. Also, as they are fixtures, they are marked on the charts. In fact, they are the only marks on the chart.

The first night out of Budapest we anchored below one of these mills in a blinding white rainstorm. The miller looked out of his back door, waved to me to come up and tie alongside. I signalled that I had my anchor down and would rather stay where I was. He was insistent – wanted company perhaps – and importuned me in Magyar. I shook my head, signalled that I had down fifteen fathoms of heavy chain. He threw up his arms and slammed his door shut. It was a comical conversation. His face was as white as a clown's. I saw smoke coming out of his Noah's ark a few minutes later; he was comforting himself with dinner. We heard the paddles grinding all night.

When we reached Paks we saw what we thought was a masquerade of some sort, a long line of people walking up and down on the Corso – all the women in long skirts. Then we realized that this was a holiday, and that these were peasants. The peasant women never will wear short skirts. A boy in a rowing-shell was racing up and down the Danube by himself. We made fast to his boathouse and climbed up the bank.

Under a promenade of horse-chestnuts was the entire population of Paks. A very fat old officer, in full rig, trailing his sword on the ground. Groups of swarthy, black-booted peasant men. Clusters of timid, soft-eyed girls. They made vivid little patches of colour — like flower-beds.

The advocate was summoned to question me — a heavy, bull-dog sort of man. He took one look at me, at our flag, and launched into a tirade about who started the war. As near as I could make out he said that England had combined with the Catholic countries to destroy Protestantism — or vice versa. A crowd collected to hear him lay down the law. They nodded soberly, and exclaimed: *'Igen! Igen!'* ('Yes! Yes!') whenever he pounded his palm.

In my best German I asked where I could buy some benzine. Instantly his audience forgot all about who started the war, and a dozen people offered to carry my petrol tins. We passed an inn by the steamboat landing from whose courtyard came the wild music of a gipsy band. A nice old man came up to me, took off his green hat, and introduced himself as a Norwegian. He said that he had lost all his money in Italy during the war, and was living in Paks. He told the advocate to leave me alone.

'He's my best friend,' he said, 'but he talks all the time.'

We had been told that if we did not stop at Mohacs the customs officials would shoot. I made a note of that in my log, 'Stop at Mohacs — they shoot.' Just as we reached that historic site of two bloody battles — Sultan Solyman killed a king and 20,000 Germans and Hungarians there in 1526 — we saw a black skiff full of peasants row out from the opposite bank. We went across to take a photograph of them. When we came back to Mohacs we could not see a customs house, so we waved and went on. That was our exit from Hungary.

We then entered the wilderness of swamp and islands in which lies Margaret Island – a hunter's paradise – and saw above this wilderness, just at sunset, the little white church on the hill behind Batina. This was Jugoslavia.

We rounded a bend, and saw a scrawny little town, running back from a shore of flat mud. A group of peasants signalled us to run *Flame* on the beach. We did so, and they said that we had to report to the police station across the river. One of them jumped aboard to conduct us. A child made a jump and scrambled on to *Flame's* bow.

Across river we ran into the mouth of the King Peter's canal. There was a Jugoslav gunboat there – a launch – with an odd crew of sailors. They marched me to the police commandant. His office was one half of a flat white inn by the river-side; the other half was noisy with peasant women and men – drinking. He asked all the questions he could think of, and then said I would have to report to the harbour-master. Like a snowball the crowd gathered size; a bevy of us passed over the canal gates, by three old Serbian wood-cutters, who turned their shaggy, long-haired heads to inspect us and, half-way to the hut of the harbour-master, the police captain remembered that their official was not at home. He was across river. Here a soldier was added to the crowd, and we turned around and walked back. The police captain pointed to the gunboat, which had crossed the river, and told me that it was in front of the customs-house. I must now pass the customs.

I started the motor again, crossed the Danube, and tied up to the launch. When I had everything ready for the night and was awaiting the customs examination, a huge man in a grey suit, spats, and a sombrero came along and told me that the customs-house was 100 yards farther down the river.

I would have to take the boat there. I started the motor again, and ran along shore at the customs. It was closed.

'Of course,' said the local Tom Mix, 'the customs closes at seven. I am the chief!'

I looked along the evil-smelling stretch of mud road, at the pigs trying to get into the drawing-room, at the refuse in the bushes all along the length of the bank, at the crowd of peasants and horses and cows on the barge being towed across river. I slapped at the swarm of mosquitoes.

'I am going to anchor out there,' I told the gentleman in the spats. 'I will be there at eight o'clock in the morning. When the customs officers enter their house, when the harbour-master returns to his home – come and get me.'

CHAPTER TWENTY-ONE

The Terrible Balkans

*

BOTH of our watches stopped during the night we arrived in Jugoslavia, so when we awoke we did not know what time it was. A peek out of a porthole showed us the customs officials sitting on shore watching us – waiting.

'They're there,' I bewailed to the Crew; 'and they have two soldiers with them.'

We held a consultation; would it be better to hide things or leave them just where they were? The latter suggestion won, probably, as the Crew sarcastically commented, because I always put things in places where no sensible person would look for them, anyway. We ate breakfast gloomily.

'That's the worst of these growing countries,' complained the Crew; 'just because Jugoslavia is the coming country of the Balkans, and knows it, she is putting on all the frills of an empire. Imagine all of this fuss about passing a frontier. Soldiers – and that man in the hat!'

The man in the hat – a Tom Mix contraption – was chief of the customs. He had moved poor little *Flame* about like a pawn the previous night – anchor here – anchor there!

'By the Pipers!' I cursed; 'if he gets stuffy I'm going to burn the wires into Belgrade.'

'Take notes,' said the Crew; 'take your notebook with you, and write down what he says. That will agitate them.'

A Bavarian tug had come in during the night, and was anchored twenty yards out from us. We heard her captain complaining bitterly: 'Why do you make all this trouble?'

I remembered a conversation in Vienna: 'You are on the edge of civilization – in Vienna.' I nicked my jaw shaving.

'Here they come!'

116

The Crew pointed to two soldiers in a black skiff putting out from the shore. I thrust my head in the Danube – might as well look decent to receive them. Twenty feet from the *Flame* both soldiers saluted. They came alongside carefully, with great care for our paint.

'You wanted some benzine last night, didn't you?' asked a black-moustachioed fire-eater in the stern.

'Yes.'

The soldier climbed into the *Flame*, pointed to my gasolene tins, and gave a quick order in Serbian.

'He will show you where to get it,' he said, indicating the other man, to whom he handed my tins. He gave me a paper: 'This is your pass for the harbour-master. He will let you go when he sees it.'

I climbed into the skiff, left Crew, who was lighting up one of the soldier's cigarettes. I could not believe it, but my eyes told me that they were chatting–and the little dark soldier was laughing. Dirty dog, he's making fun of us, I thought.

We beached the skiff beside a black barge in which was an enormous vat full of grapes. Two men were carrying these in a pot slung on a pole. They were going to a wine-press. Another man, apparently watching this precious cargo, dipped in the ship's bailer each time they left, and drank deep gulps of the fresh juice. He passed the bailer to me. The juice was cold – tasted better than wine! We crossed the deeply rutted mud road; and the soldier knocked at an archway. A burly individual admitted us into a courtyard full of trees – and washing. Yes, he had benzine. How much did I want?

I told him, but added that I should have to pay for it in Hungarian crowns. The man's face grew solemn; in the local patois he informed me that there was nothing doing in Hungarian crowns. I must go to the bank.

The soldier led me down the dirt road into a mud square, full of peasant women and horses and carts, and knocked at the door of a private dwelling. This was the bank. In a sitting-room full of deer-antlers and old chromos of the Turks burning saints, the bank director and his young wife told me that they could not buy any crowns. Hungarian exchange was too wavering. I slapped the stone walls: 'Solid as this!'

The bank director offered me a deal at thirty per cent. loss. I laughed, called him a bandit, and left. We tried two tug captains, a rich old woman – who was stripping geese feather with her three peasant servants and stuffing the white fluff into pillows. We tried the storekeeper. Batina lies on the spur of a hill – little white houses intermingled with vineyards, with a red and white church on top. We walked around and around, up and down. I began to recognize people, see them again; they bowed to me as I passed. And frequently, in the course of our travels, we passed the little stretch of dirt road off which was anchored the *Flame*.

'Any luck?' called the Crew.

'Not a chance.'

And each time the little dark soldier laughed, waved his hand to me. Drat that man!

The last time I passed I was quite prepared to swim out and choke him. I thought up cuss words in Russian – hoped they were the same thing in Serb. What was this! The little dark soldier was standing up; he was waving a handful of money.

'Exchange?' I called.

He shook his head: 'I will give it to you. You can send it back from Belgrade – or America.'

'*What?*'

Savage Europe! The terrible Balkans! Here was a soldier, who had never seen me before, offering me money. I rowed out, and he gave me 200 dinars.

'It is nothing,' he said, when I tried to tell him how kind he was.

'The customs examinations?' I said.

'I have already given you the papers,' he answered.

I nearly fell into the water. In a daze I took another one of his nice Serb cigarettes. Still feeling I must be dreaming I accepted a lift across the river in the 'grape barge' to give my pass to the harbour-master. The boatman would not take any tip! When I returned, the other soldier was on the shore, waiting for me with the little dark soldier's address. His name was Dragan A. Gligorijevic – and in the note was another 100 dinars!

'Where is he?' I demanded of the first soldier. He told me that the dark benefactor was attending to his job in the customs-house. I went there, sent a servant out for a couple of flasks of red wine. He came back with wine, some *salmi* sausage and bread.

'To your very good health!' I toasted the soldier; 'and to yours' – I bowed to Tom Mix. We drank together.

They had both been at Salonika. Nearly all the Serbs, they said, had been killed in the war. I gave a 100-dinar note to the servant. Both Tom Mix and the dark soldier jumped up – not a bit of it! This was their treat. Pressed as to the reason why they should give me money and buy me wine, they smiled embarrassedly and said – they wanted to.

I found Crew with the gasolene man and his wife. They asked us if we liked Hungary. We said we thought it was the most adorable country on earth. They gave a quick glance toward the Jugoslav customs; would we come into their house? We walked into the courtyard, under the washing, past wagon-axles, ploughs, shovels, and rakes, and entered a white-walled living-room. They produced peaches and plums and glittering wet grapes. They had been Hungarians.

They told us a pathetic tale of exile, how their children had to hear lessons in Serbian, how they had to pay taxes – which the real Serbians dodged – how they hoped, one day, to get back to Hungary. There was no sympathy, no comradeship here. We tried to put two and two together to reconcile the treatment we had received with that which they described. Somehow the two didn't fit. We told them this. They replied that the real Serbs were not so bad; it was the ones who had been Hungarians before this land was given to Serbia after the war. They were awful. We told them what a man in the foreign office had told us in Budapest:

'The Serbs are not bad as enemies. They are hard men, but they are brave, and they fight in the open.'

The wife shuddered, told how her husband had been taken out of the house three times, always at night, because he was supposed to be a political spy. Maybe he was. But he was a fine fellow, with no shilly-shallying, who looked one in the eye, and made no bones about what he would like to do to the Serbs. He was a good enemy, too.

They gave us an armful of fruit, stood on the bank and waved to us as we left. Tom Mix, the dark soldier – Dragan – the grape men, and the soldier servant waved also. We left them there in a line, undying enemies – all friends to us.

'Extraordinary,' mused the Crew as *Flame* slid round the bend, 'to think that such pleasant people can't get on well together! I wonder which of them is right?'

I lighted another of Dragan's cigarettes and ate some of the Hungarian's grapes.

'I'm neutral,' I said.

CHAPTER TWENTY-TWO

A Canoeist's Paradise

★

THE Danube is a canoeist's paradise. It combines in the 1,700 miles between Ulm and the Black Sea everything dear to the heart of the paddler — swift water, rapids, whirlpools, wide, lonely lagoons, mountains, plains, forests, and swamps. There is no place where the average good canoeist cannot take his craft, though the secretary of the Hungarian Rowing Club in Budapest told me he had capsized in the Strubel below Grein and lost everything. His own fault, he explained.

There are *Kanoo-karten* compiled by Germans that map out every detail of the river between Passau and Vienna. We had one of these for the *Flame*, but found it was really worse than no chart at all, as what is safe for a canoe is no good for a craft with any draught.

That, in effect, might be said of the entire stretch of the Danube. It is pure luck — with only a certain amount of using one's head — to take a big craft down it. There are long stretches of river where a big craft cannot go near the shore, where the ship's channel is so narrow and tortuous that finding a safe place to lie up for the night is pure guesswork. We have not seen a sail-boat since we entered the Danube, only one pleasure launch, and only since passing Paks in Hungary have we seen small motor-craft used for freight. We have seen canoeists the entire length of the trip.

I wonder that more American sportsmen do not take this cruise. There were stretches between Vienna and Novi Sad that fairly made my heart ache — I wanted to explore them. Last night we said good-bye to a party of four Ger-

man canoeists. They had written on their decks in white
paint: '*Quer durch Europa imm Paddleboot!*' 'All the way
across Europe in a canoe!' We picked them up at Batina,
where they had gone in to inquire about a comrade of theirs,
a scout, who had been drowned there. A tragic little bit of
adventure! There were two in this scout boat, one of whom
fell frightfully ill. Malaria, no doubt. They slept in the
canoe at night. And one morning, about Batina, the stern
man awoke, leaned forward to speak to his comrade and
found his place empty. That is all there is to the story – he
has never been found.

These fellows are on their way to the Black Sea. As
regulations prevent them from making a long sojourn in
Turkey, they intend to winter in Bulgaria. Next summer
they hope to make Egypt. They work as they go. I asked
them, at what? Anything, they replied. They are real soldiers of fortune. They were nearly naked, wore only singlets,
and were the colour of an old boot. One of them had a
dog – a fox-terrier puppy. That dog is certainly going to see
life.

Their canoes are flat, decked over, like Eskimo *kyacks*.
Light cedar. They paddle, sitting flat on the bottom with
their legs stretched before them. A canvas covering can be
buttoned about them casing them in when it rains. They
keep their meagre supplies in lockers fore and aft under the
covered-in wooden decks.

Up near the head of the Danube the *Flame* went aground
in mid-river. While I was labouring to get her into deep
water a flotilla of four German *falt* boats swept past. They
were students from Stuttgart, one of whom had his wife
along. We took photographs of each other, promised to
exchange in Vienna. We never saw them again.

These *falt* boats are collapsible, made of canvas, with slim, wooden slats. They fold up like a camp canvas bed. They cost about £16 in Germany. They can cross morning dew.

For the most part the Danube is an extremely uninhabited river. Except in the Wachau Valley towns are few and far between on its banks. Canoeists can camp anywhere. There are always fishermen, if a man desires company. They live in little square-cabined floats below Vienna, fishing with dip-nets. Farther down one sees them hauling the seine, or pushing along the edge of the willows hurling purse-nets. Carp, schill, and sterlet comprise most of their catch.

Old wooden barges drift past, high in bow and stern, almost level with the water amidships. A man stands on a raised steering-platform built ahead of the slanting black cabin aft. With a pole he shoves a forty-foot long tiller. Clusters of men, like galley slaves, stand amidships, straining at long, flat-toed wooden sweeps. They chant as they sink the sweeps in the water. We have seen them this way in Serbia rowing into the sunset. Their craft have changed very little since the days of the Romans.

Shepherds stare placidly at one from level stretches of bank, their dogs barking defiance at this strange intruder. We have passed little fishing-villages that looked as though they were standing in water, their men rowing from hut to hut. Nets drying on poles. The South Sea Islands in Europe.

Long, lonely stretches of river roll behind us; we enter a maze of grey willows, then suddenly see three vivid patches of scarlet. Peasant women and men, all paddling, bringing a boat-load of purple plums into market. We have seen sunsets in these grey willow swamps where trees, water, and sky melted together – and the *Flame* seemed to be sailing into the heart of an opal.

We have sat on deck in the moonlight and watched the Belgrade boat pounding past, the rhythmic thud of the paddles like distant drums in the night. We have seen lights in her saloon, the fashionable world at its dinner, white-coated stewards darting about; lights, shining silver, and laughter. Thum-thum-thum-thum! She swings down the stream; the blue light on her stern winks through the trees – goes out. The silent plain seems more lonely than ever.

No wonder that this enchanted river makes Huck Finns of otherwise industrious Germans. It was created for sport and adventure. A man could paddle his canoe, fish, shoot, and explore these wandering estuaries – and never get through in a lifetime.

CHAPTER TWENTY-THREE

Mutiny on the *Flame*

★

A PARTY of visitors to Cowes was being shown over the palatial yacht of a baronet. The Scotch captain took them into the luxurious cabins, showed them the beautiful teak, showed how, by simply pressing a button, it was possible to pass from one cabin into another.

A parson in the party smiled coyly. 'If this were not such a fine yacht,' he said, 'and did not belong to such an impeccable person as Sir Henry Gooseberry, I should say that those doors were immoral.'

'Mon,' said the Scot sternly, 'd'ye no ken that immorality is the verra backbone of yachting!'

This story has no more to do with what I am going to write about than the average funny yarn with which the after-dinner speaker kicks off his monologue. The point is – the Crew has revolted. Mutiny has been brewing for some time, though it hit me quite unawares.

I have had a bit of a time with the Crew. For instance, it has always been a hard job to make her see the reason why I want to anchor before darkness sets in. Why not go on? I explain that this is a strange river to me; perhaps we could not find an anchorage. Why not – isn't the cable long enough to reach the bottom? Yes, but – I expatiate, dwell acidly upon the question of ship's channel, rocks, hard or soft bottom. All right then, for goodness' sake – anchor.

We set in to anchor. I explain to the Crew that when I wave my hand she is to put the engine-clutch into neutral. I want *Flame* to drift backward with the current, not run over her anchor; I want to feel when that anchor has a good grip on the bottom. Of course. One night at Schoonhaven, in Holland, the Crew stuck the clutch in reverse. I couldn't let go of the cable quick enough. I was nearly jerked overboard. I said terrible things.

The Crew took them meekly, said she hoped to do better: 'I'm sorry.'

Tying dish rags in the running gear also leads to trouble. I explain that in the night one has to know where everything is on a boat. Everything must be free for immediate action. In the dark one has to act fast — in split seconds.

'I know,' said the Crew; 'I'm a perfect idiot on a boat. Do forgive me.'

When I plan the day's run, figure out how many miles we make an hour with current and wind in our favour, and then say that we will make such and such a town, several miles short of my figures, the Crew goes wild. What's the use of figuring at all? Why do I use them? Because, I explain, I must leave a margin of safety. How do we know what the wind and current will be?

'Of course,' chimes the Crew; 'how silly of me.'

Matters came to a point where I ceased to consult her. I just said, 'Do this' or 'Don't.' And the Crew did or didn't. One night, when I threw three of our dinner-plates overboard, I explained that it was dark — and she shouldn't have put the dinner-plates in the frying-pan.

'Of course not,' said the Crew.

One day in Bavaria I asked her to go ashore and buy an adjustable spanner and a small Stillson wrench. She came back without them.

'What's the matter?'

'I can't get them,' she said; 'I can't make them understand.'

'What! I thought you said you spoke German?'

'Well, I don't even know what it is in English,' she said helplessly.

126

'Don't know what a Stillson wrench is!'

'You're as bad as that matron of mine in Russia,' complained the Crew, 'who, just because I had learned the alphabet, sent me out to buy some artificial poinsettias and a frosted robin for the Christmas tree.'

She has a passion for cleaning. Every time I sit down in this cabin she moves me some place. 'Just lift up your typewriter a minute. I want to swab the table.' She's always mislaying my pipe. I wish she'd smoke one herself – she would know what it means.

In our room in Budapest I found her propping up the camera on the window-sill, several hundred feet above the swift Danube, preparatory to taking a time exposure.

'What the deuce is that you've got under it?'

'Our passport and the letter of credit. Don't touch it!' she said sharply; 'it's just the right height.'

'I ask you – !'

It's just been a steady, continuous strain of adapting the Crew to the water. It has taken a great deal of patience – and thought. I had matters just right, the Crew well in hand; and then –

It happened between Novi Sad and Belgrade. We were lying at anchor. One of those Danube towing-steamers came down the river with a string of eight empty barges. She swung around just above us to anchor herself. Watching her, lazily, I was suddenly horrified to see that she was going to swing her steel barges right in the *Flame*. At first I merely jumped up and down. It was the only act I could think of – we were at anchor. Then it occurred to me that I might brace my back against *Flame's* cabin and fend off with my feet. At least it would cushion the shock – save her ribs.

Boom! – crash! In the mêlée I was knocked over backward. I flung out a hand – felt it crash through something brittle and hard into something squashy and soft. Without looking around I knew what had happened. I had put my fist through the 'frost-box.' Our 'frost-box' – the Crew's joy! 'It keeps butter hard in the tropics!' I removed the broken clay, eggs, butter and tomatoes – looked at Crew.

Crew looked at me.

'I've always told you,' I said, 'not to leave that "frost-box" on the top of the cabin.'

'You lump!' exploded the Crew, going off like a bomb. 'Don't you dare try to put that on me! You know that "frost-box" has been there since Holland.'

She was quivering there in the cockpit.

'Hang it all!' I began; 'I'll fix it up –'

'Don't be grotesque,' she said icily.

'Well,' I said, sitting down, 'it's done – it can't be helped – it's done.'

'To think,' she said, 'what I've stood from you all these months! Clumsy, incompetent, no good on a boat!'

The more she talked, the more she seemed to find to say. As the French say: *'L'appétit vient en mangeant.'* She must have spoken to me there for nearly twenty minutes. She was slowly throwing off an inferiority complex.

She emerged, full fledged, stretched her arms!

'I'm glad,' she said joyfully; 'I'm glad it happened! You see now – I'm not the only fool on this boat. You had almost convinced me that I was.'

My prestige was gone.

'Now pull up that anchor,' she said, 'and let's get started. I'm sick of this place.'

'Yessum,' I said – and went forward.

CHAPTER TWENTY-FOUR

The Peasant Capital

★

'Oh, of course,' said the diplomat, 'it's a rotten hole to live in, but it's interesting.'

That, in a nutshell, is Belgrade. Still the old hot-pot of Europe! The old game is still on; diplomats, conspirators, spies – commercial agents with Government errands. A French investment is counterpointed by a British investment. The Italians stir up the stew with separatist clubs for Dalmatia. A colonel has a servant who is also a colonel; each watches each other. And the worst of it is, they all take it seriously.

One would think that the world would be sick of watching the Slav hatching plots.

Meanwhile, with one man in seven in a uniform of one sort or another, Belgrade is 'a rotten hole to live in.' It is one of the ugliest cities imaginable, repulsively so! It is absolutely devoid of charm! The squalor or sordidness is not that of the Waza in Cairo, the slums of Whitechapel, or the lower east side of New York – the result of great poverty and unavoidable congestion – it is a nightmare of rotten bad taste. The worst eyesores have been built since the war. It is 'hick,' the only word for it. In its way it is a terrific rebuke to one side of Socialism – the general levelling of things – for here is a capital with no aristocracy, built by peasants, for peasants, and ruled by peasants. It suits them.

The peasants are the best people in it. The grim-faced Serb from the hills is a fine fighting-man, one of the bravest soldiers on earth. Most of his brothers are under the sod. He has been refined by much suffering. He is almost spiritual, not a clod like the *mujik* of Russia. He is splendid. And it is only when he removes his moccasin-like footgear to put

129

on sharp-toed suède Western shoes, when he discards his black astrakhan hat for an abortive sombrero, when he 'tucks in his shirt,' that he becomes second-rate. He then acquires a fat neck, wastes his time in cafés, discussing *pan* this or *pan* that, and builds one of the atrocious dwellings of Belgrade.

This peasant, in his various stages of evolution, makes up the major part of this population. Add to him an intermingling of Croats and Slovenes, who strive by ingenuous ways to show that they are not such as he, and in reality differ no more than do Texans from Yankees – season with a sprinkling of chipmunk-faced Bosnians, Mussulmans in red fezes, who are supposed to be Slavs, and you have a fair idea of the people of Belgrade. Colour it all with 8,000 Russian exiles, many still in their old uniforms, and you have the picture complete – Belgrade, the capital of Jugoslavia, the coming country of the Balkans.

We approached it a few hours before sunset, after a leisurely cruise of three days down the Danube from Batina, the Hungarian-Jugoslav frontier, through the 163 miles of rich farm country ceded to the Jugoslavs from Hungary by the peace conference. The Danube is lazy and broad here – about half a mile wide where it ambles past Belgrade – almost uninhabited, with a very occasional village of white mud-houses and dirt streets. A few towns sit far back from the river on high ground. It reminded one of what the Mississippi must have been in the days of Tom Sawyer, but an old brown castle, with its wall running down over the bleak hills to the Danube, put a check to such imagery.

On the third day the right bank began to rise slightly, flattened out into a plateau that stopped short in a yellow clay palisade at the water's edge, as if cut with a spade. In places little roads wound down through the yellow mud to the Danube. Strings of low white huts fringed its heights. One town nestled in a fold of the hills where the plateau gave way. A smooth-walled church, surrounded by a wall, standing guard. An ancient church – Orthodox Greek – with a black, radish-shaped dome.

The left bank was flat as a prairie. Clumps of blue trees in the far distance. And across these, following the bends of the river, we suddenly saw the twinkling mosaic dome of the Millennium Memorial at Zemlin. Beyond that were hills – yellow, brass-coloured hills, like the bare hills of the Libyan Desert, hardly a touch of green on their slopes. These were the Serbian Mountains. Below them we saw scattered plates of white, yellow and red; a few spires – this was Belgrade.

Belgrade lies on the spur of a limesone hill where the Save enters the Danube. An enchanting situation, if they had made the right use of it. We cut off from the Danube, passing on the inside of a level morass, called War Island, and came to where a quarter-mile-wide strip of green water slipped past between us and the tawdry buildings before us.

This was the Save – a rip of little perpendicular waves dancing along, meeting with the mud flood of old Danube. We thought it shoal water at first, ventured into it carefully, killing speed. We crossed the river, made up against the placid Save along a long line of barges, floats, puffing steamers and tugs. We could find no place to anchor. Somewhat bewildered to come out of the almost empty Danube into such a hubble-bubble of traffic, we threw a line to a barge. A pimply-faced loafer, dressed in baggy trousers and what had once been a white and blue striped undershirt, bestirred himself and made fast.

I saw Crew staring dolefully at the refuse floating between us and the filthy litter on shore – at the squalid buildings beyond.

'It's all right,' I assured her; 'this is only the water-front. It will be better up on the hill.'

We dressed and struggled up the hill, through a warren of tumble-down buildings cobbled, hole-pitted streets, past dingy little cafés where greasy gipsies titivated their fiddles and painted girls screamed out love songs on the raised platform before them – where soldiers and sailors and pasty-faced 'sports' sipped their wine and black coffee. Peasants in every conceivable costume swept past us. Dark men, in walnut homespun, their cone-tipped soft shoes tied with thongs to thin legs! Little ratty-eyed men in baggy trousers, sashed waist and Turk-like in red fez! Old crones in bell skirts, struggling under head loads of kindling. Sore-eyed, dirty children that trotted after us – begging.

'That is interesting, isn't it?' The Crew pointed to one of the open-air meat shops, steaming corpses of hot pig on the counter, the proprietor extolling the virtues of each cut he hacked off and handing it to his customers, who chewed it forthwith.

I leapt across a three-foot pool of sewage.

'Beautiful!' I enthused.

Had we but known it we were passing through the best part of Belgrade. The main street was as vulgar and tawdry as a Western boom town. The dark, low cafés merely gave way to glass and polished marble, the laughing soldiers to pompous, overfed officers, the taciturn peasants to gesticulating, squabbling merchants in what they supposed was Western attire. The 'sport' shoe and low-crowned sombrero were prevalent. True, the shops no longer had painted on the door signs, for the benefit of those who can't read, all the articles which they sold. But the taste they catered to was no better. Policemen stood on every corner, waving wands to let the automobiles pass – like magicians pulling bunnies out of hats. The old joke about there being a barber's shop in front of the palace is cruel. The shop is there, but the palace is a very fine palace, rising out from the trees behind the black iron fence of gold-tipped spear points, like a fine railway terminus. It has a clock on each tower! Soldiers in blue tunics, gold facings and bright scarlet pants stand guard all round it – stamp their feet in salute to the officers who seem to stroll past every minute.

We found our way to the hotel – *the* hotel – and entered a dining-room well decorated with nudes, where the chairs, linen, and service were like those of a seaside hotel.

'We just love your Belgrade,' we heard a file-like voice trilling. 'I just won't let my husband go out alone. I've been all over this town.'

We looked at her husband – a nice old man, white hair and goatee. He dropped his eyelids in suffering, talked to his Serbian guest about politics, business. The courteous Serbian skilfully carried on two conversations at once.

A snake-like creature, with beautiful red hair – parted and cut like a man's – looked vaguely at nothing from out of grey, violet-shaded eyes. Yawned. When she got up to leave every woman in the room looked her full up and down, at her, through her, inside her. They turned to their escorts. The men didn't hear very well, because they were still – looking.

A little waiter slid up to us, pulled a package of cigarettes from his white coat.

'These are special,' he whispered.

I showed him my box of the same sort.

'Oh, no,' he whispered; 'these are different – they are made for the ministers. See.' He took one of my cigarettes and then one of his, compared the tobacco – they did look different. He looked stealthily about the room, slid back the cigarettes in his pack, showed me a blue slip of paper on which was an 'M.' 'Ministers—these are specially made for the ministers.'

'But the price on the packet is exactly the same!'

He smiled coyly: 'Of course.' He added that these 'specials' were only 20 dinars more.

I tried one – and bought them. They were 'different.'

After dinner we engaged a droshky and told the driver where to drive.

'How much?' I asked.

'Fifty dinars.'

I walked off. 'Thirty dinars,' I slung over my shoulder again.

'Forty,' he countered.

I walked on. Another *ishvoshtick* hurtled out from the line. 'Thirty dinars,' he quoted. 'Please.'

We jolted down the cobbled streets to the river front. The cafés were in full blast, little fires glowing in their open brick ovens, the music thrumming, girls singing. Staggering silhouettes contorted behind opaque window-panes. Shouts, wild music, loud laughter!

We stopped the driver, paid him, and entered a pub. We ordered black coffee – at least that had been sterilized by the flames. And these people were enjoying themselves.

'Ah, well,' sighed the Crew, 'I suppose we had expected too much. I had an idea that it would be rather fine in a simple way – like some of the old towns in Russia.'

I had just taken a cigarette – one from the second layer of the box of 'Ministers' this time. I lighted it moodily, then choked – it was as bad as my old ones. I tried another – also bad. I had been stung.

'Well,' I said to the Crew, 'in some ways Belgrade is exactly like the old towns in Russia.'

134

CHAPTER TWENTY-FIVE

Food, Music – Dirt

★

'BROOKLYN! Ah, I can never forget her!'

He was a mangy old Serb, who in the days of his youth might have been rather sprightly. But now eyes, nose, draggled moustachios, and collapsible chin had all blurred together. It was impossible to tell, from the wrinkled map of his visage, whether he was laughing or crying. Once, in the course of his seafaring career, he had been a mechanic in Brooklyn. Carelessly he had left it – and now he can never go back. It is the regret of his life. I, too, confide to him, could never get over Brooklyn. After that it was Damon and Pythias.

'Whenever I look out there at Belgrade,' he said dreamily, 'it is not Belgrade I see – it is Brooklyn.'

'Same here,' I said. And it wasn't such a lie at that.

On this rainy night – and it was not raining when we set out – he stood by as usual to haul Crew up the five feet of black iron barge we were tied to. 'All right,' he said, using one of his three English sentences, 'all right.' He nearly tore out the Crew's arm. 'All right.'

He always escorts us up the gang-planks that lead to the filthy alleyway and the cobbled road up the hill. He is but one of the many characters on that barge – all of whom are exceptionally kind to us. It is a ship's employment agency, this barge, where engineers, stokers, and so on, wait in mobs to get work. They sit in a long line like crows, and watch us washing and dressing; they comment on our dinners. I feel that it is almost cheating if I do not dress outside in the cockpit. It gives them such pleasure. And I am sure that if I did not clean my teeth in the mornings one of them would mention it. When the pompous little port captain tried to move us away, down to the port office, they objected in chorus: 'That is no place to go.' And we stuck. They have adopted us.

We feel a sense of responsibility, and always bow gravely as we pass, back and forth. On this night one of them was thoughtful enough to advise the Crew that she should have her coat – the weather smelt like rain.

The Crew knew better. And when we were up on the Knes Mihailowa Ulitca – the main street of Belgrade – the rain came and turned the city into a sort of thick, green-pea soup. Rain in Belgrade means mud – lakes of mud, and greasy, treacherous cobbles. It caught us in front of the palace, and we ran down one of the dark streets that flank that imperial dwelling until we came to a wooden archway through a whitewashed brick wall. Behind that, set in a little garden of chestnut and 'box' trees, in the Russian Winter – queer little restaurant, where you never know whether your waiter is a grand duke or a druggist; where the Russian dishes are awful and the *filet mignon* superb.

The Russian Winter is a long, low, board shack, with an uneven board floor, and a raised dais on one flank for the musicians – exactly like an old Virginia country dance hall.

Similes of the American South leap to my mind, because in many ways the atmosphere of the Russian Winter is like the aftermath of our own civil war below the Mason and Dixon line. Fallen greatness. For instance, no Russian ever talks about his home, it is always his estates. And I have met only three who admitted to rank below that of colonel. It is simple but very truthful comparison. And, of course, there are the professional Russians, just as there are professional Southerners – and this rather gets into the food of the Russian Winter and cloys things. But, one and all, they are delightful.

A girl in furs sits behind the *Zakuska – hors-d'œuvres –* usually powdering her nose.

'S'drassitcha Ivan Ivanovitch!' she greets a fat customer who comes in.

'S'drassitcha, Shura Alexandrova!' He bows over the anchovies, and kisses her hand.

A mandolin and balalaika orchestra, in white *rubaskas* and red boots, gets up from the tables where it has been reading Gogol and Gorky, shakes hands with any friends it meets among the guests, and crosses its legs to play the 'Gipsy's Romance.' A shaggy, walrus-like little man leads them with mechanical jerks – like Camp's 'daily dozen.' But they play admirably, with such spirit that some of the fat, over-emotional diners blubber into their *bortch.*

A pale, but very beautiful girl, with just the right touch of melancholy, passes the plate. She takes your money, with uptilted nose, seems to breathe: 'Only adversity makes me do this – scum!'

It is impossible to tell, seeing three men coming into the room, which of them is the waiter. We are all equally shabby. Cats and dogs prowl under the chair-legs; and one little black and white puppy – the result of a love affair between a fox-terrier and dachshund – balances himself on his absurd little hind-legs, and leaps straight up and down. He thinks he is a fox-terrier.

Flame, on the water-front, is in the toughest part of a supposedly tough city – a water-front which, in its way, is not far behind Marseilles, which is infinitely worse than Port Said, which is infinitely worse than any pure-minded man can imagine. Yells in the back streets usually mean something. We had sought refuge in a bake-shop near the foot of the black, hole-pitted streets – a bake-shop such as Gorky describes in *Twenty-six men and a Girl* – white brick oven, crawling dirt; a pimply-faced youth leaning over the hot, sour loaves. We heard yells – long, piercing shrieks – they seemed to have a certain rhythm about them. When the roar of the rain had given way to rivulets sousing down through the cobbles we went out in search.

We found the Bosfor. A squalid one-room café – a dive. An open fire of charcoal glowed in a mushroom-shaped aperture facing the door. On the left, at the end of the room, was a dais. Three gipsies sat there – teasing their fiddles. Three girls sat before them, girls in bright silk, war paint, with their hair tied in tufts before their ears – like enormous Dundrearys. Their sallow skins looked lavender under the thick coating of powder. Their black eyes were like bullets. They were flat-chested – skinny.

At the end of the row sat a wisp of a girl, not more than seventeen, her meagre shoulders wrapped in a bright shawl. She looked in the last stage of 'T.B.'

'Mercy,' said the Crew; 'look at that poor little thing. She looks like death!'

At that moment the girl opened her mouth and emitted a sound like a steam siren. The percussion nearly shattered my ear-drums. Her lungs must have been magnificent! The two other girls shrieked and bellowed by turns. They sat there with crossed ankles and hands, and simply ripped the darkness to pieces. These are the yells in the back-streets of Belgrade.

Three soldiers in the background, very drunk, were waltzing together. Some cavalrymen slapped the hilts of

138

their swords – drank some sort of blood-brotherhood in the confusion. Soldiers, sailors, and 'sports' looked glassy-eyed, shouted over their wine, argued with certain members of the oldest profession in the world who consorted among them. Way off, in a dim, smoky corner, the Crew spotted 'Brooklyn.' He was brooding over a sad little piece of sausage and a little glass of very dirty beer.

We summoned the waiter and sent him a bottle of red wine. I raised my glass amidst the blue smoke that curled under the oil-lamps:

'Brooklyn!'

The gnarled, weather-beaten features contorted. The old sailor stood up: 'Brooklyn!'

'You're comin' back, ain't yer?' the proprietor breathed on my neck. We told him we would; but as at that moment a fight broke out between the fair ladies I don't think we shall.

CHAPTER TWENTY-SIX

The Women of Progar

*

I THINK that the man with the wheelbarrow full of garbage started this trip. He used to dump a load of unmentionable things into the Save by our boat every morning.

'Let's get out of this place,' said the Crew. 'I can't stand it much longer.'

I, too, was glad to clear out. City water-fronts are unpleasant places. Sewage and smells and the crowd of parasites that batten on sailors. We were afraid to put our hands in the water; and we knew that our portholes provided a peep show at nights. Also, we had found the Serb in the country infinitely better than the Serb of the city.

We cast off, and headed *Flame* up the Save, which is a respectable, long-distance river that begins somewhere up in the Carinthian Mountains in Italy. A historic river that has figured only too frequently in the tragic story of the South Slavs, a history too complex to dwell upon, but which, for this trip, can be boiled down to the fact that the left bank was old Serb and the right was Croat — until the world war a province of Austria-Hungary. On the left bank the peasants wear a sort of curly-toed moccasin, tied with thongs to their legs; on the right they wear calf-high, black leather boots, or stuff their feet into carpet slippers.

We did not have a chart, nor did we feel that we needed one, as the Save is a deep, kindly old river with a current not too strong for our engine to cope with. We said goodbye to our cronies on the engineer's employment barge, left them hard at work on a bottle of cognac we had donated, and a half-hour later were passing under the bridge above Belgrade. The old spans of the bridge destroyed in the war gaped at us like a lot of black teeth in the water. We saw a bend to the right, leading away from the mountains, and followed it.

Flat country close to the river, and a tapering contour of bare, arid hills in the background. Sparsely settled. A steamer passed us, coming down from some place up the Save, just about sunset. We anchored below an island which must have been holding a Balkan convention of crows. They came flapping toward it from every direction – like dust in the sky. They came like long wisps of black smoke over the fast-fading mountains. They passed in squawking squads overhead, thousands of them! They fought in the trees of the island – whirled in black spray over the tossing sea of green branches – shrieking, swearing, damning everything in creation. I saw more crows in twenty minutes than I had ever seen before in my life.

'One for sorrow, and two for mirth – I wonder what a million stands for?' cried the Crew.

'Dinner,' I yelled back – and dropped anchor.

In the morning I drove *Flame* into shoal water and went overside – a thing I would never have dared do in the filthy water near Belgrade. We had hit a deadhead above Novi Sad on our way down the Danube, and the resulting vibration of a loose propeller bracket and a one-cylinder engine made us seem to be doing a Gilda Gray in *Flame's* cockpit. With a screwdriver tied to my wrist and various little wooden plugs coated with fresh paint in my teeth, I disappeared under water – and fixed things. The fact that the Save was in flood and held a certain amount of mud in solution did not help matters. Also, it was cold, tragically cold. And when I at last climbed into *Flame* the goose-flesh on my figure fetched from the Crew the remark that I looked like a cactus.

141

As if to shame me, we soon passed a bevy of peasant girls on the left bank, knee deep in water – washing. They were strong thewed, these maidens – the draught type – though their faces were rather shapely and beautiful. Perhaps they were knowing enough to realize how very becoming is a brilliant handkerchief tied under a round chin – especially if one droops the eyes. They had their brilliant, plaited skirts pulled up to the waists and a vivid little cross-stitched apron before them. They were heating water on wood fires on the bank, sudsing the clothes in tubs cut from tree-trunks, and throwing them out into the stream on the end of a string. They finished the operation by beating them to a pulp on a rock.

A Russian, who emerged from the bushes, told us that they walked seven or eight miles to get water.

'Why do you speak Russian to them?' he said. 'You haven't said one word of Serb!'

'What's the difference? They understand.' I looked at a vivid little beauty in a padded leather jacket, like a saddle. 'You understand, don't you?'

'Of course!' She flipped her brown head toward the Russian. 'Perfectly.'

I didn't try any more.

At sunset we saw the white tower and red dome of a church behind an island on the right bank of the river. As we knew it was the last for ten miles, we crossed over. Two men stood on a high, clayey bank. They looked like Italians. And this time my Russian didn't work. We followed them mutely across some quarter-mile of brambly meadows, down through a dip where bricks were being made of mud and old wheat chaff, and into a garden of corn with a sort of fantasy of white gourds hanging from the plum-trees at its

142

end. We passed into a farmyard, and the kindly Croat introduced us to his wife. She was in the back room of the
house, with two horses, some young pigs, and was busily
milking a cow. A huge vat of plums stood in the corner —
for *slivowitz* (the local plum brandy — it tastes like fire). He
opened the gate of his courtyard, and we stood in the main
street of Progar.

In the semi-darkness it looked like a long sea of black
mud. Which it was! The Croat led us to the store, a one-
room arrangement, run by a Kuban Cossack. When he
heard the familiar greeting he deserted his counter.

'Yes, yes,' he said impatiently to a child asking for change
— but didn't give her any. The customers went in behind
the counter, weighed out their supplies, and made out their
own change from the cash-till. The Cossack talked of
Russia.

He told us that the school-teacher of the village was a
Russian, the priest was a Russian, and there were seven
other Russians in Progar — Kuban Cossacks.

'And how do you find life?'

'Not bad,' he said, 'and not good. They are good people.
This is a co-operative store. He' — he pointed to the kindly-
eyed Croat — 'he is one. But I run it — I weigh out, I plan,
and take in the money. Not like Russia; but —' The
Kuban Cossack grinned at the trick Fate had dealt.

We found out the next morning that there were five
Germans in the village and five Magyars. The other few
hundreds were Serbo-Croats.

'But it doesn't make any difference,' said the school-
teacher; 'they are all just the same.'

There was an extraordinary uniformity about this simple
village of Progar. All tillers of the soil, hand labour, all

peasants. The priest and the school-teacher – the 'intelligentsia' – were each supplied with a house, firewood, and about an acre of land. The teacher gets £6 a month wages. He told me it cost him £3 to £3 10s. a month for his food. He had a wife, and baby that was always howlingly hungry. She fed him unabashed.

A romance – these two young Russians. He had been a law student in Petrograd. She lived in far-off Tiflis. The red wars drove them out. They met in Zagreb in Serbia, in a school to teach teachers. They married. And here they are, six years later, in this little village of Progar – absolutely shut off from life, content to let the great world and its troubles pass by. It has frightened them.

'If the chance comes,' I asked, 'will you go back to Russia?'

He looked up from his plate – they had asked us to luncheon – and I fancied I caught a startled look in his eyes. He shook his head. 'We'll stay here,' he said: 'It's too late now.'

A picture flashed into my mind, a scene at the dirt cross-roads that morning – four Kuban Cossacks, standing alone. I wondered if those rugged little fighters would ever settle down in this tranquil scene.

This was Sunday. Carts drove in from the outlying farms, the foals running free by their mothers. Geese marched down mud streets, herds of little woolly-haired pigs raced back and forth (the teacher had three young sickly chickens in his dining-room); men gambled with cards, squatting down on the hot dirt before the white-walled café. A band of fiddlers played in the courtyard, and bowlers threw wooden balls down a dirt alley at ninepins. All morning, until after luncheon, the women worked, cooking outside in brick ovens, serving their men, fetching water from the town pump, washing up – they are the slaves in this land. But at four-thirty – ah, at four-thirty – see the women of Progar!

Silk dresses, white gloves, umbrellas, shoes – and stockings! Yellow, red, blue, green; great creations of colour – all cut from fashion plates. The colours walk out together; two reds, two greens, or two vivid purples. They strolled with studied grace back and forth along a hundred yards of black mud – held their long skirts up daintily, made *moues* at the pigs and geese that invaded their Corso. For an hour and a half they did this. Just walked back and forth along that hundred yards of wet mud. The young men, with sickly-looking grins, strolled back and forth through them. The one-armed town crier came down on the stretch of dry ground between the ruts, beating his little red and white drum.

It was a sight to make one laugh, or swallow hard – depending upon which way one's imagination was working.

CHAPTER TWENTY-SEVEN

A Stronghold of Allah

★

IF you refer to a map you will see that Bosnia-Herzegovina – and for that matter, all the Balkan peninsula west of Belgrade to the Adriatic – is a mass of mountains. In here lies Sarajevo, the town that started the world war. In here are minarets and masked women, walled cities, primeval forests, dried-up lakes, and dead rivers. Herein is a lost world of grey mountains, with ancient civilizations behind sky-piercing grey cliffs. A country in which there were white serfs, virtual slaves, as late as the year of our Lord 1912! A dry, burnt wilderness, where every pocket of earth is locked up by stone walls – and water is as precious as life. A slag pile of Karst, where the bare teeth of the lower Dinaric Alps bite the colourless sky. And one mounts through a high, fort-tipped defile to come out and see, thousands of feet down below, the green of fig groves, olives, pomegranates, cactus, and cypress – the sub-tropical shores of the Adriatic – and the ancient grey forts of Ragusa beside the slow, peacock sea.

We set out to drive across this wildly romantic part of the Balkans in a Berliet car, though the first morning out of Belgrade made us think we had embarked in a cocktail-shaker. There is not much travel in old Serbia – yet. Bullock carts are the chief means of transport and bullock carts are built for bad roads. I think Serbians prefer them. We saw long lines of patient bullocks asleep by their carts in the deep muddy hollows, their white-tunicked drivers snoring under the acacias. There is a good deal of snoring in this part of Serbia, in the hot middle of the day, in the lazy, rich farmland by the Save. We followed this river – the old

146

frontier between Hungary and Serbia – to Shabatz, and careened into this blistering, fly-infested little town about noon.

Here, where fresh skeins of red wool are suspended before the shop-doors, where tinkers, cobblers, and harness-makers sit in open-faced booths and where a man in modern dress is almost conspicuous, we encountered the proprietor of the Grand Hotel – a Serb who had been for fourteen years an engineer in New York.

'I have travelled much,' he informed us; adding somewhat mysteriously, 'I will show you.' He led us into the garden behind his hotel, where in a sort of decorated cowshed we confronted a truly staggering pictograph of his ramblings. Each record was about twelve feet square.

'The boat-landing – Central Park,' he declared, pointing to a flat green sea and black boats, a sort of Japanese temple in the background. 'New York.'

We recognized it at once.

'The Banana Park – San Francisco.'

He whirled and pointed to another part of the wall.

'The Pyramids.' No one who had studied geometry could go wrong on these. We paused before a jungle-like plantation of immense foliage; and the Crew hazarded brightly:

'India?'

'The Boston Post Road,' he said, sternly.

He then led us into his restaurant, where he gave us a pallid lunch for which he charged Delmonico prices. 'Ah,' he sighed, leaning over our table, 'I wish that I had not left New York.'

We agreed with him.

Still hungry, we left the Save, and cut across country to the Drina, the boundary between Serbia and Bosnia. Serbia, to-day, is in one of those painful transition stages that confront the new rich. Vast areas of territory have come under Serbian sway since the war – more, almost, than they know what to do with – an embarrassment of riches. Serbia is keenly conscious of the fact that, in territory at least, she is the coming country of the Balkans. Jugoslavia is the eleventh country in Europe; in population, the tenth. The biggest cities are boom towns. Serbia stands imperiously between the East and the West, self-conscious, somewhat truculent, with a standing army of 150,000 men – more than the United States has. The talk in Belgrade is 'large.'

It was a relief, therefore, to get among the Serbian peasants. They are disturbed by no grandiose imaginings. They are simple, kindly, and courteous. Their natural good taste in houses and dress is as marked as is the vulgarity and tawdriness of their half-baked brothers in Belgrade. Their little villages, communes, are quite charming.

Each house is set off in a little fenced stockade in which, among the plums, stands a high corn-crib on stilts – or over the stable – and an outdoor brick oven, on which most of the cooking is done. The houses are smooth-walled, built of brick or unbaked pressed mud, and are either snowy white or tinted pink or pale blue. They have red-tile roofs, though some of the very poorest are thatched.

The interiors are impressive in their dead simplicity – immaculate – almost nun-like in the severe absence of decoration and superfluous objects. Four snow-white walls, beds, and a dresser. The windows are clean as a club's, but usually shut. The oblong shape of their one-storey dwellings, the relation of low walls to high roofs is about three to five, most pleasing proportions. The yards are clean and well-kept. The children are happy.

The men are lean, rather swarthy, and walk like free men. Their costume is either a white tunic – which has not changed much since the days of the Romans – and loose white trousers, like pyjamas; or the short brown jacket of homespun and tight-fitting breeches. They all wear *opankas*, soft, sort of moccasin footgear, tied by thongs to the legs. They take off their black astrakhan hats as you pass, calling out good-naturedly. They received scant courtesy from Orloff, our Russian driver – a road-hog, if ever there was one. Yet it was rather amusing to see the terrified way these renowned fighting-men piled out of their little wicker, bath-tub-shaped carts, or down off their travelling hay-cocks, and held the horns of their bullocks. Both men and animals were perturbed by the sight of the automobile. It was corn-husking time in Serbia, and groups of scarlet-clad women waved to us from mounds of golden corn. Laughing, friendly people.

It is rather disgusting to think that these simple folk are being constantly scratched and inoculated with dynastic theories – the vaccination of hate. One feels almost certain that the Balkan problem would not be a problem if the local Bismarcks and the so-called diplomats of Paris, London, Berlin, could only find a new plaything.

We drove across a foothill country, through a gradually thickening forest of oak, toward a range of blue mountains. We reached the Drina, about forty miles above, where it empties into the Save, went up among the stony, trickling bed of the river, reached a bronze gorge, and there – fantastic, Byzantine in the golden powder of sunset – were the minarets, mesreybiahs, and high-pointed roofs of old Zvornick. Turbaned men stared at us across the narrow strip of green water. The stronghold of Allah – Bosnia!

It was extraordinary, the transition in crossing that

stream. A step from the West to the East. We drove the car off the little float ferry, climbed up the beach, and entered a different world. Tarboosh and turban, scrolled lattice, high, wedge-shaped roofs, sickly, sweet-smelling bazaars, coffee-stalls, hammered brass. At the bend, where the Drina curls like a green plume between two pinnacles of grey rock, we saw a woman in white. She turned – a black mask.

'Golly!' the Crew gasped, almost frightened.

The sinister mask had the same startling effect upon me – though I had lived more than a year among veiled women and the nomads of the desert. But this was no yashmak. There were no languorous kohl-painted eyes behind a cylinder of carved brass. This woman was hooded like a Taureg. Not one particle of her flesh was visible. It stunned one.

What was even more startling was the thought that if she spoke it would be Serbo-Croat. For all we could tell she might have been ravishing – one of those luscious blondes which the Mohammedans seem to go in for – but all we saw was a blind, black mask that turned to follow the car. Over a third of the Bosnians are like this – Mohammedan Slavs.

Ever climbing, we followed the Drina, and then through a darkening trail up the forest slope of the Drinaca, a purling little tributary. Always the same wedge-shaped roofs, the eaves overhanging dwarfed walls, blue smoke rising out of the smoke-holes cut in the long, snake-scale shingles! Bizarre-shaped roofs – like gnomes' hats. We saw squatting figures beside the red glow of fires, like red-bloomered tots. Two women, in a cornfield, peeked under their masks, clutched each other timidly – hid their brazen faces. We saw women in the pack-trains ahead drop their masks, huddle close to the little over-burdened, dwarfed mountain horses. We saw red-fezzed men rush to drive them indoors. The queer secretiveness of the East! Minarets against the gathering gloom of pine forests. White Mohammedans.

We came upon fields, little patches of land where hay was so precious that each stack was raised from the ground, or protected by a barrier of wickets. They looked like Tartars' hats. As the sun went down we came upon a donkey standing, apparently alone, on the road, and then, beside him, we saw an old Mussulman on his knees, bowing toward Mecca. Probably not a dozen cars a year pass over that stretch of wild road, yet the old Mohammedan did not turn his head. The donkey, however, jumped into the woods, pack and all.

We climbed to where one could leap across stream, where the tiny water-mills were so small that one wanted to pick them up and run off with them. If a little band of dwarfs had suddenly emerged from the forest we should not have been surprised. It was that kind of country. The stars came out. We saw lights at the foot of another wall of high mountains – we came to Vlasnitca.

A mountain guard, his short Steyr carbine on a strap over his shoulder, regarded us apprehensively. Where had we come from? We told him, and, finding we could get a room, took out our bags – left him. He walked off slowly, as if wondering whether it would not be better to ask further questions.

In the little Gostina, in a dim room where Mohammedans – sad defaulters – drank *slivowitz*, we ate some sort of mess made of eggs and meat fried together. It was too dark to see it – which was fortunate. We climbed into hard beds (you do not rent a room in Vlasnitca, you rent so many beds), and, with the fresh forest air in our lungs, fell asleep.

The light of our lamp awoke me a few hours later. I saw Crew sitting in the middle of the board floor — like a Yogi. Her bed, she wailed, was alive.

'What is it?' I asked, 'fleas or — '

'Both,' she said miserably.

We had found the real Balkan problem.

CHAPTER TWENTY-EIGHT

Cross and Crescent in Bosnia

★

ORLOFF, our Russian chauffeur, came to my room last night and gave me his money. 'There is a strange man in my room; he did not look sympathetic.'

I asked him how he had slept.

'Poorly. They drank and sang all night.'

An odd lot these Mohammedan Bosnians; although the women out-muzzle the Mussulmans in the completeness of their shrouding and sinister masks, the men defy the Koran and drink *slivowitz*. I told him that it was probably Ramadan – there had been a fine crescent moon. I, too, had had a bad night, I informed him, my tormentors – bit!

Orloff dismissed the bugs with a shrug. '*Nitcehvo*. You will get used to them.'

He had been up since five o'clock going over the car, fixing spare tubes. I saw two oil-cans full of water in the front seat, and an extra rope tied around our reserve gas-tank on the running board.

'From now on,' he explained, 'it is mountains.'

I had the idea that we had had mountains the previous day. But when the Russian hurled the car around the cliff above Vlasnitca, and I saw the little minarets of the town on its ridge far below, and, towering before us, a tumbled wall of green forest in a sky-line of blue peaks – then I knew that Orloff spoke the truth. These were mountains.

The road zigzagged up the mountain-side like a streak of pale lightning. On some of the sharp, hairpin turns the car could not make the turn; it was necessary to back, which Orloff did with a blood-curdling sang-froid, backing the rear wheel to within a hand's width of the precipice and giving me an excellent view of the scenery below. Usually, however, he managed to make it by skidding the rear wheels around. I am not sure which method appealed to me least.

The forest was beech, studded with oak, very beautiful and utterly wild. I have seen its counterpart in New York State and British Columbia, and was wondering how unforeign it seemed, how much it resembled American woods in the fall, with the leaves turning colour, when we shot over a ridge into a clearing. At the far side was another sheer wall of mountain, jagged cliffs on its ridge, cloaked in almost a black-green forest of spruce. And against this cold northern background I faced the yellow logs of a cluster of high-roofed Bosnian huts, a woman in scarlet bloomers, who hurriedly dropped her black mask, and two men in white with red sashes and fez, chopping wood. A girl crawled out of the roof of the house nearest me with an armful of hay. She turned her head so that I might not see her face.

Imagine Turkish villages in the Rockies, or in the high uplands of Switzerland, windswept plateaus, where, through the clouds, one gets glimpses of vast depths of valley, the tips of towering spruce, cows, with bells, browsing among the autumn crocuses; little sharp-roofed chalets. Picture minarets on the sky-line of the Catskills. Let the cold, swift wind of north land fan your cheeks, and then see, coming down the trail, a pack-train of dwarf mountain horses, golden corn in their panniers, and a little baggy-bloomered Turk at their head. This is Bosnia, a country as complex and confused as is this description, a land of Orient and Occident, where blue-eyed girls stain their hands red with henna, where minarets are often made of pine slates, and the Cross meets the Crescent in the depths of silent pine forests.

For more than 400 years the Turk held this wonderland. He did not get out until 1878. And while he was here, you may be sure, he was not celibate. He left more than his religion to the Mohammedan Slavs. He left swarthy features, hawk-like eyes, stiff, black hair, and an astonishing luscious legacy of blonde, shapely women. His turbaned tombstones dot the hills like white forests. Yet he left a civilization and a system that was still operating in 1912, the system of overlord and white serf – *beg, beglouk*, and *kmet*. He left this within twenty hours of Paris.

The Austrians, when they formally annexed Bosnia in 1908, made a pretence of abolishing this. In reality they encouraged the Turkish landlord, the *beg*. They wrote the ordinance so that the Serfs were freed by 'mutual consent' – at their own expense. They even provided a Government loan from which the Serf could borrow enough money to free himself. But as the Serf had no way to make money above that actually required to keep him alive, the loan had no appreciable results. The *kmet* tilled the soil of his lord, received one-fifth of the fruits of his labour, and in addition had to render personal service when required. All this was going on about the time you and I were being taught what a fine world it was – back in college.

The Jugoslavs, when they absorbed Bosnia and Herzegovina after the world war, abolished this feudal system. They have established 111,102 *kmet* families as owners of the land they had previously tilled. There they are to-day, happy as ticks, having a hard time to make both ends meet – this is a wild mountain country – but free. They are no longer *rayahs* – dogs for the Turks. Yet still – 'a muezzin from the tower calls' – at the sinking of the sun more than a third of the Bosnians bow their heads toward Mecca.

A strange, beautiful, fantastic country – the past projected into the present – where the Romans left old forts and stone bridges (like the beautiful arch over the Narenta at Mostar), where the early Slavs gave the tongue and Cyril the alphabet; where the Austrians brought a culture, the Roman Catholic religion, and good roads, and the ineffaceable Turk left his imprint on everything.

The peasants live in the *poljai* fields between the clefts of high mountains, altogether outside the age of machinery. We dropped down through the forests, where the air was cold and damp, into one of these sunlit, broad valleys – probably the dead bed of a lake. Cattle, sheep, and goats browsed on the short mountain grass. Woman shepherds were spinning wool on hand distaffs, swinging the thread on plummets. Men in white were driving horses around a gold disk of wheat – winnowing it with wooden pitchforks and shovels in the fresh morning air.

Inside one of their primitive log huts we saw mounds of fresh fluffy wool, the women carding it with rude combs. They had a stone stove going at full blast to dry the white, snow-like hair. The smoke curled out through a niche in the roof. Farther on we saw tiny water-mills like toy music-boxes over the singing, green mountain streams. Wood-cutters peered at us from the forest, their straight-handled, ancient axes exactly the same as those their ancestors used to part a man from his head.

We swung one high ridge, looked out over a petrified sea of purple mountains, and in the far distance saw the glistening minarets, white domes, and houses of Sarajevo in the trough of a wave. A queer little town, with its eyes pointed west, but unable to overcome the romantic influence of a hundred white mosques and a Scheherazade of Turkish bazaar. El Raschid bought his coffee-pots from such tinkers as these, and I think he would have appreciated the beautiful Oriental jewellery from Vienna.

In the fountained garden of the old Husref Beg Mosque we confronted a dreamer. Could we, dogs of infidels, pass through that sacred archway? We could, and for some peculiar reason a woman also could enter. The Crew and I pushed our shoes into slippers like snowshoes, flapped across the spotless grass matting inside the quiet walls, and listened to the beauties of the mosaicked archways above us, of the gorgeous winter carpet – now rolled up for the summer – extolled by a devout catfish-whiskered Mohammedan in German.

One notable thing about Sarajevo is its cooking. I have eaten toasted possum in Virginia, boiled chicken heads in Hungary, the *shaslik* of Tartary; but the cuisine of Sarajevo stands alone in its frightfulness.

We were glad to get out in the open country again. In the afternoon we met streams running westward. High in the hills we found the Narenta, the old Roman frontier, crossed by Scipio in 156 B.C., when he subdued the Dalmatians. He could have jumped across it where we found it – a trickle among the grey stones. We drove down its valley, crossed it on old Roman and Turkish bridges, where little towns held the banks – minarets and tall poplars.

We found a new brand of peasant – beautiful broad-eyed women, who parted their black hair in the middle and wore gold coins on their foreheads. We followed the green ribbon into a fat farm land, drove for miles under an archway of walnuts and then came to a wilderness such as can be compared to no place on earth – a perfect orgy of rock, where it seemed as if the Creator in the making of things had suddenly become annoyed with His task and smashed things every which way. We entered a narrow defile, where some of the battered crags were 6,000 feet high.

The moon peered down at us beside the white, rushing water – made the world cold and dead. It sank over the mountains, and we looked up to see just a jagged, black contour against a gun-metal sky. The lights of the car played on a bull's-eye of white rocks. A race out of this gash in the mountains and we came into the Turkish streets of old Mostar.

From the round windows we looked down on the Narenta, still rushing in its rocky gorge through the town. We saw bright lights across it, a broad street, cafés, girls, and soldiers – tall poplars, minarets, reaching wistfully to the star-studded sky. A muezzin called from the tower:

'*Ya Allah! Ill' Allah. Wu Muhamud. Razul Allah!*'

His voice floated to us from the cold background of hills, whining, petulant; it broke on a high note, as if in rage at these infidels in the streets of Mostar below.

CHAPTER TWENTY-NINE

The Lost World of Herzegovina

★

THE gentlemen who embarked in their steel globe in Mr. Wells's *The First Men in the Moon* could have stayed on earth and seen the same thing in Herzegovina. This country is not like the world that Americans know; it is lunar, and the race that lives in it seems to belong to another planet, or, at any rate, to a civilization very remote from our own. Chaldeans or Assyrians in the moon craters would just about fit them.

Geologically, the 3,500 square miles of Herzegovina is spoken of as a Karst-like formation. I have forgotten what Karst is, if I ever knew. All I know is that it looks like a chaos of gigantic grey cliff and mountains made entirely of pumice. There is no colour, no water, and practically no vegetation, only a few stunted thorn-bushes that seem to grow independently of soil or moisture from the very rock itself. The only wild things we saw were some green lizards and a beetle that, with his hind-legs, rolled a ball of dirt up a rock. He also had an idea of the value of soil.

Earth is as precious as gold in Herzegovina. Every little pocket, collected through centuries in the rocks, is almost fortified by high walls of stone and cultivated with a pathetic eagerness. There is no place too small to be worth while. Every yard is precious. High up in the mountains we would see little squares of corn or millet, hardly bigger than a bedspread, which must have taken hours of climbing to reach. The poor huts are built of stone, with only one object in view – to obtain a shelter against the blinding white sun, or the rains – when they come. The men, although they are a fierce fighting breed (which is to be expected in a country like this), destroy the dignity of their beautiful blue and red clothes with little 'Happy Hooligan' hats.

However, they wear this suit only on Sundays or fête days; their other suit being a tragedy of tatters and patches. And it is to be noted that in this nondescript costume they are still the same splendid men. When Orloff, pursuing his mad career in the mountains, ran into a pack-train, I expected to see the flash of long knives. The small mountain horse was unable to get up under the heavy load of wheat. He lay there philosophically, almost under our mudguard.

'Now,' I said to myself, 'this is where Orloff "gets his."'

I had no wish to protect him. But the two Herzegovines were fascinated by the fact that the Crew was taking a photograph of them from the back of the car. Orloff misunderstood. Perhaps he did not see the level glance they gave him from out their bold mountain eyes. He rushed on.

Soon, on a high stretch of road, with a sheer precipice down one flank, we saw another pack-train ahead. Orloff blew his horn, held the speed, yelled at the Herzegovine in the lead to clear off the road. The Herzegovine, with his hand on his horse, stood perfectly motionless. Orloff jammed on the brakes, we made a sliding stop, almost on the mountaineer's toes.

'Stop!' commanded the old man. 'You will stop!'

Orloff bellowed at him to move to one side.

'You will wait there,' said the old fellow. 'You do not own this road.'

As he spoke he moved steadily toward Orloff. I have never seen such implacable determination in any other man's face. Neither had Orloff; he waited. And from then on to the Adriatic he was a changed man – Orloff was no longer a road hog.

Strange people. Later on in the day we saw – oh, miracle! – fig-trees by the road. Fresh figs in this frying-pan of grey rock! We asked a man if we could buy some. He leaped up on his wall, filled our hands with the soft, purple fruit. We ate to bursting. I handed him money. He had been laughing, smiling up to that moment, like a great child, but then his face froze. He stepped off a pace and bowed gravely.

'Please!'

A courtier could not have made a more dignified protest. He then jumped the four feet of wall and pressed more figs upon us. This is a country where every twig, leaf, or grain of wheat is of value – where they shuck the corn in stone platforms so that they do not lose one grain!

We drove for hours between sheer walls of rough limestone unrelieved by one spot of colour, where grotesque fields of boulders swept up to the sky, and came out through a niche to look down upon Popovo Polje – one of the strangest sights in the world.

Popovo Polje is a lake, about twenty-five miles long, holding about fifty feet of water in winter and bone dry in summer. Its fertile, flat bed provides the granary for nearly all south Herzegovina. We saw people moving about on its surface, little clusters of workers, and what looked like a great carpet of disks and squares in yellow, brown, and bright gold. When we came near we saw that the golden disks were ripe corn, and we saw long thin men beating it with long sticks! The lighter, yellowish patches were of corn already broken up – cracked – and we saw women toting this off in sacks to the waiting horses. It was tribal, very primitive life. The brown squares were millet. There, on the floor of this valley, was the food supply of these people for the long winter months.

One wondered what tragedy would take place if the rain should come on a few days too soon. The bare hills would not hold it. Popovo Polje would almost instantly become a lake. And, strangely enough, I had this question answered. I passed Popovo Polje six days later, after three days of rain, and much of it was already covered with water. In the moonlight I looked at the silent huts of the sturdy Herzegovines. It pleased me to know that this year they had won their race with the water – they had their corn already in.

We climbed to the last sky-line of hills. White forts on their peaks showed that this had been a hard-held frontier. To our left loomed the raw mountains of Albania and Montenegro. We shot through the gorge, and there, thousands of feet below, were the green shores of Dalmatia, groves of olives, pomegranates, oranges, and figs, and an old square-rigger coming into the port of Ragusa across the blue lazy sea.

An hour later the Crew and I sported about in salt water, swam down to the white-pebbled floor, opened our eyes, and saw shoals of fishes dart between the rocks. The burnt slag-pile of Herzegovina was already a mirage.

CHAPTER THIRTY

The Return of the Native

★

'THEY mos' drive me crazy. I tell you, I'm bughouse.'

Thus a returned Dalmatian spoke of his country. He had been twenty-five years in America – for eighteen years a miner in the Copper Queen, Bisby, Arizona – and had come back home to live on his grub-stake.

'But I ain't got a chance. Dey find out every cent you got, and some way, somehow, you bet your life, dey're going to get three-tirds of it!'

'Who will?'

'The high mucka-mucks – these Serbian – ' (The last is alliterative.) 'Last year I pay an income tax of 25,000 dinars. I say, "You tax me twice more like dat, an' I'm broke. See?" I tell 'em; "Looka here, you give me passport".– (he had not taken out American papers) – "you let me take my dollars I bring from America – I go back."'

'Well?'

'They say: "You ain't gonna get no passport. You stay here."'

'Why?'

'"Cause I got money. Mister, you doan' understand. Dis country all right come and take a look at – stay a few days. You come an' live here – try dat.'

I told him I should like to; I had found it most beautiful.

'Ha! Rocks – you call dem good-looking?' He waved a great paw toward the crags holding Cattaro; 'Dis is a dam' poor country. No land, no cattle – just rocks. No place for a ranch.'

'So it seems. But you don't need much money to live here.'

'Dat's right – man can live here for a dollar a day, but how

163

in hell's he gonna get dat dollar? Man here's gotta work ten hours for six bits.'

He explained that while it costs much less to live in Dalmatia (now part of Jugoslavia) than it costs in America, it was relatively harder to get even that modest amount – and when a man got it he did not live as well.

'It's like dis: mos' men here are poor men – eat black bread. Little better guy – he eats bread ain't so black. High mucka-muck, Serbian' – (alliterative) – 'he's the only man eats white bread.' He waved his arms around the café: 'America – every man eats the same stuff. Got four bucks a day, Copper Queen, Bisby – pay buck and a half for my board – live like a king, bet your life.'

'So, even if you did have enough money here, you would rather live in America?'

'Say – Mister, I'd be the luckiest man on earth if I could see New York again. Better grub, better clothes, better people – dey leave you alone. I'm home dere.'

He said that Dalmatia might be all right for one who had never left it – didn't know anything better – but for him it was 'damn rotten hole.' He had two houses, he said, to rent, but –

'You ain't boss in your house here. Dey is. Dey tell you who to take, an' how much you get. Huh! An' if a boarder leaves, see? – and you don't tell 'em, take another, see? – by gosh! – dey put you in jail!'

He banged the marble table in the Business Men's Café – awoke most of the 'business men' – and went on.

'These Serbian – ' I listened to a tirade against Serbian officials, the high mucka-mucks, how they found out every cent a man had and how they eventually got it. I asked him if it had not been the same under the Austrian regime.

'Course not,' he declared; 'it's these Serbs. In the old days things was different.'

Of course, things always were different 'in the old days,' infinitely better. They always were. And he had been out of Dalmatia for twenty-five years. It would not be fair to burden the Serbs with all this man's discontent. Still, he was a Serbo-Croat himself and miserably unhappy. Slav officials, charming enough as equals, do not make such pleasant superiors. And there was enough smoke here, for a certain amount of fire.

Here was a man who, though he had been twenty-five years in America, could speak only broken English; had probably lived in almost a transplanted colony of his kind; yet in the dirt and sulphur fumes of the copper mines he had found a freedom he could not find in the old world. That was the interesting part of his story.

Cattaro is one of the most beautiful spots in the world. Maria della Scapello, white walls and cypress island in a sapphire fjord, is as unearthly and fantastic as a Persian poet's dream. A paradise. Yet the ways of his kind, the petty restrictions and customs, had made this a purgatory for the returned emigrant. The ring of grey mountains seemed a prison.

'It is – so help me Christ! I am lost!'

I paid for my round of black Turkish coffee – left him; and three minutes later was buying some paper in the book-shop before the old Venetian cathedral.

'Gee! I'm glad to hear that!'

I looked up, met the blue eyes of a man about my own age and size. 'Hear what?'

'American. I have been there.'

Here was another native – returned.

'And why did you come back?'

'My father. He wrote me; he said things were different.'

He, too, had been in Bisby – a truck driver, delivering groceries – and, although we walked back and sat down at the same table which the disconsolate miner had left, these two men did not know each other. I asked him why so many Dalmatians went to Bisby.

'Why not? I have a friend; he writes, "Come over here, and make money." I go. I write my brother. He writes his friends. Bymby we all meet in Bisby. Some of us make lots of money.'

He mentioned Medigovrich, a Dalmatian wholesale groceryman in Bisby, now retired to live near San Pedro, California. 'Gee! That's some place.' He told of other Dalmatians, heroes of emigrants whom the natives talked of by the shores of Bocche di Cattaro. Pioneers, adventurers in the new world – men to follow!

He told of his own pilgrimage to America. How at first he was unhappy – 'Everything upside down.' He told how his own people made it hard for him: 'Now you've got to work like hell' – how they took advantage of him, the low wages they paid. That was the first year and a half or two years – when he was washing dishes in a mining camp. Then he learned a trade; he became a truck driver. 'Gee! I lived swell. Got four dollars a day and my keep.'

'Well, you're a truck driver here – what's the matter?'

'Say – you don't understand.'

He drives the post coach between Cattaro and a town in the fjord, for which he gets 40 dinars a day – about 3s. 6d. He pays 20 dinars for his luncheon, and 20 dinars for his dinner.

'Figure that out,' he demanded; 'where do I get off?'

166

'But you don't have to pay 20 dinars for your lunch.'

'Sure, I know; but I don't want to live like no dog.'

In America, he said, he had saved £600 in five years; he could not save that much in 100 years in Dalmatia. That was the trouble here – no one could save. It was work till you dropped. The meagre farms, won from the rocks; the small groves of olives, figs, pomegranates; the tiny vineyards – these barely kept a family alive. The good grape land was owned by a few wealthy landlords. Labourers got less than 15 dinars a day. A skilled, first-class mechanic could make only 60 – about 5s. All the young men, he declared, would leave at once for America if they could.

'Well, why do so many come back?'

'Ah, you know, we was born here – an' we got our people. Guess we kid ourselves, you know; think things will be better. We forget. Most of the guys come back with a pile to try and start business.'

But this doesn't seem to work out.

CHAPTER THIRTY-ONE

Among Mountains and Clouds

★

'YOUR MAJESTY, we pray that you will see to it that every man is permitted to emigrate from this country.'

Sad and startling words for a Montenegrin to utter. The little bantam-weight country that licked or helped to lick so many of the heavyweight countries of Europe — and used to beat up the Turk for a pastime — is now off the map. It now no longer exists. In 1918 it deposed the king, Nicholas. In 1922, when the old king died in exile, the council of ambassadors in Paris recognized its union with Jugoslavia as a fact, and in 1925, when Alexander, King of the Serbs, Croats and Slovenes, came to Cetinje, a Montenegrin stepped forward and made this pathetic demand.

Where are the Montenegrins of yesterday? Has the old breed died out? Have the present inhabitants thrown up the sponge? I asked myself these questions in Cattaro. Above me, beyond the fort-tipped wall of the ancient Venetian city, towered the awesome bulk of Mount Lovcen. A majestic frontier! Beyond those cloud-drenched peaks lived one of the fiercest fighting breeds on earth. War was their pleasure; and when the men went to war the women went with them. The entire 200,000 went to do battle. What had happened to them?

'Very kind people, Montenegrins,' said an old dock walloper of Cattaro; 'very good to their families. When their families are hungry they take their guns and go out, and wait till some one comes along the road. They don't let their families starve.'

Evidently the old breed was still there. Other people had

told me that until a few months ago a band of bandits had worked the Cetinje road; but – now that the king was coming – soldiers had been sent to ' clean up.' Another man had sworn to me that all this was bosh, and that a man and his purse were as safe in Montenegro as they were in Chicago. So you can see how things stood.

The road over Lovcen is a masterpiece of mountain highway engineering. It climbs, for the most part, straight up the side of a very steep mountain. It goes up like a snake, or a jagged streak of lightning. There are twenty-seven switchbacks in the zigzag up the rocks. Always as one goes up, one side of the road hangs over the blue and there is a precipice on either side of the zigzag route. The outer edge is protected by a low wall of limestone or stone posts, until you reach the old Montenegrin frontier at 3,000 feet. After that you are saved by thorn bushes from going over the edge. And people say that if you fall 3,000 feet you are dead before you hit the ground, anyway.

I went up it in a lightning-storm – with a Russian. We could not see the top. It was somewhere in the clouds. When we got into the clouds we couldn't see anything. The mountain guards, however, saw us. A group of them appeared at the Montenegrin frontier and stood there among the barbed wire staring at us, rifles hung on straps over their backs, their heads in sharp-pointed hoods. This was wartime barbed wire and marked the gallant battle Montenegro put up against Austria. They are using it now on their poor farms all over Montenegro. It's an ill wind that doesn't blow some good to Montenegrins.

We dropped down out of the black heart of the clouds into a high mountain valley that was strangely like a savage and very, very desolate Scotland. In fact, there is an almost uncanny similarity between this fierce mountain kingdom and the wild clan country of the Scots. Grand, hard country, the same cheerless, stone huts; the same dignity and pride – and the same hard-hitting free men. The Montenegrins, too, have bagpipes. It is impossible to depict the naked barrenness of the country. The valley, tufted with thorn and scrub oak, was rimmed by almost a rough sea of sharp little peaks. Two of these held small but grim forts; others, commanding the road, had tiny roofed-over watch shelters. A nasty country to take!

One wondered that anyone ever wanted to take it. Yet this eagle's nest practically broke the heart of the Turks; was for centuries the stronghold of Serbian liberty and guardian of its traditions, and under the masterful will of the late – and now much lamented – King Nicholas even aspired to leadership of the Balkans. It formed alliances with the great powers of Europe; co-operated with the English to drive the French out of Ragusa; was the pet of Russia, and provided a beautiful queen for Italy. In the world war they had the Homeric sport of standing on their peaks and hurling bombs down into the Austrians in Cattaro, 6,000 feet below.

'It was awful!' said a citizen of Cattaro, throwing up his hands; 'they just stood up there on the top, and pitched them over. They couldn't miss us!'

A very sporty country! Behind Cetinje they have a little round tower on which they used to mount the heads of the Turks – hunting trophies, so to speak.

We saw this from the top of the next pass, and the straight white road running across the flat green bed of valleys at the end of which were the low white houses of Cetinje. In the distance were more mountains, grey and menacing, the silver waters of Lake Scutari, and the 'accursed mountains' of Albania.

In three and a half hours' hard driving we had done exactly twenty-eight miles.

There is a room in the Grand Hotel kept for the Standard Oil man, but as that hotel was under repairs we went to the Hôtel de Paris, where we had a fine lunch, with huge Montenegrin grapes, in the cellar. It would take perhaps fifteen minutes to walk around this remarkable capital. In the square under the horse-chestnuts I saw the market going full swing; peppers, walnuts, chickens – hobbled in pairs – eggs, cheese, figs (from Cattaro below) – a great deal of barter and bicker. The clothes of the women were shabby and black; those of the men were sometimes even tattered; although here and there was a beautiful personage in gold and red embroidered jacket, baggy blue breeches and queer white leggings laced with brass up the back. Strangely enough I saw fewer peasant costumes in Cetinje than I did, relatively speaking, in Belgrade. And even the fiery old picturesque warriors, with revolvers sticking out of their belts, came past in Burberrys – holding umbrellas. It is an intensely clean, respectable little capital.

Orloff, our Russian chauffeur, noticed other things. '*Bozhe moi!*' he exclaimed, 'it is true! They are the most beautiful in Europe!'

He pointed to some of them coming past; dark, wide eyes, silky black hair, tall, slender and graceful – the maidens of Cetinje. I caught my breath – I knew why the Turks had fought for 500 years to take Montenegro.

I stood in front of the simple two-story old palace, gazed at its shiny slate roof – a plain country home.

'Yes,' said a Montenegrin who came past, 'that is the

palace.' He sighed. 'But it is quite empty now, and they have taken everything.' He accused the Serbs of having taken the art treasures away.

'Well,' I said, 'you deposed your own king.'

'I know, I know – we did it.'

'Well, what are you kicking about?'

He explained that it was the result of Serb propaganda; this was a hard country to live in; they thought that Montenegro would have autonomy under Jugoslavia; things would be different. He pointed to probably the biggest buildings in Cetinje – the Serbian regiment's barracks:

'And now look what we've got!'

I thought of gallant old Nicholas and how at nineteen he had defeated Omar and Derwish, two of the best Turkish generals; how he had doubled the territory of Montenegro, won for her a port on the Adriatic and a recognized place among the nations of Europe; had given the Montenegrins a good public life, improved laws, and good schools; how he had wheedled, cajoled and extracted money for Montenegro from the reigning families of Europe. And these people, for whom he had worked almost miracles, had denied him.

'It was on the promises of Wilson – ' said the Montenegrin.

'Not so!' I retorted; 'it was on the principles of Judas.'

Whatever happens to the Montenegrins – they have it coming to them.

CHAPTER THIRTY-TWO

Entering Roumania

*

No one but the most fatuous admirer would call Belgrade a pleasing town; yet nothing will ever make us forget the kindness of its people. After two weeks' absence and a motor drive over the Balkans to Montenegro we got back with trembling hearts as to the fate of our *Flame*. She had been left alone on the river front.

'She's afloat, anyway,' cried the Crew, who had rushed on ahead.

I saw the stars and stripes floating under the stern of the employment barge. And not only was the yawl intact, but our friends on the barge had even taken out the cushions, tools, etc., 'In case some one should come while we slept.' An offer of money was refused indignantly. We shook a dozen friendly hands before we cast off. Our travels through the Balkans to the Adriatic had made us realize what a powerful empire this little war-worn capital represented. Perhaps, if she gets time enough between wars, she will rebuild herself more beautifully. At any rate we gave her a respectful salute as she dropped over the stern.

Fall has come to the Danube; the early mornings are shrouded in a thick white mist, like steam. This blew off above Semendria to reveal the low wooded shores of the island on our left, the last of the Serbian mountains on our right, and, ahead, an imposing army of tall grey towers.

'Grain elevators,' I said to the Crew.

'How do you know that?'

'By their shape; anyone can tell grain elevators by their shape.'

'Oh,' regretfully; 'I thought they must be a fort.'

They were a fort! The most astounding array of battle-ments conceivable. We bore down upon an expanse of serrated walls, high-flung fighting-towers – a veritable whale of a fort! A spray of black crows swirled over the fighting-tops.

George Brankovic vs Turks – 1492!

Eventually the Turks had swarmed over it, destroying it in parts – we saw gaping sides and broached lancet windows as we passed – but there was enough of it left to be almost unbelievable. The present has formed but the thinnest of layers over the past of the Danube. In England one is shown a heap of dirt, and is told: 'That was an old Roman barrow.' At Szinice, in Roumania, one whirls through the rapids, catches a startled glimpse of three yellow towers standing on a queer doughy-looking rock, and knows that they *are* the old Roman fort.

Over the whirlpools in the Greben defile we saw the road of Tiberius cut through the crags in A.D. 33. As we lay at Coronini, the six towers of Golubac would gradually appear to us each morning, as if the mist blown away by the sun had been the veil of the past. Shooting out of the gorge of Kazan we saw postholes, the deep cut belt road in the cliffs and the inscription of Trajan:

IMP. CÆSAR DIVI. NERVÆ F. NERVA TRAIANUS AUG.
GERM PONT. MAXIMUS

His Dacian campaign!

On the left bank was an ever nearer page of history which might be said to be in writing to-day. This is the Banat, that fertile belt of farm land that stretches from the Theis to Orsova on the north shore of the Danube. Until the world war this was one of Hungary's most precious possessions.

In the days of Brankovic it had been colonized by the Austrians with Serbs, Germans, and Czechs to be used as vanguards against the Turks – the Serbs, in fact, formed the granica – the frontier guard – being almost janizaries to the Austrian and Hungarian armies. Eastern Banat held large colonies of Roumanians. Since the world war the Banat has been divided between Serbia and Roumania. This part of the world to-day is an ethnographic museum, and one shudders to think of the peace conference that was daring enough to try to figure it out.

The first night we lay on the left shore of low, long and apparently uninhabited Temes Island. Great flights of mallard pitched down through the willows. A silent night; a huge lopsided moon, silky water – and the green of buoy lights far below.

We woke up in the morning to find two men on the bank. They had guns.

'We are Magyars,' they said in answer to my question. In that part of the river I knew they were subjects of Serbia. And I knew that they came from the left bank because that had been Hungary.

After an hour under way we raised the blue bulk of the Carpathians. At a point some sixty-two miles below Belgrade we passed Bazias and knew we had entered Roumania. The right bank, however, would be Serbian for the next 150 miles.

The Danube here is about a mile wide, flanked by rather bare sandy mountains that, both in shape and colour, are much like a moth-eaten camel's back.

'What is it?' I asked. 'Serbia or Roumania?'

The Crew wanted change. 'Let's try Roumania.'

Most of the villages were set far back from the shore on

account of the high water of the Danube in the spring, but at noon we came to the little village of Omoldova near the water's edge. It looked irresistible – and we dropped anchor for the first time in Roumania.

Sixty feet away, across a sloping, pebbly beach, stood Omoldova's most imposing building, the guard-house. Its glaring white arches vomited a stream of swarthy little soldiers. They fetched up short at the rail and clustered there, talking excitedly. Most of them had rifles with needle-like bayonets slung over their backs. Farther along the beach, in gorgeous blotches of colour, were peasants unloading barges packed tight with bullock carts and gold corn. Rough dirt roads wound down the slope to the edge of the beach from a bank fringed with fruit trees and little white cottages. And above them, of course, rose the paternal tower of the Orthodox Greek church.

We had been warned against the Roumanians as we had been against the natives of each successive country since leaving Holland, and went ashore well fortified with passport and letters. As usual, the warning was calumny. A polite little official barely glanced through our papers and told us that we could lie off Omoldova. He seemed strangely preoccupied, which we understood later, as he was arrested that evening for taking bribes to pass contraband. He had been doing this systematically for three years, and had kept a book of the names of the people with whom he had divided the spoils. The discovery of this had cast a gloom over the official circles of Omoldova. And the Government spy would not divide!

The peasants, I think, were rejoicing, because, outside of officialdom, the soldiers and a stray storekeeper, the men of Omoldova were all Serbs. I doubt if their costumes had changed one bit from those worn by their ancestors, brought here by the Austrians, 400 odd years ago. Man after man, as we passed, took off his black sheepskin hat and wished us '*Dobra dan.*'

Back on the *Flame*, I pointed to a crowd of children who had lined up on the water's edge to inspect us – peasants in miniature.

'What price Roumania?' said I to the Crew.

'It's Roumania, all right,' she exclaimed suddenly.

The soldier on guard was driving the children away.

CHAPTER THIRTY-THREE

St. Louis on the Danube

*

'HELLO, Sport!'

These words greeted me as we dropped anchor off Omol-dova, our first port of call in Roumania. I nearly fell into the Danube. I had expected things below Belgrade, all sorts of things, but not this. The speaker wore a pair of black and grey striped trousers that had probably been part of a morning suit, and a baggy blue coat. His black felt hat was peaked 'Montana' fashion. He was a rough diamond at first sight – and a pebble when I got to know him. He was rolling a smoke.

'Better lie up there,' he poked the cigarette toward a spot in front of a white-arched building on shore. 'If you don't they'll make you.'

'They' were Roumanian soldiers, a group of them – rifles, with long pointed bayonets, on their backs – arguing excitedly and pointing toward *Flame*. I moved on.

'Well, well,' he said, pointing to our flag; 'old U.S.A.! What are you doing here?'

'What are you doing?' I countered.

'Me? – I was born here. Right back there.' He pointed to a few white houses on the slope of the Carpathians.

'Oh – you're Roumanian.'

'Hell – no! I'm a Serb.'

I rubbed my head. A Serb in a Roumanian village, which until this war belonged to Hungary, talking an unmistakable brand of American. I told him to elucidate. 'Me? Sport, I been twenty years in America. Kept a saloon in Medicine County, Illinois – Eighth and High Street – right

across from St. Louis. My woman, L – P –, she runs it.
I'm over here now and can't go back.'

'Why?'

'Ah,' he wrinkled his nose, flung out his arms; 'I can't
get in. Gotta wait two years until my boy gets twenty-
one – then I'm father of American citizen. My woman,
she writes – '

A bayoneted soldier came to the rail of the guard-house
and called down to him.

'I gotta go,' he said; 'they tell me I gotta stop talking
to you. These guys – !' He swung up his shoulders.
'Say – I see you later.'

To my astonishment he walked off and left me. The
soldier and I faced each other across a strip of pebbly beach. I
felt the hairs on the back of my neck start to tickle. What the –

'Say!' Another man in Western attire had come down to
the water-front with a soldier. 'Hey, mister, how long you
going to stay here?'

I told him I did not know – a day, perhaps two – how
could I tell until I saw what Omoldova looked like?

'Well, they want to know.'

'Tell them four days.'

He translated this to the soldier. 'Hey, mister, what's
your name?'

I told him. Also I answered questions as to where I had
come from, whither bound and why. I answered them fully
and truthfully as this was a frontier – Jugoslavia was just
across river – and they had every right to the information.
It did not seem enough for the soldier, but as he could
think of nothing further to ask, he left. He did not salute.

'Hey, mister. Ever been in St. Louis?'

'Yes, have you?'

'Sure. Work there eighteen years. Hospital. Fine place – St. Louis.'

Nearly every family in Omoldova, he said, had relations in either St. Louis or Detroit, or some one who had been there. 'I show you the pictures in the houses.'

Simple, low, dirt-floored peasant homes! Here, in this primitive village in the foothills of the Carpathians, I had come upon one of the bed-roots of two of the greatest American cities. No railroad, no street lights; the church was by far the biggest building in it.

'I come home to retire. I'm fifty-five – I got a little money. Don't work any more – just fish.'

'Ever catch any?'

He said that he had caught one last week. He was quick to tell me that he was a Serb and that practically all of the inhabitants of Omoldova were Serbs. 'Before the war,' he added, 'we used to belong to Hungary. Now we are Roumanians.'

'I suppose you find things just the same?'

He made a grimace which might have been interpreted in any number of ways: 'Mister, when you go to the ball you got to dance to the music they play.'

I thought it politic not to inquire just what sort of dance tunes the Roumanians offered.

But the ex-saloon-keeper from Medicine County orated freely. Not against Roumanians, but just the futility of life in the old world. He was waiting for me at the crossways where the dirt road from the river traversed the even more dirt road that was the main street of Omoldova. He pulled me into one of the doors in the continuous flank of one-story whitewashed dwellings. This was his stamping-ground – the saloon.

'Look at these duds!' he whined, plucking at his shabby blue coat. 'Cost $25 in America – cost 3,500 lei here.'

'Well, that's only about $20.'

'Say, Sport, you got any idea what a working man gets here? Forty lei a day is good pay!' He plucked at his trousers. 'Got to work two months to buy a pair of pants.'

A peasant came past in the street in a white tunic, red cloth bound round his legs, a black sheepskin hat – a sensible, rather attractive costume. 'Sport' looked at it with contempt.

'That guy's got one of the biggest farms here – thirty-five acres – and he don't eat meat twice a month.'

I felt like saying that the peasant looked none the worse for it. But it would not have gone well with 'Sport.'

'Say, in the old Jefferson house I used to blow $200 a night.'

Perhaps that was the trouble with 'Sport.' At any rate, he feels an exile in his birthplace. Another tall glass of wine and his story came out. His wife had been born in Golubac, across the Danube, and they had gone to the new world together. They prospered – had three children. In 1921 he felt a desire to see the homeland, and asked his eldest son to go with him. 'Nothing doing,' replied that youth, who had been in high school in St. Louis; 'they live darned poor over there.'

'You go first,' urged his wife; 'then if things are all right, we'll all come.'

With $2,500 he came to Omoldova. The new immigration quota came into effect, and he found that he could not return. To-day the $2,500 is gone.

'My woman, she send me $650. Then she send me $100. Then she say: "That's the last. You marry over there – I marry over here!"'

He made a pathetic gesture: 'My boy I work my hands for – he's big now, got a fine house. My heart, it is no good I want to see him.'

That night we dined with the priest whose housekeeper had worked in the Morris packing plant in St. Louis. She showed us an insurance certificate. 'I have missed my chance,' she said; 'I am too old to go back now.' As we went about the streets one person and another came up to say that they had been in St. Louis, or had relatives there. One woman asked us to mail a letter for her in another town. 'I can't understand,' she said; 'I write my sister again and again, and she does not answer. I think the postmaster must be keeping my letters.'

St. Louis! St. Louis! How they speak of you here – fine, free, wonderful, bright-lighted St. Louis! I fell asleep that night in a brain haze of Roumanian soldiers, simple peasants, electric lights, the obsolete truth in the Monroe Doctrine, and the last words of 'Sport'!

'First thing I do when I see America again – stand in New York – I get down on my knees and I kiss the ground three times.'

CHAPTER THIRTY-FOUR

Slivowitz

*

THIS is the way the peasants of Omoldova, a little Serbian village in Roumania, make plum brandy. First they build a hut of wattles and clay by the side of a little stream, and in one corner erect a cone-shaped oven of clay. They behead this cone about two feet from the ground, and in the four-foot broad top insert a huge copper vessel like an enormous squat vase. They mud this up, leaving only the mouth open, and put thereon a large copper globe, connected by a two-inch wide pipe of that material with a copper worm, which is submerged in a great oak vat of cold water. They fill the copper pot with hundreds of pounds of blue plums, build a fire underneath, wait four hours – and *slivowitz* runs out the other end! *Slivowitz* is plum brandy. What could be simpler?

I held a cup under the tap and got some of the first run. Hot – in both senses of the word!

I think that if some great catastrophe should suddenly shut this village off from the world things would go on just the same. It is the closest thing I have met to the Swiss Family Robinson. Its black and white sheep are sheared periodically, and the women wash and card the wool. Then, while they are watching the flock as it grows a new fleece, or their curly-haired pigs, which look more like sheep than any pig ought to, they spin the wool on hand distaffs. These are of two kinds – one, on which the wool is plucked in little tufts and rolled into thread with the fingers; the other, like a long-pointed top, which they press against their legs and with a sharp shoot of their hands set spinning in space. This form seems an improvement – almost a modern invention. Probably brought in by the Romans.

183

When they have prepared a large skein they take it to the wool-dyer, whose house is just up the road from the *slivowitz* mill. He weighs it, gives them a receipt for so many pounds of wool, and then takes it into the back of his house and pushes it into a vat full of the colour selected. The dyes, I regret to say, are not made in Omoldova — they are supposed to be of the best German quality — and the red usually comes off when the peasants wade to tow their barges out into the Danube, so that they look as if they had been walking in cranberry sauce.

The wool-dyer's house has a perpetual rainbow under its eaves of yellow, green, red, and purple skeins of wet wool. The floor of his bedroom is under a snowdrift of fresh orders. At one time he was a gunner in the Austrian navy, but a bullet in the diaphragm and an edict of the peace conference turned him into a wool-dyer. One can see that he has travelled because he wears a felt hat and his trousers reach to his ankles.

The other peasants wrap their legs in red cloth strips, which their good wives make from the wool I have just been discussing. Their shirts are also made by their wives, as are their trousers and the red sashes they bind round their waists. Styles change slowly in Omoldova, the last to be noted being the blend of Dacian with Roman. The trousers still have the wide, free Dacian swing and look like modern pyjamas. The belted-in-tunic, buttoned at the throat, reaches to the knees. It was introduced to the Danube by Trajan. A suit, therefore, does not date in Omoldova, and can be passed on to the next generation.

Shoes may be pointed or blunt-toed as the owner desires, but, in any case, are almost square bits of soft leather, laced across the foot with thongs and bound to the calves with broad leather straps. They do not have the cone tabs, such as one sees on those of the Serbs across the river. For that matter, neither are the leg wrappings a sort of Scotch plaid like those worn by the Roumanian peasants at Coronini, five miles below. Yet these are inessentials, slight departures in dress – and 1,000 years have attested to the value and practicality of this simple footgear.

The style in hats is unborn lamb, black or white – in the shape of a tea-cosy.

The women, although usually bare-legged, are bright as humming-birds in intricate coloured embroidery. Where these designs originated I do not know, but they are almost Arabic in their richness. For dress, scarlets and yellows are the colours most favoured, or a beautiful clear emerald green. Imagine these peasants on a barge-load of golden corn and bronze pumpkins as they come singing across the pale Danube at sunset!

Corn – *kuckrutz,* they call it – is the all in all to the peasants of Omoldova. They seldom eat meat. The corn is grown in little clearings in the Carpathian foothills or on the low sandy sweep of Moldova Island. The peasants usually own some land in both places, as well as a small slice of grape-land. These little holdings lie alongside one another like matches laid in a row, and are worked on the communal system, like the old Russian *mir*. The average farm is between five and ten acres per peasant, although some of the wealthiest have perhaps thirty-five acres. The peasants all live in the village, and go out each morning to work in the fields.

Most of the corn is grown on Moldova Island. When we dropped anchor the harvest was in full swing. Nearly all the life of Omoldova was centred on the little pebbly headland sticking out in the Danube about half a mile above the island. Before dawn we heard the peasants arrive with their bullock-carts. Much yelling and shouting as they hauled their stubborn bullocks on the long, low, black barges. Chants as they strained at the sweeps to row out in midstream. The cabin doors of *Flame* made a frame for one of the loveliest vistas I ever wish to see. In a strange sort of one-dimension effect of light the shelving beach of Omoldova seemed to float in a transparency of water, land and sky. Faintly in the background was the blue sweep of the Carpathians. And floating like a cloud on the glassy river were the yellow sands and tableland of Moldova. Barges, in silhouette, drifted downstream. The rising sun brought out the colours.

We went down on one of these barges, landed before the mob of peasants fighting about their carts on the long, flat, sandy shore, watched them struggling with their loaded carts of gold corn, and, stripped to the waist, wade nearly a quarter of a mile into the Danube to tow the laden craft against the current. Then they jumped aboard, and, with a queer, rising leap, jumped against the sweeps to win the Omoldovan shore. They were swept down until they won land nearly a mile below, and we saw them hitch their bullocks to the tow-ropes and tow the barge loads upstream.

Other bullock-carts plodded toward us through the white dust of the long island roads. Sweating, hairy men strained at the wheel-spokes in deep sand. Clouds of dust showed the presence of more bullock-carts toiling over the sky-line. There was something epic, a saga, in the labour of these simple men. They took no more notice of the Roumanian soldier stationed there to guard and annoy them than they did of the faint clouds above.

The corn is ground in two little mills turned by the same

186

stream that cools the *slivowitz*. A little ratchet stick, clattering against the notched upper stone, feeds the kernels down one by one.

We went into an old peasant-woman's home after sunset – three rooms. The best, bulging on the street, held her bed, table and chair, and two coloured mats on the walls. The floor was of dirt, and we could reach up and touch the beamed wooden ceiling, above which was the winter supply of unshucked corn. The centre room was really all a part of her stove. Its ceiling was a blackened funnel of bricks, across which were some black sticks. These held chains that dangled over a mud oven. One of these held a black pot. The old crone took off the lid, and we saw nothing but a mess of leaves and a pathetically small bit of cabbage – her dinner.

'Oh, no!' she exclaimed. 'I have more.'

She led us into the other room, where, beside another frowsy old bed, was a board, and on it two flat round loaves of corn bread. Not the cornpone that you and I know, rich with butter and eggs – just corn-flour and water.

'You see!' she said proudly.

We nodded silently, wished her good night, blew out the match – and the village of Omoldova was in darkness.

CHAPTER THIRTY-FIVE

A Priest of the Banat

★

'*A MOMENT of life is sad —*'

We heard his voice, like a deep bell, in the bare dirt streets of Omoldova. It seemed to challenge the rustic placidity of this Danube village in the spurs of the Carpathians. It was a lonely voice. A few minutes later we passed him, sitting at his harmonium, his superb head and shoulders outlined against a whitewashed wall. Sharp-bearded, high-cheeked, with a wave of greying brown hair, it was the face both of fighter and poet. A brown, healthy face set off by a thin band of white above a black soutane. '*I see everything darkly —*'

'That is the Serbian priest,' said the Roumanian port captain. 'He is very intelligent. He speaks Roumanian, Russian, German, and Hungarian.'

I said I thought he would have need of all those tongues in such a chameleon-like part of the world as this. The port captain, a bald-headed young man, did not smile.

'These Serbs,' he said, 'are better than the Serbs across the river, because they have had the benefit of years of Austrian culture.'

He pointed to the little fishing-village, hidden behind willows on the flat Jugoslavian shore: 'They live like savages there.'

It was only a few minutes' walk to the end of the main street of Omoldova, and on our return we encountered the priest. He was sitting on a bench before one of the low, whitewashed houses, chatting with an old man in shabby black coat.

'That is an Austrian general,' whispered the port captain.

Another unexpected anomaly in this little village – but I had eyes for no one but the priest. His extraordinary personality seemed to lay hold of one. He kissed the Crew's hand like a courtier. We fell into step, almost automatically, and went down the street. I found myself telling him the history of our trip. I said things to him that had been almost secret thoughts. He seemed to understand everything. He stopped before a heavy wooden door.

'I live here. Won't you come in for awhile?'

The door opened, not into his house but into a courtyard where stood several stacks of hay and an incredible quantity of drying corn. 'Part of my salary,' he laughed. 'I have sixty-five *jochs* of land on the hill over there, and I have four Berkshire pigs. I have 300 more *jochs* near Temesvar, so you see I am not poor.'

We learned later that the entire proceeds of his Omoldova land were distributed among the poor of the village.

People talk about empty rooms, but few ever have really empty rooms in their houses. All the priest's were empty – two of them entirely so – and the third held a chair, a table and his harmonium. I sat on the window-sill, the Crew took the table, and the priest pulled his only chair over to the harmonium. 'I will sing to you,' he said.

The deep tones boomed out through the dust of the street and seemed to ring into the Carpathians. He stopped abruptly, laughed: 'For six years I was in opera in Budapest.'

This extraordinary priest! He vanished, to come back with his housekeeper, who was carrying a tray of glasses and a flagon of red wine – freshly pressed wine and rather sickening.

'I live all alone here,' said the priest, 'but I have my meals in the house opposite. Won't you have dinner with me?'

This was his housekeeper's house. She put her best foot forward for the occasion. But even so, the dinner consisted of one small chop each and some cheese. There was nothing else. The priest talked of America.

'Chicago,' he said, 'is very musical. You have a good orchestra, haven't you?'

'Yes,' I said smiling, 'but I did not know its fame had reached here.'

'I haven't always been here, you know,' he said, a trifle tragically. He held up a finger: 'Hsst! Do you hear them? I have a choir here of seventy-five voices.'

We suddenly became aware of the low hum of voices coming from his house opposite – some of them were 'tuning up.'

'Yes,' he said, in answer to our look of amazement; 'they will sing for you.'

A choir of seventy-five voices in the Balkans, and across the river men carried knives in their belts! He dashed out to prepare them. The Crew and I followed him in a sort of daze across the dark street, entered his room and saw, above a sea of primitive faces, his two upraised hands. They waved –

The song broke like the crash of heavy surf on a beach. A booming chant of the old Orthodox Greek Church. It swayed one like the high winds; it faded into the clear, beautiful voice of a girl, and boomed again from out the deep, hairy chests of the men.

Here, in white tunics and sheepskins were the same peasants we had seen that afternoon on the beach, struggling with their bullock-carts of yellow corn, wading waist deep in water to haul their heavy barges up against the stiff flood of the Danube. Under the upraised candles the men held aloft we saw faces that had been wild, primitive – almost savage. They were strangely civilized now.

'We are all peasants here,' said a shaggy-faced man, sorting out some of the priest's hand-written sheets of church music; 'you must excuse us if we don't sing very well; we have been working all day in the fields.'

Old inhibitions concerning peasants and the Balkans were casting loose in my mind like the breaking up of a bad cold in the head. These people were primitive, almost uncouth. The girl before me had on a little leather jacket studded with brass; a stocky little creature, like a pony. And yet there was a warm feeling of sociability in the room that one associates with sophisticated people. They were essentially gentle.

'In two years,' the priest whispered aside to the Crew, 'we shall have an opera here.'

Two years! He had told us, at dinner, that he, too, had tried to go to America. He had had an invitation from Youngstown, O., to go there as a priest, and a professor of music. He had been a bit impatient about things, and offended his bishop.

'He is my best friend,' said the priest; 'but he sent me here as a penance.'

The hope still burned. I looked at him now. Metaphorically speaking, he had his coat off and was 'working' with his people. Budapest, the opera, were laid aside; his big house in Temesvar stood empty; books and friends were out of reach – he was part of the life of these people.

Now this is the sort of thing that doesn't happen in life; and I don't suppose you will believe it, but it happened in Omoldova the next morning. The priest got a letter. We heard him calling us from the beach:

'*Dobra! Dobra!* It has come!'

I fetched him out in the dinghy. He was so excited that he nearly upset us.

'I go to America!' he said.

The bishop had written him. He had three days to make up his mind. There was a deputation in Belgrade, some kind people from Steubenville, O., who would take him over.

I looked at the peasants, towing their barges of corn up the Danube. There will be no opera in Omoldova.

CHAPTER THIRTY-SIX

Good Father Bufanu

FATHER BUFANU, of the little Roumanian village of Coronini, had asked us to breakfast. 'These are the things you must do,' he said, as we sat down before the boiled turkey, cavaire, and coffee: 'I have made notes':

1. Get a small dog to give warning when the Bulgarians attack you.

2. You are on the edge of a very dangerous part of the Danube. No one is allowed to proceed below Drenkova through the rapids, the gorge of Kazan, and the Iron Gates, without taking a pilot. You must be sure to get a good pilot.

3. When in Bukarest you must see the queen.

'Bless her!' said Father Bufanu, closing his eyes and raising his hand. 'She is very good to all of us.'

We had had an odd prelude to our meeting, Father Bufanu and I – two dreams. Coming down river from Omoldova, we – the Crew and I – had dropped anchor, as it happened, immediately below his garden. (Coronini snoozes on a hill.) And I, looking up from the anchor chain, had seen a lean black priest on the bank; quite old – his hair and eyebrows looked like tufts of fresh snow. He saw, he said, the yellow-haired sailorman he had dreamed of the previous night.

'As a priest of the Lord, I swear to you that I dreamed I was flying over the earth – so!' – he raised a lean hand in benediction – 'and I blessed a man just like you.'

Usually I do not take much stock in dreams, but I started when Father Bufanu said this. Perhaps *Flame* has made me superstitious. I, too, had had an uncanny dream. I dreamed – how frightfully real some dreams are – that, off the Newfoundland Banks, I was before the mast on a fishing schooner officered by grey monks.

'You can't see dreams,' explained Father Bufanu, 'neither can you see the wind – yet it blows over houses and ships.'

Therefore, over this cheerful though rather amazing breakfast the next morning we felt like old friends. Father Bufanu and his wife lived in one enormous long room. In one end were their beds and the stove. At the other end was a very formal parlour-set of stamped velvet, placed around a round table with a big bunch of white paper roses on it. Looking down upon this were three confusing pictures of saints in Prince Albert coats. Down the side was an altar, rather touchingly arranged with burning candles, a taper guttering in a cup of fluid, and some little offerings of flowers in front of a shrine.

The house saint had a position of honour on an easel. Between the high windows, looking out through the plum trees on to the curving Danube below, was a very official-looking desk containing the records of all the souls in his keeping. He opened it, showing us the 'reforms' he had made during the previous years – scoops from the Roman Catholics. He also showed me a charred tract which an anti-Christ, from New Moldova, had thrown into the fire. In a little tray he had a collection of all post or visiting-cards anyone had ever sent him – about six in all. The breakfast-table was placed in a very *gemuthlich* fashion at the foot of their beds, and they had spread before us the best, if not all, of their Sunday's provisions.

A Roumanian captain – white tunic and Charlie Chaplin moustache – came in with a private who held a two-foot-long bayonet. They took off their caps and stood very embarrass-edly while Father Bufanu showed them our papers. This done, he solemnly shook hands with us, as did the uncomfortable soldiers.

'When our Queen came past with the princess, on the way to her wedding in Belgrade (when she married Alexander, King of the Serbs, Croats and Slovenes), we had three pipers who sat on Babakai Rock and played the "Abchied's Lied." Both our Queen and the princess wept,' said Father Bufanu. 'Our princess was leaving her people.'

He went to the window and beckoned some one. A smiling little peasant, square, with moccasined feet, green-embroidered black coat and fierce moustachios, entered the room and took off his tea-cosy hat. He placed a wooden flute to his lips and produced a series of gurgling, shrill squeaks that squirmed like worms in the air. A bitterly doleful lament.

'Roumanian songs are sad songs,' said Father Bufanu, 'because they are always about battles – which we have lost.'

I looked at Babakai, standing up in the Danube like a spear at the head of the cataracts; no wonder the emotional Queen and Princess Mary had wept.

We went out into a crisp, yellow fall morning. Two peasant men struggled up the hill in front of us. They were both very drunk – arms around each other's necks – and their lace-fringed panties looked strangely debauched.

Father Bufanu (he looks very much like Admiral Sims, by the way) made a gesture of impotent rage: 'The tavern!'

He rushed us into the white sanctity of his tiny arched church. The peasants were already assembled – a gorgeous cluster of women and girls standing in the back of the church – and greatly to our regret we were placed in the quadrangle of oak seats, set about the walls for the elders of the village. Father Bufanu came out from behind the white arches and stood before the bough-decked altar like a gleaming canary in his bright yellow robes. A smell of candles and incense slowly sifted into our thoughts.

'*Gospodie.*' Father Bufanu broke into swift intone, the choir of three peasant men boomed out the response. A woman behind us bought five candles and the peasant man clipped the tapers into tips with his finger nails, gave them to the woman to light, and walked across the cement floor to affix them to black steel trays. He wore a rough suit of white wool, green designs on the front of the thighs. Another woman fed her baby to silence its cries. A girl behind me, wide-eyed, stood with beautiful slim gauntleted wrists folded over her breast – transfixed. In the prayers every one got down on hands and knees. We heard our names – as well as those of our family – being prayed for by Father Bufanu. He prayed for the safety of *Flame*.

A black arm appeared from the recess of the arches, and Father Bufanu walked, swinging the burning incense around the beech leaves holding the altar. The blue vapour moiled upward through the shafts of wine-coloured sun.

'*Gospodie. Gospodie.*'

The service was ended. We stood among the knots of the peasants outside, and, as is the case with every Christian town in the world, Sunday morning was church parade for the people of Coronini. They stood about like exotic little parrots among the trees. Coronini has no railroad, no post office. Boats do not stop there. Coronini is conspicuously primitive even in a primitive country. We were as much of a curiosity to its people as they were to us. They came up and fingered our clothes. One, timidly, offered a little bunch of flowers to the Crew. The girls here – I do not know what ancestry started it – wear little vivid aprons, embroidered like rugs, fore and aft. They are dark, rather slender, with a great breadth of eye – untroubled steady eyes, quite unlike the shifty ones one sees in the larger towns. They had necklaces of huge silver coins, many of which were old Roman. Some had wristlets of coloured velvet worked in beads. As in Serbia, the ever-becoming, brass-studded leather jackets and coloured handkerchiefs tied round the head still held good.

The men's fashions, though not so gay, were more striking. Over rough *opankas*, soft leather moccasins bound with thongs to their legs, they wore white cotton pants, reaching just below the knee and edged with white lace and embroidery. Embarrassingly feminine.

'I would give my eyes,' said the Crew, pointing to a girl in vivid sapphire blue and flame-colour shot with gold, 'to have a costume like that.'

But they are not to be bought in Coronini. Each girl makes her own, lovingly and laboriously, through the long winter nights – weaving, spinning and embroidering to her heart's content. In fact, there is no store in Coronini – they have to walk seven miles to get the simplest commodity.

As we passed Babakai Rock and entered the throat of swift Klissura Gorge, we saw Father Bufanu, standing alone on the headland, raise his hand.

CHAPTER THIRTY-SEVEN

Islands of People

★

EIGHTY miles below Belgrade the Danube widens, and, in a gourd-shape flow, passes Moldova Island. At the foot of the island stands Babakai Rock, and there the river undergoes another of its startling changes, suddenly contracting to pass through the Carpathian mountains in sixty-five miles of rapids.

Encircling Moldova Island it is as placid and wide as a lake. On the shores of this calm stretch of water are other islands – not of land, but of people. There, intact, in their setting, are villages of Serbs, Roumanians, Czechs and Schwabians, who have been Hungarians until the close of the world war, and are now Roumanians. These are within seven miles of one another on the left bank. The right bank is Serbian, and here is another little island of people. Vince – a fishing-village – where the men carry knives in their belts.

'The people over there,' said the Roumanian port captain of Omoldova, 'live just like Africans.'

We Americans have so effectively annihilated distance with train, trolley, and automobile that it comes almost as a shock to hear a village not quite a mile away spoken of as if it were on a different continent. I could hardly believe it when the port captain said that 1,000 yards up the hill from Coronini – five miles below us – there was a village of pure Bohemians, St. Helena.

'But they must mix with you,' I said.

'Oh, no. We see them only when they come down to sell butter.'

I had seen for myself the strange anomaly of Omoldova – a village of pure Serbs in Roumania, who until the end of the great war had been Hungarians. I saw Coronini – pure Roumanians who for centuries had maintained their individuality under Magyar rule. And we sailed across to the village of Vince, crossed from Roumania to Serbia in ten minutes, and into a different world.

We dropped anchor off a low mud shore backed up by a wide band of scrub willows. The only signs of life were some ragged-looking men in one of the flat fishing-skiffs beached on the mud. They were baiting trot-lines for sturgeon and sterlet with white grubs they had been kedging out of the mud – horrible-looking things like small dragons.

In Omoldova the peasants would have stood up and wished us good day. These shaggy men merely stared at us sullenly. Some children, who had been playing under the willows, ran and hid under an overturned skiff. In spite of its primitiveness, the village of Omoldova had had a certain civilized touch in regularity of outline. The roofs – just the roofs – had reminded us of an old New England town. In Vince the huts were straggling, like native huts. There was nothing definite in the plan of the village. A few paths of dust wandered through it, but none seemed to have more importance than any other. The village seemed entirely uninhabited, yet as we strolled about we had the uncanny feeling of being watched.

We became conscious of an incessant tapping, as if there were woodpeckers in the fruit-trees shrouding the small, white mud huts, and, looking over a split-wood fence, we saw a bare-legged woman beating a grey fibre against the sharp edges of a cleft log. This, we discovered, was hemp. Other women, sitting on the ground, were shredding the fibre over little blunt-tipped pyramid frames topped with sharp spikes like a comb.

As I wanted some cigarettes I set out in search of a store. There was none, but eventually I found out that the two women I had seen beating hemp sold cigarettes. One of them, a cackling, toothless old dame, went into her home, produced a box where cigarettes and greasy dinars lay mixed, sold me six Cabà. I inhaled the first puff and nearly blew out a lung. When the two soldiers of the Finance Control descended upon us I gave them each one – to start pleasant relations.

'Ha!' one of the soldiers grinned, and held up the cigarette to his mate, 'Cabà!'

'Have you any good cigarettes?' asked the other.

'No, I am looking for some.'

'Well, you won't find them here. This is the worst village in Serbia.' The little customs official, who evidently detested his billet, insisted: 'This place is awful.'

They were so absorbed in telling their troubles to that gift dropped from heaven – a visitor – that they forgot all about asking me for my papers. I gathered that, although the Serbian village of Golubac was less than ten miles away, they were in positive exile. One of them had the bloodshot, muddy eyes of a man who starts the day's round of drink before breakfast.

We came upon Crew, who had a fierce-looking gentleman, with a long knife in his belt, posing before his front door for a photograph. He glared at me as if to say: 'Now, don't push in here and spoil things.'

Another knife-bearer, who was making some repairs to a corn-crib, hung like a wild man of sorts and glared at me. They both grunted a cordial good-bye to Crew.

The two men from the Finance Control and I got a skiff and went after sterlet. These skiffs are made of hand-cut planks of about eighteen feet long with long overhangs on both bow and stern to enable them to reach solid land in shoal water. They look something like cigars cut in half lengthwise. Two men sit in the bow and row with thick oars tied with loops of willow wands to a thole-pin. A third man sits in the stern and alternates between paddling and steering. They are always ankle deep with muddy water.

We rowed out in the Danube to where a gourd bobbed in the current, and hauled it aboard. At the end of about thirty feet of rope was a rock, and from this, lying on the bottom, was a long fishing-line with hooks baited with grubs about every ten feet. We hauled in over a hundred feet of untouched hooks.

'There are no sterlet,' sighed the Finance Control; 'the river is too muddy.'

'No,' said the fisherman, 'they have gone over to Roumania.'

It is exemplary of the reduced mental state of the exiled Finance Control that when I asked if the sterlet took their passports with them he guffawed with mirth.

'Do you hear that?' he cried, beating his comrade on the back. 'He says, "Did the sterlet take their passports with them?" Ha! Ha! Think of that — sterlets with passports!'

They told the fisherman, and he rubbed his head as if wondering if that was a new regulation or something.

The next gourd and trot-line hauled up produced a vicious-looking little sterlet of two pounds or so — a sturgeon in miniature. He had a head hard as steel, a line of those star-shaped, hard scales on his back, another line down his sides, and two little lines on each side of his tummy, like bilge keels. I suppose they are fortification against the rocks in swift water. He had a skin raspy as a shark, and a shark's mouth underneath.

'Ugh!' exclaimed Crew when I climbed into *Flame*. 'Eat that!'

'That,' I said, 'is perhaps the most delicate fish in the world.'

We were having macaroni and cheese for dinner that night; but after one bite of the boiled sterlet the Crew began to think of nothing but fishing.

'I can't see why you don't keep us supplied with fresh fish,' she said. Neither could I.

There were no lights to be seen in Vince after sunset. A complete silence on the other side of the willows! I put up a riding-light as we were lying well out in the Danube – and something might come down the river – and along about midnight I was glad we were so far out. Blood-curdling yells came from the darkness of Vince – wild bellows. Sounds of struggle. Wee! Yow! The price of one fresh fish at least was in the tavern-keeper's till.

CHAPTER THIRTY-EIGHT

Flame Rides the Rapids

★

FLOWING between Serbia and Roumania the Danube cuts in a series of rapids through the seemingly impenetrable wall of the Carpathians. This sixty-five miles of adventurous water is known as the 'cataract region,' the river falling over six distinct ledges of rock. Great grey and purple mountains imprison a frantic pent-up flood of rock-ripped waters. Though the river is over a mile wide at Bazias, there are not 80 yards between the sheer precipices in the gorge of Kazan. The stream widens then to flow softly past Orsova, swoops round Ada Kaleh, the old Turkish island, and races in a white sea through the black teeth of the dreaded Iron Gates. A very nubbly stretch of water!

'There, at any rate, you will have to take a pilot!'

The Crew and I had heard this warning so often that it rather put our backs up. A director of the D.D.S.G. in Vienna had even suggested that we tie to one of his steamers, and be towed through it. But we felt we owed it to *Flame* to take her through on her own, and one thing which we would not have was a stranger's hand on the wheel. I clung, perhaps foolishly, to an old captain's utterance.

'You took your boat down through the rocks of Vilshofen at low water, didn't you? Well, then, you have nothing to fear from now on.'

I was glad of that, because the frantic guess work of negotiating that nasty bit of water above Passau had put one grey hair in my head. And I think that Crew and I stalled about an extra day above Babakai Rock for much the same reason that bathers linger on the beach when the water is cold – we dreaded the plunge. We went over the mighty fortress of George Brankovic, which glared at us almost intact from the Serbian shore; we learned the history of Babakai, how the Austrians once threw a chain across the Danube at this point and practically annihilated the trapped Turkish Fleet, how only an old *baba*, named Kai, remained clinging to the sharp pinnacle of rock which now bears her name. We examined the water-filled caverns of Golubac, from which are supposed to issue the poisonous Golubac gnats. At two-thirty one sunshiny Sunday we decided that honour demanded a start.

We cleared Babakai, approached an apparently unbroken wall of mountains and swung sharply to port to enter Klissura Gap. The current picked up speed at once, but not an unusual speed, and we had passed Stenka, a submerged ridge of rock nine hundred yards long, without noticing it. Once or twice we felt little tugs on the rudder, when *Flame* shot through some water swirls, but most of the run down to Drenkova was an exhilarating, swift passage through clear water, and mountains whose forests were a glory of vivid yellows and reds. But the fact that the mountains rose sheer from the water prophesied the formidable gorges ahead. In the crisp autumn sunset we dropped anchor off Drenkova, a strip of low houses flanking the Szechenyi road.

A man on the bank advised us to lie farther upstream. Another in the crowd told us to lie farther down. We compromised and remained where we were. When I went ashore to report to the port captain I found that the first man was a pilot, a Hungarian – this part of the Danube used to be under Hungary – and while we were waiting for the port captain to emerge from his snooze I asked a question: Was it really such a bad stretch of river from now on?

'Well, yes.'

'Do I have to take a pilot?'

A smile. 'I will have to telephone to the commission at Orsova, anyway; I will ask them.'

The International Danube Commission now controls all traffic on this part of the river. No boat can go through without its permission, and it is obligatory for every craft over ten tons, or a metre in draught, to take on a pilot.

The grey-haired Hungarian – he looked more like a successful banker than a river pilot – picked up the phone in the pilot's quarters.

'There is an American up here with a boat that draws 78 centimetres who wants to come down without a pilot.'

A pause. Then the answer: 'Yes, on his own responsibility.'

The Hungarian pilot, being a sportsman, then carefully indicated on my *Donaukarte* the spots which were difficult. As this chart is something less than one-half an inch to the mile his warnings were something like this: 'There are two rocks here, sticking up in the stream; as soon as you leave them bear hard for the Serbian shore.' I hoped fervently I would recognize the two rocks. 'And remember,' he said, as we shook hands on the beach, 'cut sharp to the left after Greben.'

When we woke up a grey storm was piling up the clouds on the peaks below Drenkova. A black Danube towing-steamer was getting its anchor aboard just above me, and I had the futile idea that I might chase it through the first stretch. I saw it swing round a sharp cliff just as *Flame* lurched into the whirlpools off Kozlatelep, whereupon I forgot its existence.

Flame fought with her rudder like a horse trying to take over the bit. The engine slowed down almost to stopping, and then raced as if our stern were sticking out in the air. *Flame* wobbled and shook, and then straightened out to streak past five red buoys. This is the sensation of taking a craft of this size through a whirlpool. It is neither more nor less. It is like a succession of mechanical disasters — as if something had gone wrong with the ship. She strains, the steering gear doesn't answer, and the engine goes crazy. We swung round to face an engine-turned strip of grey water, on which I saw the Danube towing-steamer — broadside to me in the stream — cutting for the Roumanian shore.

But I felt better now; a grave doubt had been answered; *Flame* had shown that she could fight the 'throw' of the current.

The mountains closed in behind us; grey cliffs locked jaws over the swirling waters ahead. I saw two rocks 'sticking up in the stream,' and then — oh, mystery! the silhouette of a buoy. These buoys are a tragedy; they are flat steel plates — like frying-pans — upright on the ends of long, floating logs. They are painted black or red, as such buoys should be, but coming down on them, unless a vivid sun is behind one, it is impossible to tell which is which. I guessed this one correctly, left Izlas Ridge well to starboard, and streaked it for Serbia.

Only when we had passed it did we see the long, white waterfall which crashed all the way across river from the narrow channel to the far Roumanian shore.

The great rock of Greben loomed ahead. This has been partly blasted away — 1891 — and beyond it the Serbian peasants have built little heaps of rocks to trap sturgeon. We saw the gourd floats of their trot-lines bouncing in the white water as we swung away from the deceitful smooth water above. The Danube here races in a whirling flow past

Brnica, a little fishing-village on a high gravelly bank with rickety platforms projecting over the water. Below these we saw the three towers of Trikule, the old Roman fort, on their queer, doughy-looking rock. And there, after a sharp swing to port, reared the grey rocks of Kazan.

Their height – Sterbez rises sheer from the water 2,240 feet – made them seem nearer, and we were astonished at the time it took to cover that fast swiftening pathway of water. Here again we felt the same uncanny sensation of rushing at an apparently unbroken wall. Then the mouth of the gorge opened out, and we saw with a start the narrow belt-road and post-holes of Trajan's road (cut through the precipices of this otherwise impassable defile in A.D. 103), and the sun disappeared. We saw some fishermen in a black skiff – Kazan is famous for its sturgeon – and made the resolve that at Orsolva we would for once eat our fill of fresh caviare. Aside from the fact that the water is swift, this gorge gives no anxiety; it is 250 feet deep.

The Roman road, however, was troublesome; the men who had crawled out over the whirlpools to cut those post-holes in the rocks had been dead nearly 2,000 years. It was a low gallery they cut – built for small men.

Then, as if the road were not startling enough, we faced the inscription of Trajan, clean cut in the rock:

IMP. CÆSAR DIVI. NERVÆ F. NERVA TRAIANUS AUG. GERM PONT. MAXIMUS TRIBI.

His first Dacian campaign!

We shot out into a widening flow of smooth water, and dropped anchor off the horse-chestnuts of Orsova. Three days – and our fill of fresh caviare! and we swung down to the little Turkish island of Ada Kaleh, saw islands ahead, a line of seven black buoys, and then little leaping waves of white water – the dreaded Iron Gates!

What would they be like? I think our only sensation was that of overwhelming curiosity; these gates had been an obstacle even back in Chicago. There they were, like black teeth, a long line of rocks tearing into a splashing torrent of water. I clawed the wheel hard to starboard; *Flame* fought away from the down-rushing suck of the rapids, won the curved end of the stone-walled channel cut through the gates – and we shot down a swirling cascade.

The Germans used locomotives to tow steamers through here during the world war. It takes a special towing-steamer, hauling itself up on a cable, two hours to climb this downpour of the Danube. We shot it in something over six minutes.

The only things we lost were some cups and saucers, which a sudden gust of wind hurled off our deck. In a rising gale we looked our last on the dreaded Iron Gates. Romans, Turks, ancient Serbians, mountains, whirlpools, and rapids – possibly some of the most awe-inspiring sixty-five miles in the world lay behind us; but not so dangerous as vaunted.

For that matter, nothing could be.

CHAPTER THIRTY-NINE

In the Roll of High Seas

*

BELOW the Iron Gates a new series of obstacles reared up before *Flame* – the fall storms. It was as if failing to trap us, the mountains and rapids had said to the winds: 'We have given them a run for their money, now you take them on!' The very gale that whisked enamelled cups and saucers out of our cockpit as we shot the last stretch of white water below Orsova was the messenger of the high seas to come. We yawed into Turnu-Serevin with yellow seas pushing the transom. . . . Spray on our cheeks.

Below the Carpathians the Danube changes completely. The river widens out, slows, looks like a lake – it is miles wide in spots. Light buoys appear. Tugs – ocean-going! Barges deepen and broaden, and we see fleets of the big 1,000-tonners that change their cargo into the 650-ton barges that climb through the Iron Gates to the swift Danube above. These 1,000-tonners, however, draw less than ten feet. This new Danube between Turnu-Severin and Sulina on the Black Sea is a shallow river full of sand bars. We saw tows slinking past islands, men in the bow taking soundings.

Lights on the high plateau of the Bulgarian shore stand out like points at sea. The Roumanian shore is low, swampy, speckled with lakes.

The winds – they blow sometimes for six weeks – howl across the flat Roumanian marshes, shrill down the bare, bleak slopes of the Bulgarian highland and churn to froth the yellow flood of the majestic Danube. It is like the seas off Ledge Light or Six Fathom Bank when a sou'-easter piles up against tide in the Delaware Bay. They have a name for these winds here. I have one, too, but no good newspaper would print it.

They are cold winds. With an army shirt, vest, two sweaters, tweed coat and a Burberry I still feel the goose-flesh tickling my garments. My arms feel smaller – weak. Crew, in a thick rubber sea-slicker, has stuffed everything underneath. The winds blow the tobacco out of my cigarette and leave me sucking a burned tube of paper. *Flame* lurches and dives.

'How about it?' we say. 'Can we make this long stretch to win the lee of that point? What about sliding in between that island and anchoring?'

Crew sways and squeezes into the cabin to look at our chart.

'The river bends sharply to the left after there; we ought to make Corabia to-night; there is mail at Bukarest that I am simply dying to get – let's try it.'

We go on. . . . Wumph-whumph-wumph! Three seas bashed against our blunt counter. *Flame* rolls like a drunken sailor. Crew comes pelting out.

'What on earth has happened?'

'Shoals.'

'Well, there go our plates!'

'Hang the plates – the potatoes went overboard a few seconds ago. Put the 'Frost-box'' down here.'

I watch the point. That point, at the moment, is the most important thing in my life. If I can win that point, then – well, nothing else matters. I nurse *Flame* over the big ones; bit by bit I edge across river so as not to have to cut across broadside to the sea when we come to that point. The seas, as the white horses race past us, grow higher. The wind is getting a great sweep to play with the river. I begin to have doubts. Sug! Without rising at all *Flame* has struck her nose in a comber. Curse those letters in Bukarest! I should have made for the island – the world wasn't built in a day – the letters would keep. We swing round a red light buoy, its 'blinker' flashing a thin cylinder of light (they burn them day and night!) – leave it 'pumping' behind in a smother of seas. Ah, well, it is not so bad; *Flame* is a good little boat; I am winning the point.

I round it. There, in the hollows of a cold, barren cliff, are horses and cattle and goats. Two Bulgar shepherds jump up from behind the rock they were sheltering under. A soldier comes out from the frontier post on the crest of the bluff, stands there, rifle in hand, staring down at us. There is some small shelter, not much, in the lee. Shall we anchor?

The Crew and I look at each other – nod. But not to anchor. We go on. And at nightfall we run inside the sand bars off Corabia. The anchor goes down; we have made our objective, and we are laughing about things now. Thank goodness that duck soup didn't go to the way of our plates! What about a spot of Cointreau as a warmer? . . .

This is a sample of one of our days. I could give you another sample – when I went down the wrong side of an island – could not get back against high wind and current – and *Flame* rolled in the seas off a point until everything inside her was shambles. A day when we contemplated spending that night – and more days – on an uninhabited island, and I took out the insurance policy covering *Flame*, 'Navigators and General,' and buttoned it in my back pocket. Days when the wild geese skimmed in black lines over the wave crests.

Fine days – to talk about afterward. There was a daybreak off Turski-Cibar, in Bulgaria, when in a peach-coloured dawn I looked upon minarets drenched with rain and

Mohammedans in ragged red turbans fishing for sturgeon in a yellow-green sea. Minarets drenched with rain. . . .

The night off Radujevac in Serba was as black and ominous as a tiger's throat. Then for some reason the stars came out, and from the black silhouette of foliage on shore we heard the squirling music of flutes – and the drums going. There was a savage eastern rhythm to those drum-thuds – like a tom-tom.

Long windy nights, when we slept to a long length of cable and *Flame* rolled in the seas.

CHAPTER FORTY

Three Danube Nights

*

In the last three nights, without even packing a bag, we have slept in three different countries. We blew in before a stiff gale to Turnu-Severin, Roumania ; rolled the next night off Radujevac in Serbia; and on the third evening watched a new moon tip the minarets of Bulgarian Vidin.

In Turnu-Severin we saw dandified officers in French blue with painted cheeks and red lips. (Be it noted, in the Roumanian Army no one below the rank of major is permitted to use cosmetics.) Most of the crowd in the street wore western clothes, or what had been sold as such, and the cafés were not littered with peasants. But the cafés were dirty, the streets were poorly lighted, and the whole place seemed down-at-heel. The atmosphere was – Europe, badly in need of repair, model French.

The Roumanians refuse to be Balkan. They speak of their country as being south-eastern Europe – 'an island of Latins in a sea of Slavs.'

The Serbs and Bulgars are essentially Slav, with a slight dash of Turk. They care little for Paris. And the trip down the Danube and across to Radujevac on the Serbian shore is a retrogression in some respects and progress in others. Serbian towns are essentially peasant. Even in Belgrade one man in three wears the soft-soled *opanka*. In Radujevac the cafés were crowded with peasants, the officers did not paint their cheeks – or, for that matter, shave – and there were no lights in the streets. People stared at one stolidly. But they did not put out their paw for baksheesh when you asked them the time.

It is difficult to tell the difference between Bulgar and Serb. (It is not polite to say this to either of them.) Physically

213

the Bulgar seems blacker and bulkier, and it is said he has more Mongol blood in his veins. It seems that the only obvious difference is in the uniform of soldiers and slang. The Bulgarian soldier looks like a Russian. He wears the same long, belted great-coat, although blue, that reaches down to the wrinkled leather of solid black boots. He cocks his flat-crowned hat at the same cocky angle, and when he trots toward you on a horse, one hand on his hip, toes turned out, straight-legged, rifle slung across back, you think you are seeing Ivan again. But whereas the women of Serbia are usually laughing, those of Vidin seemed grim. It was very noticeable. And, of course, in Bulgaria there are minarets.

Minarets! See them as we saw them above the forts of old Vidin. Slim, white minarets, like sticks of chalk! Minarets made of brick! Watch the muezzin call out, hands cupped on either side of his mouth, to the four points of the world:

'Ya Allah il' Allah –'

See the Danube steamers lying beneath him. The fat Germans on the B.L., Bayerischer Lloyd barges, the blue sailors on the Bulgarian gunboat. See little *Flame*, being made fast by a kindly Magyar under the lee of his barge (Vidin has no harbour) and, Crew, spotting a crate on her deck, bargaining with the Hungarian barge-wife for eggs. See the soldiers, sailors, merchants, and – yes, Turks – on the sea-wall, pushing, jostling, trying to stretch out their necks so that they could see into our cabin. Come ashore with us – because it was not chickens the Crew saw in that crate, but geese – and watch us try to buy fish.

The streets are awful, just as if freshly bombarded, and a Czecho-Slovak waiter from the Grand Hotel trots along beside us importuning us to come to his hostel – 'Everything is dirty in this town,' he tells us. We do; but the Grand belies its name. The Turks puff sleepily before their stores, move as if selling things were an affliction – and stare at the Crew. We find the fish-man. There are two familiar fish faces on the bench before his store.

'Catfish! Ye gods!' I summon the Crew.

But they are not catfish, hornpouts, bullheads, dear old bait-eaters – they are wels. They have the face of the fish that helped to make waffles famous in the inns on the Schuylkill; they have the hard spur in each fin by the jaw; but there is no back fin, and from amidships down the wels is an eel. By these surprises lay two sterlet. And to show that there was caviare inside them, the fish merchant had cut a slit in their sides. There they lay, panting and puffing, fresh caught, and the fish-man pointed into their interiors. 'Nice caviare,' said he.

The Crew is now letting me eat all the caviare.

These are impressions from three nights on the Danube. The Bulgarians asked us what we thought of the Serbs; the Serbs asked us what we thought of the Roumanians; and the Roumanians asked us what we thought of the Roumanians.

We gave them the answers they expected – the Crew and I are not taking sides.

'It's like this – all people are nice. It's only politicians that set people crazy.'

And, saying this one night, it suddenly struck me how true it was – especially in this part of the world. They are nice. If a Roumanian official holds out for baksheesh, that is only to be expected when one realizes what his salary is. A captain of port in a big river town gets slightly less than £6 a month. He is expected to graft, and the sleek man behind the banker's desk in the city grins over it. Why not? If a thing is forbidden by law, how convenient to be able to break that law by paying sixpence or so! How cheap, my dear sir!

So much for most of the trouble one meets with in Roumania. If a Bulgar shoots at one from the river-bank, and that seems to require a lot of explaining, it becomes almost clear when one realizes how he has been educated to the belief that everything on the other side of the Danube is anathema. When the man in the Press building in Belgrade refuses to take you up in the elevator because it is *for ministers only,* you understand that it is not surliness on his part, but the inability of a fresh-hatched set of officials to get a decent sense of perspective. These things one understands – after a time.

They have not made a permanent 'set' in the character of the people, because about 80 per cent. of the people are peasant, and will be somewhat unconscious of this. But in the cities one feels it. And the cities reek of the diseased ideals that have turned this pleasant part of the world into the cockpit of Europe.

CHAPTER FORTY-ONE

Freeze-out with the Guard

*

SHOT at in the morning and given a banquet in the evening –
what more could a man ask in one day?

It was off the Island of Baloiul, about five miles below
Roumanian Corabia, and we were cruising down mid-channel
– a hundred yards off the Bulgarian shore. It was a beautiful
day – blue morning mist, ducks sleeping on the silky ribbon
of water.

'Moo-o! Moo-o! Bl-oo!' I heard shouts from the Bulgarian shore, saw five soldiers with their guns pointed at us,
and another man waving his arms to signal us to come in.

'Well, well,' I said to the Crew; 'look at the Bulgarians.'

'Take no notice,' said the Crew, who was deep in *The
Smiths*; 'international waterway.'

Whack! – a bullet ploughed the water not far behind us. I
saw a puff of black-powder smoke.

The Crew dropped *The Smiths*.

'They can't have!' she said.

'But – they did.'

A red rage descended upon *Flame*. We put about, charged
for the little Bulgarian guard-house. Miraculously, all the
Russian curses I had known came back to me.

'Idiots!' I brandished my fist, and pointed to the American
flag. *'Chort praklati –!'* And our little old glory, as if knowing that she had been foully insulted, lifted on the still breeze
and fluttered indignantly. Fifty yards off the low, shelving
beach I dropped anchor, and, taking my camera with me in
the *pram* dinghy, rowed ashore. When the *pram* grounded
I stood up and took a photograph of the wild Bulgars rushing
toward me.

Three of the soldiers were in red-faced khaki and those queer white boots striped with black leather. One was in breeches and a dirty black shirt. They all held rifles, and their eyes were bloodshot and muddy.

As tersely as I could put it I told them just what I thought of them, and what it would mean to them for (1) having fired on a ship coming down the mid-channel of an international waterway, (2) for having shot at the American flag. I then said that I was eventually going to Sofia, at which place I should do my best to make them wish they had never been born.

They stood there snarling, like a lot of lions when the trainer beats them over the nose.

I then very nearly made the mistake of a lifetime. They had been accusing me of trying to run contraband. A flat-faced official appeared in a filthy black shirt, and to him I foolishly showed the *laissez passer* I had received from the Bulgarian Government in New York.

'*Kak!*' a nasty grin spread over his face; '*talka korespondent!*' I was only a newspaper correspondent.

'*Ya-a-a-h!*' Their ringleader, a sallow degenerate with a head like an egg-plant, charged at me with his rifle. He jabbed it into my stomach; and, looking at the plunger-bolt, it seemed to me cocked.

'Break it – break it – break it!' he raved, jumping up and down and waving a free hand at my camera.

I shook my head. The camera was in the stern seat of the *pram*, which had grounded in shallow water four feet from dry land. I interposed myself between that and the dirty frontier guard. More jabs in the stomach with that devilish rifle. The eyes over it were maniacal – the mud spreading over the whites.

It was the worst few minutes I have had to put up with. At first I thought it was a great hand of poker – freeze-out – and they did not know the strength of my hand. But now I saw that it did not make any difference what position I held – these people were half idiotic with rage – and drink.

Fortunately, there was a split of opinion. The officer began to feel worried: 'Give me the photograph – and you can go.'

We had the photographs of the Iron Gates in that film pack – priceless. I shook my head.

More jabs with the rifle. The egg-plant-headed idiot pranced back and forth on the sand, jabbed his heels in, stiff-legged – an imitation of marching. They were going to march me away.

'How far?' I asked. They replied, 'Twenty-five kilometres.' '*Neit!*' said I, 'tell the captain to come here.'

In the deadlock which followed the faint-hearted official evaporated. Egg-plant went off to cool his malformed skull in the water. I lighted a cigarette.

'Well,' called out the Crew, who had been watching all of this breathlessly, 'what is going to happen?'

'I don't know – so far it's a draw.'

The soldiers had collected again a short distance away. They had left one to guard me. He had a rifle in one hand and a spade in the other, and as I strode toward him he suddenly pushed me away and drew back the spade in indication that if I took another step he would brain me. A tableau!

Then they cracked. The spokesman of the group nodded: 'You can go.'

Freeze-out! Two deuces against four knaves.

They held their rifles on us while I started the engine; I

did not feel free yet. 'Go inside,' I ordered the Crew. 'I think they're going to take a pot at us!'

'Not I!' she flared – and I think it was just as well for these particular Bulgarians that *Flame* bore their worst enemy away.

That evening we saw across the bleak Persin Island the straggling roofs, minarets, and climbing streets of Sistov. As we made fast to a barge below the old Roman fort a man in a Burberry appeared.

'I am the Chief of Police,' he informed us. 'We have been expecting you.'

'Oh, Lord! It's a nice town you have here,' I said.

'Yes – may I show you around it?'

I removed the five days' growth of beard – at least I should look well for this ordeal – and, wonderingly, Crew and I followed him up the strange streets, past Turks, Bulgars, and a withered, grey little man with only one ear, whom the C. of P. said was the old Russian general, Fok. (He had come to Sistov as a *propersheik* with the Russians when they first crossed the Danube in 1877. He has come here again – as a refugee.) The smiling Chief of Police pointed to a vast, gloomy building:

'Won't you stop by the Government? They would like to see you.'

Yes, we would stop. And, after a tense walk past stiffly saluting police, we were ushered into a huge, unlighted room. A black-moustached man rose from the solitary desk in the corner, was introduced as the Prefect of Police. He shook my hand. Smiling! Other people came in. They stood off in groups in a corner, talking, whispering, pointing at me, and then at the Crew. 'A trap?' she breathed. It was very uncomfortable. Every time one of the Bulgars caught my eye he smiled.

'Ha!' The Prefect of Police disengaged himself from the group and advanced toward me solemnly:

'Ha! Gospodin Farson, we have been expecting you. We invite you to dinner.'

He cleared his throat again, handed me a newspaper clipping, the *Vidin Mir*:

'Yesterday,' I read, 'an American, James Negley Farson, arrived here with a boat from Holland without incident, down the Rhine and Danube to our shores. His wife . . .'

I bowed low. The Bulgarians bowed and smiled. They surrounded us, led us out through the fast-darkening streets of Sistov, and gave us the feed of a lifetime.

'I am sorry,' said the Prefect of Police, as we faced the course of rapturous eggs and cheese after consuming steak, sausage, and wooden bowls of fresh salad, 'that we give you so little to eat, but you must excuse us, as this is impromptu.'

'Yes,' I said, 'it is a light meal.'

They roared with pleasure over this very small joke – ordered more wine – told the orchestra (a Roumanian gipsy and a Russian refugee) to play the 'Gipsy Romance.' The waiter bore down with a heavy tray of glistening, wet grapes.

With a bull's-eye light they escorted us down the black cliffside to the *Flame*. We had never mentioned the shooting affair of the morning, but when they had gone, the Crew held up the newspaper clipping:

'. . . arrived at our shores without incident.'

Hardly!

CHAPTER FORTY-TWO

We Dine with the Iskarskaya

*

'THERE! . . . There! . . . There! . . .' – the officer holding the wreath pointed to Roumania, Serbia and Turkey – 'thousands of Bulgarian soldiers are lying in unknown graves. And the union of officers, faithful to its trust, holds this day sacred.' He placed the wreath on the rough shaft of granite.

'Now, may God forgive them for their sins – and remember them,' he added devoutly.

The Iskarskaya regiment in company formation stood immobile – little brown blocks of men on the shelf of upland overhanging the Danube. We sank on our knees, and, looking over the bowed heads of the people of Sistov, I saw the yellow flow of the river – shoals, islands and sand bars – and the misty blue and ochre plains of Roumania. A day dark as an etching, with only the scarlet flags of the Iskarskaya waving against a leaden-grey sky.

Before us, under a canopy of oars, sailcloth and crossed rifles, under the sinister guard of machine-guns – and festoons of cartridge belts – were the ikons of the regiment. Six priests, two of them Russian, in robes of yellow, green and salmon pink, stood before them like gorgeous scarabs. They held burning beeswax candles, and as they swung the incense their old voices intoned a bitter lament.

A sudden surge of almost savage grief swept among the people. Grim-faced old women put their hands over their eyes – the widows of three wars wept around us. The gnarled men bit down on their sorrows, stared dry-eyed at the ikons, their jaws twitching convulsively. The colonel of the Iskarskaya bumped his head against the heel of his hand. Beside me, upright on his knees, was the Russian general,

Fok, incredibly ancient – his grey head trembled from side to side like a toy. Weeping perhaps, over the folly of all wars! The stump of his left ear marked when he had fought beside the Iskarskaya in 1877! He kissed the cross.

Rat-ta-tat-tat! . . The drums of the Iskarskaya beat a tattoo.

'Bulgars!' An old Bulgarian general strode across to the flags. There, before a thin line of greyheads – all that was left of the lads of the war of liberation – he hurled out a savage defiance – 'Bulgaria. . . . Bulgaria!'

The tension broke – a hoarse cheer burst from the regiment. In the sudden movement and voices I discovered that the colonel of the Iskarskaya and I were shaking hands – vigorously. 'My men . . . my men! . . .' He suddenly seized his scabbard amidships and dashed off to take the review.

First, followed by his aides, he walked down the regiment. Before each company commander he stopped – gave a sharp, stiff salute – 'Your health!'

'Health to the colonel of the regiment!' barked the company.

'*Dobra!* Good!'

'But we will try to do better!' barked back the soldiers.

He went thus, past the pontoon company, past the machine-gunners, down the brown blocks of infantry, and then past the Boy Scouts of Sistov, the Girl Scouts, the gymnasts in white tunics and red-topped white sheepskin hats – and at last saluted the organization of fishermen.

'Your health!'

'Health to the colonel of the regiment!'

'*Dobra!* Good!'

'But we will try to do better!' barked the fishermen.

'Braaa! – Braaa! – Boom-boom-tiddy-boom!' The band

crashed into a fanfare, whirled into a soul-twisting march (there is something devastating about the drums of a regiment; it turns a man upside down), and the Iskarskaya came swinging past.

(It must be remembered that this was October 30, and the Greeks were still in Petrich, where they had slain some Bulgarians. There was a feeling of war in the air!)

The Iskarskaya is a composite regiment. The pontooners were from southern Bulgaria, and they marched stiff-legged as in the old German goose-step. Their smart officers flashed beautiful sabres in salute. The Boy Scouts also did the goose-step – huge steps to keep up with the soldiers – and executed a savage 'Eyes right!' As every man had to serve either two or three years in the army in Bulgaria, the fishermen also marched well, with rather a conscious pride of their organization. The non-coms. of the reserve came swinging past, and at last, a slow pedalling file of six cyclists. The bicycle corps! And then – how the Bulgarians cheered – a stubborn handful of veterans, who had fought to make Bulgaria a country – only forty-eight years ago.

A good review; good soldiers, clean rifles, smart officers – and the barracks, which we inspected before dinner, were as clean as the ones I had lived in at Aldershot.

Dinner was served in the open on long tables stretched along the edge of the high plateau overhanging the Danube, so that we could look up from our wine and see towns miles back in the plains of Roumania. Great wedges of geese winged overhead. The widows and children of the dead soldiers were the guests of the regiment.

With great courtesy the colonel placed the Crew and myself on either side of him. General Fok was on the left of the Crew; the Deputy of Sistov and the mayor sat on my right. Opposite us were the six priests – one with a mane of red hair like a lion's – the head non-com. of the reserves, the old fighting Bulgarian general, two other Russian generals (these three Russian generals are now pensioned by the Bulgarians in remembrance of their services in 1877); and beyond, at tables that stretched off from the main table like the teeth of a comb, were veterans, widows, children, officers and wildly hilarious soldiers.

The dinner, soldier soup – a marvellous concoction, hot and strong, full of meat and vegetables; great roasts of veal and cabbage baked together in big tins like the lids of trunks, was carried out from the open-air cookhouse by the soldiers. Casks of wine had a steady stream of soldiers running back and forth with tin mugs. Two dozen bottles of a twenty-year-old vintage were uncorked before the colonel. Pies, pastries and fruit descended upon us in showers, and the head of the gymnasts came up frequently, saluted, and handed us an apple, already peeled, on an extended bayonet.

Speeches! The old general surpasses himself, fights the old battles again, sits down in a fury of cheering – suddenly leans across the table and kisses the colonel. (None of your anæmic Latin embraces, but a good sound kiss on the mouth – smack!) One of the old veterans got up to say something, forgot what it was, but was cheered just the same. A young, dark-eyed officer makes a passionate plea.

And the band, skirling away at our backs, plays the old songs of the regiment – its battles. At each ending they play 'The Attack.' When they played the charge of Tutrakhan the soldiers went crazy – they rushed to the colonel, chaired him, and carried him around the square on their shoulders.

He lands on his feet, mounts a chair, and we hear our own names and *Flame*! Bulgarians, he says, have a great respect for America. My sincere and deep-felt reply is translated. I look out across a sea of unsophisticated, honest faces. They are rushing toward me, I feel hands gripping my legs, I am shot up into the air, and carried around the square of the regiment.

The band plays 'The Attack.' The soldiers run in a mob around me, laughing, cheering, waving their hats. Over the rough sea of bobbing heads I see the Crew and the colonel standing side by side, waving. Something pops somewhere inside me — I seize a hat and yell wildly.

Still dizzy with the whirl of it all I shake hands one by one with the veterans. A soldier shows me a post-card he has just received from Ohio. 'Do I know . . . ?'

We were marched into the town, through the autumn trees to the streets; and before the monument there the regiment links hands, and dances the Horo. . . . A wild leaping circle.

'Do you think that the Bulgarians are savages?' asks the colonel.

There is no need to translate my reply.

CHAPTER FORTY-THREE

A Dance in Bulgaria

*

CREW and I climbed up from the river front through the dark streets of Sistov to attend the annual dance of the Iskarskaya regiment. We entered a big casino with a stage at the far end of the parquet floor and rows of cane chairs along the other three walls. The regimental band held the balcony.

'These are the people,' said the deputy, fearful lest I might think I was gazing upon the élite of his city.

'These are the people,' said the mayor, leading us to chairs.

I nodded. They were nice people. I recognized two of the fishermen I had seen parading that morning. I saw several unmistakable peasants. I saw the richest girl in the town – we had had preserved walnuts with her that afternoon. And one defeated-faced little youth smiled as he passed me, bending back so stiffly in the 'correct' embrace of his partner. In him I recognized the Russian refugee who had played such reveries on his guitar for us two weeks before. He nodded and nodded until he had satisfied himself that I had seen him.

There was more tragedy in those nods than in most people's tears. He was not a Russian aristocrat. He was a molecule, an atom, precipitated out of the Russian confusion. He landed in Sistov, and there, with a Roumanian gipsy, he plays divine music while other people eat. If he could get away from Sistov to America, Germany, where people pay high prices for talent! But he can't, and this dance was his one big night in the year. He wore a little brown Norfolk jacket – just a touch of 'not-peasant.'

His partner – he danced with no one else – was evidently a gipsy. She had made a green dress – just like the fashion-

227

plate – and he had probably taken her shoes to a Turk to get them that violent red. But red shoes, black cotton stockings, ill-fitting dress – none of these counted when one saw her face. Radiant! Cream and jet black!

The colonel of the Iskarskaya did not say, 'These are the people.' He came up, clicked his heels softly, and whirled Crew away in a waltz. He wore only one medal, and was the least official-looking man in the room. His officers were magnificent.

Their uniform of greenish khaki whipcord had facings of scarlet. Their tunics were wasp-waisted. Their breeches, tight at the knees and then very puffy, made their legs look like lamb chops. Their black patent-leather boots gleamed like polished ebony.

They stood in a herd in the centre of the dance floor, and each bowed to an intended partner twenty feet distant, took hold of her gingerly, danced one turn round the floor, 'unclutched' her before her chair, and bowed off. The girl never smiled during the whole of this ordeal.

There were the 'two-perfectly-wonderful dancers' – a slim young man with his hair pasted back and a *svelte* young thing with a shingle. They danced as if some one were holding a bad egg under their noses. They glanced furtively sidewise – to see if others were getting the benefit of their art. His shoes were long and sharp – looked as if they bent upward with his toes. He must have sent all the way to Paris for them – a man-of-the-world's shoes ! Her dress had those plain, simple lines!

The peasant women looked healthy, though they tried to disguise it, and danced decidedly.

The room was hot, the dances were long, and there was a buffet where wine and sandwiches could be bought at the side. This was packed. During the one-step it was jammed.

Waltzes cleared it a little. The young bloods among the officers coursed up and down it like greyhounds in order not to lose a partner for the 'dreamy ones.'

But there was not much love in this dance in Bulgaria. It was a formal affair. The girls didn't chat – and slay each other in clusters; there was no *deux à deux* on the stairs. The men did all the talking – together.

A dance was a formality – only once around the floor.

'What have I done?' bewailed the Crew, after six officers had given her one round and dropped her.

'It is the custom – watch me.'

I then took a girl over the course for two laps. She was fiery red when I left her.

'You have compromised her,' said the Crew.

I did not answer – I was having woes of my own. The colonel had just left me with a wallflower – a very important-looking lady.

'May I have this dance?'

She shook her head vigorously.

I have had turndowns, but never before one that came so flatly. Also she was smiling.

I sat down. She looked at me strangely.

'It's a nice dance,' I said.

Again the same vehement shake.

'Mercy,' I thought, 'what's this?' I then suggested some wine – and pointed toward the buffet.

She nodded and gave me a glare.

'Dancing?' said the colonel, who had just dropped a partner.

'Er – apparently not.'

The lady then became voluble. The colonel looked startled, smiled and said to me gravely: 'I think you have made a mistake. In Bulgaria, when we shake our heads we mean "yes."'

I shook my head vigorously and gave the lady three rounds.

After that, the colonel, the mayor, the deputy, the Prefect, the good lady, the Crew and myself trotted off to the buffet, I shaking my head vigorously whenever I was offered wine. (Imagine that!) The Crew, who had not caught on to the signals, did the same—and was forced to eat a Bulgarian sausage.

Suddenly the buffet was empty. Colonel, mayor, deputy, Prefect, lady, Crew and I raced through the door. They were dancing the Horo!

We linked hands and tagged on to the leaping line which was curling about the dance floor like a coiled strap. We skipped sidewise quickly, putting our left foot over our right, stamped and leaped gaily into the air toward the centre. We then flung up our hands, skipped in the other direction, stamped and leaped gaily upward. The line then curled furiously. The music went faster and faster. Circles formed within circles. All Sistov was in that leaping, laughing, stamping throng. One ceased to think – and just felt. It was a delirious revel, the very essence of joy.

My dud leg gave out. I broke the clasp of the colonel, ducked under the arm of the mayor, dived between the Russian refugee and his lady, and fell on a seat beside an old sergeant, whose gold and silver chevroned arm showed that he had fought in three wars. They had spoiled him a bit for the Horo. But he was beating time.

I saw Crew in the centre circle – the fastest – going around like a whirligig. The adjutant had her by one hand, a fisherman by the other. The mayor was trying to outdance a peasant. The richest girl in the town was swinging hands with a soldier.

These were the people, and this was their dance.

230

CHAPTER FORTY-FOUR

Land of Itching Palm

*

WE left *Flame* beside the Roumanian navy at Giurgiu and took the train up to Bukarest. Soldiering and sailoring being white men's jobs, we felt that she would be safe. Giurgiu, the old San Zorso of the Genoese, and for some three hundred years a stronghold of the Turk, might have been beautiful in its day. But that was a long while ago. The exotic little thoroughfare to the railway station, where every conceivable form of peasant ware is displayed on the pavement or hung on trees before the open-faced booths, is the only bright spot in it. The rest of it is as dull, dreary and dirty as the usual Roumanian town.

There are no check-rooms in the Roumanian stations. The porter takes your bags into the restaurant, where, metaphorically speaking, you sit on them. Half of the people about you are peasants, in great sheepskin cloaks that make them look like strange polar bears, with funny little soup plates of felt hats on top. There are a few contemplative Turks. (They always seem to be looking on at life!) And the rest is a medley of fat-lipped, overdressed, loud-voiced 'business men.'

The restaurant serves cognac, wine, Turkish coffee, *twika*, and a few greasy dishes – on a cloth which, if boiled, would make a thick soup. Boiled eggs are the only things eaten by the initiated. They are strange people – the travellers on the trains in Roumania.

'Baksheesh,' demanded the porter as he put down my bags.

'What for?'

'For carry you bags.'

231

'All right. I will pay you when you put them on the train.'

'Train no come – give baksheesh now.'

I explained that I should not run away and that he would probably find me, gassed, by the table on his return.

The boy waiter, a Bessarabian, had a napkin tied around his head, under his chin, the tips of the bow projecting upward like rabbit's ears.

'Teeth?' I asked.

'No,' he said, 'a man hit me on the head with a bottle.' He dived in the filth behind the counter and brought out the broken fragments of the weapon.

A crowd of stupid-faced soldiers slouched in – there are soldiers everywhere in Roumania – and dropped their shabby gear on the floor. The numbers of their regiments were merely strips of cloth pasted or stitched on their caps.

Breathing as little as possible, I finished my coffee.

It is about forty miles from Giurgiu to Bukarest – across a yellow, monotonous plain. The train takes three hours – or more. And the Roumanians, on this line at least, have a neat way of converting second-class into first-class carriages. This is done by painting over one of the Roman numerals. One from II leaves I – is it not? Yes – it is not. But in Roumania –

The price is printed on the ticket – but the man behind the wicket always writes another price on with a pencil. An argument sets every one in the station screaming at once. As the punch-on-the-nose is almost unknown to Roumanian boyhood, the men grow up to be awful fighters – with their voices. They have nothing to fear – except that the other man will yell louder. To watch them boarding a train, fighting for places, is to see a verbal carnage indeed.

I squeezed into a carriage for six which held eight men and a girl. The girl was the only one standing. One of the business men was reading a business letter out loud. He halted when the ringing of bells, whistles and the tooting of horns announced that we were about to start. Then he carried on, telling the compartment at large how he was 'swinging a deal.' And the flashily dressed, powdered-faced men lolled at their ease, listening to this national lullaby of Roumania – the making of money. In the fading light he showed them two shirts he had bought. Wonderful shirts for a man of affairs – purple and pink!

Darkness came and I was not surprised to find that the car light did not work and that we were supposed to see one another by means of an oil smudge. Roumanian economy! The conductor came along the outside of the train, swinging from door handle to door handle through the night! He had a lantern strapped to his breast. Before that he examined our tickets. The men snored, their heads drooping like dying cabbages – or Mestrovic's bas-reliefs.

Getting the train out of each station was accompanied with the fuss attendant to launching a battleship. It seemed an event to reach Bukarest.

'One hundred and fifty lei,' demanded a flivver driver. He said that petrol cost nearly a dollar a gallon in Roumania.

Now, as it happened, I had bought lots of petrol in Roumania – and if there is one place in the world where it is cheap it is Bukarest. I quoted him the price per litre.

'Eighty lei,' he said immediately, looking at me angrily. How did a stranger, coming in on that train, know the price of petrol in Roumania! It wasn't fair!

Bukarest is a false-face of Paris, or a great masquerade, or a gold-plated Ingersoll. Things are never as good as they look. At first you think you've found a real city, then you know it is Hicktown – painted up. There is only one hotel worthy of the name – and that you can't get into, as the guests hold the rooms by the year.

The other, almost-hotel, is an ornate, deceiving affair. The price for the rooms seems cheap. But as there is a tax for heat, a tax for light, and a tax for – Well, it is not so cheap. There is even a tax for each time you use the elevator – and when people come to your rooms. A government tax leaps on top of all that.

You shower tips like the rains of the spring. If you don't, the people come up and ask for them. You tip the elevator man as you come down in the lift. If one porter brings in your bags another porter helps put them down on the floor, a third picks them up and a fourth brings them upstairs. Your floor-man then takes them from him and brings them into your room. Then they all stand holding out their hands – to see whether it will rain or not.

The tips are not much, and after you get over your first revulsion of always shelling out – even for asking the time – you might be as tolerant about it as the Roumanians are. If only you got something from them! But rudeness seems the chief stock-in-trade of the menials of Bukarest.

I went to the post office to send a wire to London.

'When will this get there?' I asked.

'To-morrow – some time,' without looking up.

I dropped twenty lei on his desk.

'When?'

'It should be in London in two hours.'

Twenty lei is ten cents!

People say that this subservience to tipping is due to the fact that all employees, Government or otherwise, are woefully underpaid. And it does make one rack one's brains to see how a garrison commander can support wife and family on six pounds a month. It would take almost a saint of patriotism, or a fanatic, to keep pure on that sum. Living is infinitely cheaper here than it is in America — but not as cheap as that. Honesty has its elastic limit as well as everything else. And as people get so little for the toil of their lives, it is but natural that they give little in return. Even courtesy has its price.

CHAPTER FORTY-FIVE

Breakfast in Bukarest

*

'What time is it?'

'I don't know – my watch is still at the jeweller's.'

'Well, look at the clock on the church.'

'I have – but it's stopped.'

'Then look at the one on the landing.'

I made a sortie in my pyjamas, to find that the time-piece said half-past three. I knew that we could not have slept as late as that.

'Get the maid,' I said to the Crew; 'the one that speaks German.'

The maid came, said '*So fort!*' and vanished.

Furious ringing of the bell brought the boots and a frightened little second maid, who mewed something, and dashed out, and finally the maid who talked German.

'It is half-past eight,' said she.

'Good! Tell the waiter to bring our breakfast.'

'What shall we do,' asked the Crew; 'wait for it, or get dressed?'

'I think I'll shave—wish you'd asked the maid for hot water.'

I rang the bell, got the second maid, who did not understand anything, not even sign language, and then the frowsy boots. He nodded. Disappeared.

A knock on our door. 'Ah,' exclaimed the Crew; 'there's breakfast.'

It was not. One of the army of porters who infested the hotel lobby below stood before our door with a note. It was from the British Legation:

'. . wanted to make sure this would reach you. . . . Dinner at 8.30. . . . Our man will wait an answer. . . .'

'Oh, bad luck!' said the Crew; 'we're going to the Whatsisnames' to-night.'

The Crew wrote a little note and gave it to the hotel servant: 'The man is waiting below?' she asked. The hotel porter nodded. 'Please give that to him at once.'

Ten minutes later another knock and a dirty little waiter shuffled into our room, bearing a tin tray on which were two cups of hot milk, a jug of suspicious-looking coffee, some grey bread, and butter that smelt like cheese. The tepid milk in the cups was covered with a thick scum.

'Save us!' gasped the Crew; 'tell him to take that away.'

'Get the maid that talks German,' I said.

The maid came in, after a time, and the Crew explained to her how we wanted our coffee – two jugs of hot milk, two jugs of hot coffee – *café au lait*. The maid translated this to the blank-faced little waiter. He nodded. Disappeared.

'Heavens! You would think that after three days they would know what it was!'

'You would think so. You would also think they would know better than to put strawberry polish on tan shoes.'

I held up my brogues, which the boots had succeeded in dying a bright Turkish red. They had been nicely broken in, too.

The Crew sighed: 'My poor hair will never grow back – look what they did to it yesterday!'

She turned her head, and I saw a lopsided shingle which looked as if it had been done with an axe.

'Where the deuce is that breakfast!' said I – not wishing to give an opinion on that ghastly shingle. As in answer, the fusty little waiter appeared again, bearing two cups of milk.

237

'Great Cæsar's aunt!' said I, preliminary to really expressing myself, 'where's the coffee?'

The waiter nodded – scowled.

'Get the maid that talks German,' I commanded the Crew. 'No' – to the waiter – 'you stay here.'

The maid came in, in five minutes, and, without the slightest trace of expression on her always-bleak face, duly told the waiter to fetch the hot coffee, the bread and some butter which was not in transition to cheese. The waiter walked out.

One half hour later he came back with two saucers of plum jam!

'That's enough!' The door had hardly slammed on the waiter before the Crew was furiously dressing. 'I'm going out for my breakfast. I'm going to have *café au lait* – jugs of it.'

'Are you?' I asked, crawling into my duds, 'get me some, too.'

In the lobby we asked if there were any messages for us. They said 'No,' without looking. I suggested that they look. Deeply insulted, the desk-clerk peered in my box – and brought out a card. It was from a prominent banker of Bukarest, asking me to call on him before luncheon.

The Crew and I walked down the Calea Victorei, the Fifth Avenue of Bukarest – a strange street with narrow pavements. It widens and contracts and wanders around like a stream. It is always thronged with people who never seem to be going anywhere or doing anything – just strolling. In the morning it is merchants, clerks and girls that one sees; in the evening it seems to be a Peacock Alley for highly rouged officers. Horse carts plod across it; droshkies and French automobiles file down it in two slow-moving lines. Where it widens out in the squares one confronts the white expanses of the palace, the Military Club, and the Prefecture of Police – all looking very similar. The shop windows are a false-face of Paris.

'Why is it?' I said to the banker, 'that one can never get anything in this country?' I told him of our difficulties – of the breakfast we never could get.

He rubbed his thumb and forefinger together. 'To-morrow morning when you ring for the waiter, give him the tip – first. Then tell him what you want.'

'And the desk-clerk also?'

'Of course.'

'And the post office?'

'Naturally – it hastens telegrams, too.' He smiled benignly: 'It is the custom.'

He explained that foreigners were always angry about this at first, but they got used to it.

Lunch was an oasis – Capsa's! – one of the most famous and best restaurants of Europe. Cold breast of chicken, stuffed with *pâte* and woodcock! A bottle of Dealu Mare 1907.

After that we felt that nothing could depress us. 'By Jove!' I pointed to a huge arch on our drive out to the Country Club; 'that's rather impressive, isn't it!'

We drew near the high yellow structure, saw the carvings and figures – quite an arch! Then we learned that it was made of papier mâché. Gaping holes showed a hollow inside. The Country Club – only three years old – was falling to pieces.

'Oh, we have ripping times here!' said the Whatsisname at dinner. 'People never go home until five o'clock in the morning.'

'You must have some wild times?'

'No, it isn't that, but you see they hear that in Paris people keep going till then. They think it is not a good party if they go home earlier.'

After some sultry bridge, we went home at eleven. In the hotel I remembered the banker's advice, and, giving the desk-clerk twenty lei, I asked:

'Anything for us?'

'Oh, yes,' he said, brightly, and handed me a note.

With a start, I recognized the handwriting – it was the Crew's. It was the note she had written that morning to the British Legation!

By our beds stood a small jug of coffee and two cups, half full of milk, all stone cold. Breakfast had arrived.

CHAPTER FORTY-SIX

In the Dobrudja

*

THE *Flame*, at Giurgiu, had been moored with hemp warps between a river gunboat of the Roumanian navy and the shore of Ramadan Island. Some time, along one of these lines, came a mouse. I saw him that night when we were well down the river, sitting upon the bread tin, staring at me.

'A mouse!' I cried to the Crew. 'I shall kill it.'

'Yes, you will!' she said, laughing.

Mousey and I had a chase around the duffle-bags in the fore-peak. The mouse won.

'I think I'll let him live,' I said. 'After all, he's a small mouse.'

And so we took him down river, and we knew that, come next morning, whether we put him ashore on the right bank or the left he would still be in Roumania – because we were now in the Dobrudja. If you look at a map you will see that the Danube, after flowing in a south-easterly direction across Europe, suddenly straightens out to flow almost due east to separate Roumania and Bulgaria. Then you will see that for no apparent reason Roumania has spread across the river. This part of Roumania lying south of the Danube is the Dobrudja.

There is a strange story about it, hitherto unwritten, which I have by word of mouth from a diplomat. But, as it involves the name of a fair and very clever lady – now dead – I shall skip some of the details. Roumania had always wanted that section. She claimed that it straightened out her frontier. But unfortunately it was held by the Turk. In 1877 Russia came down to push out the Turk. Russia had other ideas in mind than ousting the Turk – some of which didn't exactly please England. Therefore, the Russian ambassador in Bukarest and the head of the Roumanian Foreign Office formed a secret agreement. In return for certain considerations, Roumania was to permit Russian armies to march through Roumania unhindered.

This was a secret agreement between Russia and Roumania, and this was where the beautiful lady came in. She was the wife of a diplomat – and she came into the case and went out with a copy of the secret agreement. This was sent post-haste to London, where it found a resting-place in the desk of Disraeli. Then in his time, and quite unaware of this very secret agreement, the Roumanian ambassador in London came to the great English Prime Minister

'What position is Roumania to take, sir, in case the Russians march on the Turks?'

Disraeli reached in his desk. 'Why come to me?'

He handed the appalled ambassador a copy of the secret agreement. The ambassador resigned forthwith. And Disraeli, in the treaty of San Stefano, saw that Roumania got the Dobrudja – but, as he never forgave her, he saw that Russia got Bessarabia. The Dobrudja, rich in the south, is almost a bleak country – Bessarabia is a land of gold corn. The world, which knew nothing of the secret agreement, has been puzzled ever since that, in return for her help to Russia, Roumania had to lose the rich Bessarabia in return for arid Dobrudja. But from time to time Roumania enlarged the Dobrudja holding at Bulgaria's expense – until it now includes the rich lands of southern Dobrudja. She has also got back Bessarabia.

The Danube, below Giurgiu, is a wide flood ambling through a network of islands, against which the high right

Dobrudjan shore stands out like a hard sea-coast. Tutrakhan is the first big port in Dobrudja, a corn port, where, on the fringe of a shelving mud beach black lighters take on their golden cargo. Turks trot up and down the gang-planks bearing sacks on their backs. The children who came to peer into *Flame* all spoke Bulgarian, but the expressionless soldier who clumped up and down with a gun on his back and the port officials sitting on the destroyed Bulgar cannon let us know that we were in truth in Roumania.

A deadly dull little town, but with a water-front brightened by picturesque Turks and a most extraordinary collection of boats. In shape, these boats were identical with the American Indian canoe. But they were made of heavy wood, painted vivid scarlet, green and yellow, and two men sat in the bow — rowing. Other men fished with queer nets, like cupped hands, or a duck's foot, for skippering little bright silver fish like sardines. Low-browed black buffaloes pulled the corn carts.

That night we lay in the scant lee of a wild bit of headland. The wind hauled, and *Flame* tossed about like a leaf. I lay in my bunk thinking of conversations back in Chicago — the exhilarating free life of the wanderer — my bunk was hurtling about as if lashed to a broncho, and our dinner consisted of one Oxo cube each. And our blankets were wet. Even the mouse was depressed by this state of affairs.

Directly one gets out of Hungary one feels that life is getting more and more raw. It is like driving out from the main part of a city into the back lots. And then you come to a part where people chuck away their tin cans — this is the feeling one gets from the Dobrudja. It is neither city nor country. You feel that great civilizations have been here one day and that this is the refuse. You feel that the present unjoyful inhabitants are saying: 'Well, we will stay here and work this place for all there is in it. We will cut down the forests and throw our refuse in the streams, and we will get all the corn we can out of the soil, and then we'll get away from this place.'

I saw a sick Turk squatting before a sunny wall in Silistra. He had a sick child in his arms. Its miserable little features were the colour of an unripe tomato. He did not even ask me for baksheesh, or smile when I gave him some. I saw him later, walking in a dazed way through the vile-smelling Turkish quarter, and his face had the absolute blankness of a man who has nothing to live for. I saw the same lack-lustre gaze in the faces of the Roumanian officials.

'Oh, we are only the official class,' said one, 'and we will be moved on in time.'

The Dobrudja seems to have no nationality. People without patriotism or partisanship for any country. People with feeble ambitions and no pleasures. I know of no place in America – even the raw mining-towns in Pennsylvania – where life does not hold infinitely greater enjoyment.

Of course, this is Dobrudja as seen from the Danube, where it is a bare, yellow, almost devastated part of the world. And what the interior is like the world will probably have a hard time finding out, because, except for the single railway crossing it from Cernavoda to Constanza, on the Black Sea, it is almost without communications.

It was with a sense almost of shock that we saw a range of blue mountains rising out of it opposite Galatz – sharp, very jagged, peaked mountains that seemed to thrust up like a sheet of broken blue glass on clear days; secret mountains at which one cannot look for long without a desire to penetrate; mountains which the Crew and I mean to reach.

CHAPTER FORTY-SEVEN

Where Life is Cheap

★

THE causal manner in which Sofia accepted the assassination of its mayor, George Madjarov, is typical of Balkan mentality.

'There are two bodies lying over there in the Levsky,' said the waiter, as he put down our breakfast. 'A man just shot the mayor and then killed himself.' He pushed the plates about, making room for our bacon and eggs. 'You can see them – if you want to.'

I looked across the green square between us and the War Ministry. It was only a few minutes past eight o'clock; people were crossing the square on the way to their work. A few, very few, clung to the steel railings, peering at two motionless forms sprawled on the yellow bricks of the Levsky. Soldier-like policemen were diverting the traffic.

'Oh, I don't know,' frowned the waiter, when I detained him to ask the reason. 'Colonel Tomov used to be the director of public baths – the mayor dismissed him.'

'And so Tomov killed him.'

'Yes – he said he would.'

I went across. The limp forms were just being removed. A man crossed the street with a bucket of water and slushed the blood pools from the bricks. Little clusters of officers and civilians stood about, discussing the scene, pointing to the blood pools and arguing dispassionately. Nothing like the outcry that would have been occasioned by an argument between cabbies! People shook their heads and moved on.

Twenty minutes later the Government buildings had unrolled their black flags – they seem to have them in readiness – and at noon the city was placarded with black-rimmed

245

little announcements of the death of George Madjarov. They plastered these on house walls, bill-boards, and even trees. In several places I saw, under George Madjarov announcements, similar mourning announcements of Colonel Tomov's death side by side – even as the two had lain in the flesh! Sofia seemed to make no discrimination between them – this was a personal affair.

'Nevertheless,' a foreign diplomat told me, 'I shall not go to the funeral. This might be bait – you know the way they killed General Konstantin Georgiev – to lure high officials into the St. Kral cathedral.'

In that dreadful massacre 178 were killed, among the number twelve generals, nine colonels, five lieutenant-colonels, two majors, four captains, two lieutenants, three non-commissioned officers, four members of the *sobranje*, and four private secretaries to Ministers.

I shuddered. 'I can't understand it,' I said; 'these people aren't savages – they seem to be extraordinarily decent. Why, look at So-and-so.'

'Yes, one of my best friends – knew him in Paris. But I can imagine that in the heat of some political battle – everyone's blood is up – he might also run amok.'

'The old story – force answering force,' he added moodily. 'But it doesn't seem to get them anywhere.'

He looked at me steadily. 'That's where you're wrong – it does!'

He pointed out that every political change in the Balkans was occasioned by force, accompanied by force, and maintained by force.

'Look about you,' he said, 'and contradict that. Why, my dear fellow, that's all there is to it. It's in the air.'

A Bulgarian high official had already confirmed this

statement – regretfully. 'Young George Madjarov had a great career before him. He had everything. He was the son of our former Minister to the Court of St. James. And now along comes this' – the official shrugged his shoulders – 'this idiot, and kills him. He had a grudge, yes, perhaps. Why kill, you ask? Because it seemed logical – here.'

The official – he had served his country in various parts of the world – gave the background from which had sprung the reasoning ability of Colonel Tomov. 'Wars, wars, wars – five hundred years of Turkish domination – and then more wars! Wars external and civil! Political assassinations! Death is commonplace.'

So it seems.

The previous night we had come up on the train with Mencia Karniciu, the Vlaach Macedonian patriot who had shot a traitor to the powerful Macedonian party in Vienna. She shot him in a theatre, during a performance of *Peer Gynt*.

'I selected that,' she told us, 'as I knew it would create the most talk.'

She was like a long thin knife. And, contradictory as it may sound, she had both charm and beauty. She was ill and had come into our *wagon-lit* compartment wrapped in dressing-gown and Burberry. Her laugh was hoarse – like a man's.

'But surely – I mean to say – what will you gain?'

'They must give us our freedom. We shall never let them rest till they do.'

'Have you no way of getting it other than – er – making trouble?'

Her fine lips curled, she looked at me – the innocent stranger.

247

'Of course not!'

And she was speaking the truth. The Macedonian question, background of all Balkan disturbance, seems to receive attention only in proportion to the trouble it makes. At times, when it has turned those fertile valleys and fields into a very hell on earth, it has even aroused the sluggish mentality of the great powers. When it seems quiet, it is forgotten. Meanwhile, a formidable party of Macedonian patriots has been formed which counts nothing lost, even life, if it furthers the cause of Macedonian freedom. Mencia Karniciu picks a performance of *Peer Gynt* in Vienna to kill a traitor – so that her shot will ring around the world.

Perhaps the great powers are too much enmeshed in their war promises to Greece and Serbia to pay heed to that shot. They didn't see, of course, the bugler who stood on the bank as our train climbed out of Rustchuk, the crowd that had waved good-bye to Karniciu; they did not see the laughing men, the smiling women who climbed into the *wagon-lit* at every station *en route* and the masses of flowers in her cabin. They did not see, among the hilarious crowd that mounted the train as we pulled in to the misty hills round Sofia, the Bulgarian general, who clanked his way down the corridor and entered her compartment. They did not hear her hoarse laugh. Macedonian patriots – and, mind you, the man she had killed was a Bulgarian!

And, perhaps, because for so long their ears had been closed to shots like those of Karniciu, we arrive in Sofia on a bright November morning to find that the mayor has had an argument with a dismissed assistant – and paid for it with his life.

CHAPTER FORTY-EIGHT

Turks on the Danube

★

BEFORE Kemal Pasha chased the Greeks into the sea the western world had an idea that the Turks themselves had been pushed out of Europe. Now we know they are back. Officially, they are held below an irregular line stretching from Enos on the Ægean to Cape Iniada on the Black Sea. Unofficially, they are all over the Balkans. They are the bootblacks, the water carriers, the stevedores, the shopkeepers. They are Roumanian Turks, Serbian Turks and Bulgarian Turks. In Serbia they are indistinguishable from the Mohammedan Slavs. But in the other two countries they are quite unmistakable. A Turkish Turk would not smell any sweeter.

They seemed to be leaving and yet they are here. In Vidin the mosques are falling into decay; the windows are broken and boarded; a bootblack rubs shoes under an Arabic arch; the plaster is dropping off the old minarets; and the muezzin has a crack in his voice. Yet at Vidin, Sistov, Tutrakhan, Silistra, all the big corn ports, the water-front is pure Turk. Wild-looking men with gaudy rags bound around their fezzes, trot up the gang-planks and drop golden corn into the holds of black barges. Little girl Turks in pink bloomers drive whacking black buffaloes away from more sacks. Turkish water-carriers come down at night and fill their brass jars from the filth of the river. Vendors of sweets trot past with fly-covered, sticky pink trays on their heads.

'Ya Allah . . .' A peevish whine comes from a dozen slim minarets. But nobody seems to listen.

Perhaps the Turks are too busy. In the old days it was

249

the Christians who were the rayahs, dogs, who did all the work. Now it is the Turks. In some towns it seems as if the Turks run the show. In Tutrakhan, in the Roumanian Dobrudja (that part of Roumania lying south of the Danube), sixty-seven per cent. of the inhabitants are pure Turk, twenty-five per cent. are Bulgarian, and eight per cent. are Roumanian. In Silistra seventy-five per cent. are Turk, twenty per cent. Bulgarian, and five per cent. are Roumanian. The Roumanians are the over-lords, officials, port-captains, police (secret and otherwise), soldiers, and tax collectors. They live in a few official houses and fairly clean dwellings; the rest of the town is an odoriferous maze of Turkish bazaars.

In Vidin the Turks live within the old fort. Their mosques are neither more nor less than minarets sticking out of ordinary rectangular houses. The richer Turks wear Prince Albert coats and their women have discarded the yashmak. The veil is still worn, however, shrouded around their faces and closed over their mouths. The upper teeth usually bite it. That gives them a queer sort of no-jaw effect. The poorer Turks, and they are poor, wear anything they can get. The bloomers of both rich and poor are quite tight around the leg, the only bloomer part being seat. Very baggy!

Silistra, from the river, looked most imposing.

'Ha, ha!' cried the Crew; 'we ought to be able to stock up here on provisions.'

Cheered by the thought of white bread again — even butter — we bore down upon a hillside of great minarets, many-windowed white buildings and a great grey pile with a statue on top. A maze of shipping lined the river-front. Had we been passing by on a steamer we would have gone on believing what the steamship company's guide-book said:

'Silistra is a Bishop's see, and besides the Greek church and four mosques it has a handsome Government building.'

We swung about, headed up behind the lines of corn barges – Ali Baba and his forty thieves, with red sashes and corn sacks held in headslings, trotting barefooted up and down the gang planks – and made *Flame* fast to a Greek. (What these Greek barges are doing hundreds of miles up the Danube is a puzzle to me.)

The minute our lines were fast the inevitable Roumanian soldier appeared – an insolent-faced youth. While he muddled about with our passport I inspected the shore. Hundreds of Turks were running about under heavy backloads of corn; another hundred were building a house; another hundred were bossing the work – shouting. Turks in the foreground and Turks in the background. Turks arriving in carts.

'Bang goes your white bread,' I said to the Crew: 'we're in Turkey again.'

She knew what that meant, and walked with me dolefully into the city – toward that 'handsome Government building.'

Now the Rue de France in Alexandria and the Muskie of Cairo are unquestionably Arab streets. I had prated to the Crew of their charms – the eye remembers what the nose forgets. I spoke of the *guhargi*, cross-legged, beating his gold; of the sellers of brass, of sundowns, the smell of the desert, the call of the muezzin on star-dusted nights. I had built up a rather romantic picture, forgetting, meanwhile, that the British had cleaned up the place. The

British have given Egypt a bath. The Roumanians have not done that to Silistra.

They have not even built streets. Dirt roads, wonderful hog wallows, wandered among the clay buildings. That 'handsome Government building' – a painted, tawdry affair – was like the ring in the cannibal's nose. Across from it hideous, mange-naked scavenger dogs tore at some carrion. That sweet, sickly smell of over-ripe fruit, hot bread, sewage and sweetmeats surged over us. A seller of '*halva*' sat behind a fly-moving mound of pressed honey and nuts. Glistening coils of entrails hung suspended from trees, waiting to be stuffed full of sausage. Shanks of yellow-red meat hung outside the butcher's.

All the shops were open-faced, their wares hanging on their exterior – sprawled on the pavement. Rows of black sheepskin hats, like black eggs, were parked out in their wood moulds. We bought some glistening, sticky pears from a fruit vendor (we boil them), and he weighed them out with a hand balance.

Tinsmiths hammered away at their pots. Clusters of Turks sat in the coffee-stalls appraising the women who passed. Turks sat in barbers' chairs having their red fezzes pressed while being shaved. And through it all, bumping, jolting, yelling for the crowded street to make way, wild Turks in buffalo carts, horse carts and bullock carts, Turks on donkeys, raced back and forth. Over this from a rickety minaret a muezzin leaned down, put his hand to the side of his head and wailed dolefully.

'Are you a Turk or a Pomak (Bulgarian Mohammedan)?' I asked a great red-bearded, blue-eyed Turk in a buffalo cart.

'Turk!' he answered in Bulgarian, as if to say, 'And a

jolly good Turk.' He was the head man of a gang I had employed to beach *Flame* on the morrow. He turned up with as wild a lot of ruffians as any robber could wish, but they did a good job and laughed like children over the smallness of *Flame*. They all shook hands with me when I paid them. Friendly lot!

These are the pukka Turks, out of bounds in Europe, but there is an even more isolated nest of them 600 miles up the Danube. This is Ada Kaleh, 'the island that men forgot.'

In the conference of Berlin, 1878, this little island, two miles below Orsova, was overlooked, and when the wise men had done sitting, it was discovered that there was an island of Turks between Serbia and Hungary. In the compromise it was allowed to maintain its identity; tobacco and supplies were sent there from Turkey. It had its own customs-house, and the Austro-Hungarians had one on the shore by its side. They even had a little market where the Turks could come to the mainland and sell things. But they charged duty on anything a tourist brought ashore with him.

The Turks are still there, although the island now belongs to Roumania. They drowse behind high fences in their queer little refuge, wander about the old fort, its moat zigzags all over the island, and have degenerated into sellers of souvenirs. They are tourist bait. We wandered about the ruins of the old fort, and felt sad for such exiles – marooned by the ebb-tide of Turkey!

CHAPTER FORTY-NINE

The Roumanian Swamps

*

STRAUSS did this noble river a great deal of harm when he wrote 'The Blue Danube.' It is not blue; it is a wild, spreading, sullen, yellow flood – and for 1,000 miles of its course it flows through the most primitive part of the white man's world. It is no ball-room river. In the Roumanian swamps it seems desolation incarnate.

Harsova, the last bit of high land on the right bank, in the Dobrudja, stands at the head of these swamps like a headland at sea. And as if the land wished to make a last mighty boast it suddenly thrusts up here in grey withered rocks. The wide yellow waters, which have been flowing for hundreds of miles between the flat Roumanian shores and the high clayey cliffs of Bulgaria, are suddenly torn by submerged ledges of rock. *Flame*, barging into these uncanny whirlpools, shot under the old ruins of the castle, and we had all the feelings, as we let go our anchor, that the next morning would find us at sea.

Certain pictures symbolize countries – a drinking moose for New Brunswick, the fox-hunt for England, cactus for the alkali desert. A vulture on an old withered tree will do for the swamps of Roumania. These ill-omened birds rather got on my nerves. They swooped down over dead yellow flats, tore at something dead on the shore line. They wheeled in the pale, washed-out sky. They watched us, like wicked old men, as we nosed our way through the wilderness.

The Danube suddenly seemed to have forgotten its course. It wandered, curled, twisted through a maze of grey mud flats. Expanses of colourless water seemed to float off and

254

merge with the sky. On our chart we saw that great lakes lay all around us. We saw flights of geese and ducks rising and pitching again into some hidden water. And like some animal hidden in the scant cover of bare willows we came upon the mud huts of a village. Pathetically primitive! Under a tree I saw a peasant shaving his son's head – he sort of held the boy down and scraped him.

Another peasant, looking like a shaggy black bear in his great cloak of sheepskin, sat there as a spectator. Their houses were rimmed by fences of plaited willow wands. They had their corn-stalks and hay inside the enclosure in thatched cones. Some horses galloped free over their island. Other peasants emerged from the mud-coloured huts, stared at us blankly. They did not answer our wave.

Near some of the thicketed islands we saw black skiffs pulled up on the mud – a sort of cross between a dug-out and American-Indian canoe. They were collecting firewood for the winter and we saw them at sunset under loads of small sticks. Floating downstream they looked like little islands themselves. Great mounds of thin sticks which no one would have bothered to pick up in any other country.

We saw a fishing-village at noon. A very much advanced village – they had whitewashed the walls of their mud houses. They had plaited the willow wands in a wavy effect for their fences. Evidently they had a motto, 'Keep our city beautiful.'

Now this is a part of Roumania where there are supposed to be bandits. We had been warned not infrequently about the queer characters we might meet in these swamps. And the previous night we had had an uncanny occurrence. We were tied up behind an old wood-barge in an apparently uninhabited part of the river. It was a fine cold night, with a half-moon – so cold that I had rolled myself in a thick cocoon of blankets and was deep in sweet sleep. I woke to the Crew's low voice:

'*There is some one on the boat!*'

I sat up in my bunk – held my breath. The seconds seemed to stick in the passage of time. Absolute silence. The moon cast pale shafts of light through the hatchway and ports. I shook my head. Then bright in the moonlight against the last port I saw a naked foot!

'*There!*' whispered the Crew.

My lurch to escape from the blankets nearly pitched me to the floor. As I reached the cabin doors I heard a thud of feet on our deck. *Flame* rolled as a figure jumped from her bow. I was alone in a moonlit, empty world.

The deserted wood-barge was a honeycomb of black shadows. The only tangible evidence that we actually had seen a foot was the fact that our bowline had been pulled to the barge bitts, so that *Flame* lay almost under her stern. I cast off, let *Flame* drift down with the current and anchored out in the stream. Our visitor evidently thought that we would be sitting up to receive him – which we were – and we were not troubled again.

The Crew says it was a big foot!

With this experience quite fresh in our minds we bore down on the village.

'We ought to investigate one of these spots,' said the Crew. 'Let's visit this one.'

We anchored off a cluster of huts whose front doors overhung the water. A crowd of men basked on the hot beach in the sun. One of them cried out excitedly, but as it was in Roumanian we could not understand. We got his signals, however, which told us that we did not need to anchor but could run up to the sharp bank. At once the question presented itself. Should we leave our boat? We decided to chance it and left everything as it was.

The village was one long street of mud huts. Each hut had its willow-wand fence. Each yard had its stacks of hay and corn-stalks, and in most of them men and girls were shucking the corn. We saw one man, with arms full of reeds, on a ladder, thatching his roof. The windows of these huts were rather beautiful, as they were all set skew-wiff, just panes of glass pressed in mud. One hut – goodness knows where they got it – had a tin roof. We saw a fish-net covering an open window in the roof and fish hanging behind it. Smoke, curling hot, showed that the winter's supply of smoked fish was being prepared.

People smiled at us and asked us to look into their homes. This village had beds, ornate beds, and beautiful hand-woven covers and rugs. The interior of each hut was whitewashed and the mud ovens had black-painted iron doors. A fat old lady commanded us to sit down and have coffee. It was served in thin china cups.

The rumour went around that there were professional photographers in the village. We were besieged. One girl raced off and put on her stockings; a very shaggy little man insisted that we walk to his house and there posed his wife. They had an idea that all we had to do was press the button and then hand them a tintype. One man drove up with a horse and new cart – a beautiful cart, hand-painted with big bunches of roses on a green ground. Almost frantic sign language on our part to prove that we could not do what was expected.

We left this little oasis of culture and vanished in the wild swamps again. If possible, they seemed to grow even more desolate. Sunset was a glow of red embers over a sky-line brushed with bare willows, and then –

'B-o-oom!'

We heard the deep voice of a steamer – a salt, deep-sea sound. 'B-o-ooom!'

We rounded an island, saw a sudden pale cliff of land, hundreds and hundreds of black barges lying out in the stream, the twinkling lights of a city, and the great black funnels of the ocean fleet anchored off Braila.

We had crossed Europe, 2,500 miles, to deep water again. There they lay, the tramps of Europe. *Padmore*, Liverpool; *Wright*, Stockholm; *The City of Naxos*, Chios; *Taxiarchis*, *Gastein*, Trieste; *Naperedak*, Split; *Arta*, Bremen; the *Leonidas* from Antwerp. Grim, great, rusty with the salt of white seas. And to these royal tramps came the *Flame*, and Germans, Greeks, Skowegians, Limies and Wops looked down from their bridge wings on the newest flag in their midst.

CHAPTER FIFTY

Three Merry Brigands

*

DURING the last of her cruise through Roumania *Flame* was in the bad bandit country – the land of Cocosh and Varlan, of the terrible Litchinski and romantic Terenti. We were of two minds about meeting them – one, the hope that we might face such picturesque brigands; the other, a fear lest we should. Although redeemed by a great sense of humour, their methods were likely to be crude.

There was one rogue, for instance – I've forgotten his name – who operated about Bukarest. One wild, rainy night he stopped a motor-car on its way to Sinaia, the royal summer palace. There were two men in the car and three women, who subsequently arrived at Sinaia without one stitch of clothing. Can you imagine a more embarrassing ride?

Terenti once defied the whole Roumanian army. He didn't like soldiers anyway and killed one whenever he got a chance. He didn't like the navy either, because he had run away from that. This twenty-five-year-old terror operated opposite Galatz. I saw his stamping-ground. No one could catch him – and he isn't caught yet.

He had a collapsible boat, this fellow, which he could carry under his arm. He also had an actor's wardrobe of costumes. He would turn up as a peasant, a sailor, a soldier – and sometimes a colonel. He liked himself best in his dress suit. When he felt inclined to put this on he always did something devilish. One night he heard that a relative of his was being married in Braila. Putting on his dress suit he stepped into his collapsible boat and rowed across the river to the big Roumanian grain port. In all his glory he entered the house.

'Allow me,' he said, 'to introduce to you Mr. Terenti.'

Consternation! Some of the guests tried to jump through the windows.

'Now look here, boys,' said Terenti, 'I'm not going to kidnap the lot of you. Be calm. Though I wouldn't advise you to follow my life – it's dangerous! Now what I suggest is that you bring in a bottle of campagne and one of vermuth, and I'll drink the bride's health.'

They did. And Terenti, after a jolly evening of wine, turkey and ham, got up to leave them: 'Good night, gentlemen – I leave you in peace.'

Then he stepped into his collapsible boat and rowed across the river.

The next night he was in a cabaret in Galatz. This time he was in full rig of a Roumanian naval officer. He declared who he was, took charge of the cabaret and, after a pleasant evening, cleared out.

And, as I said, he killed a soldier whenever he caught one. He had been badly treated, he said, in the navy. Things got to a point that at the mere mention of his name soldiers dropped their rifles and ran. This, of course, endeared him to the peasants. Also he used to split with them half his ransoms. He was as hard to lay hold of as smoke. Here, there, everywhere – soldier, sailor, peasant, prince – and pop! goes another dead soldier. The Roumanian Government thought it was time something was done about it. It brought in 5,000 soldiers and surrounded Terenti's haunts. And it only cost them more soldiers. They were easier to hit in a bunch.

Then Terenti disappeared, and the Press reports him living the life of Riley in Hamburg. The Roumanian Government swore that it would drag him back.

'Oh – don't!' pleaded other Roumanians; 'please don't do that! He will escape, and then the trouble will start all over again.'

Terenti was a Russian, a Lipovane – one of the strictest religious faiths – and a bit of a dog with the women. In fact, had he not been such an outrageous caveman with them he would be remembered as the great peasant hero. But no young fellow's sweetheart was safe with Terenti.

Litchinski worked the marsh land of Sulina. It is an almost indescribably desolate country. Miles and miles of water-soaked reeds! He, too, was 'nuts on soldiers.' He used to go out for a day's shooting over them – bag a few – just for sport! Naturally the peasants adored him.

One day he saw a peasant woman leading her cow to Sulina. 'Where are you going with that?' asked Litchinski.

'I am taking my cow to market to sell it,' she answered, crying.

'Why?'

She told him that she had to have money to pay her taxes. They were 200 lei, she said.

Litchinski gave her 200 lei.

Another time he held up the 'post-cart' and got almost ten thousand dollars. This treasure was guarded by two soldiers and a Sub-prefect of Police. It was on the lonely stretch of beach between Sulina and St. George. The soldiers dropped their rifles and ran.

'Halt!' cried Litchinski. Then he made the Sub-prefect and the soldiers wait while he rifled the bags.

'Now,' he said, driving off with the cart, 'you come back here on Monday, and you will find your cart. I will not steal your horses, gentlemen.'

They sent a small army back for the cart, which was there.

The famous Cocosh was a humorist. He stopped a peasant woman on the road outside of Tulcea. She had a cart full of pottery.

'Break it!' thundered Cocosh.

Raining tears, the poor woman smashed up her pottery.

'Now count the pieces,' ordered Cocosh. And when the woman had fearfully counted every small bit he gave her a lei – about half a cent – for each piece.

Another time he told a woman to go into town, enter the stable of the richest man there, and bring him two horses. 'Give him a receipt,' said Cocosh, 'from me. I will deal with him later.'

Excerpt from a letter written by an Englishman in 1924:

'The writer was obliged to drive to Tulcea and back, a distance of about eighty miles, in an open cart, as there is no other means of communication. The journey occupied twelve hours each way on a very bad road. He was escorted by a Roumanian soldier, as the intervening marshes are infested with wolves and bandits; a case of "hands up!" ending fatally, having taken place three days ago just outside Tulcea.'

The sound of oars in the night always made us prick up our ears in that part of Roumania. A great bandit country, where anything might happen – even to bandits.

Witness the end of Litchinski. Having exhausted the fun in his own beat at Sulina, he thought he would try his luck around Tulcea. There he fell sick, and, as he had always done, he repaired to the hut of a peasant.

'I am ill,' said Litchinski; 'give me shelter.'

There was a woman in that simple hut. She took him in. She cared for him, made him comfortable, and saw him to sleep breathing easily. Then she sneaked out and informed the Roumanian police.

They came, set the hut on fire, and shot the half-blinded Litchinski as he staggered out through the flames.

Our Last Town

The most striking thing about Galatz, if we can forget the fact that it is the big Roumanian grain port, is the eunuchs. These queer, rather 'baboony' creatures are self-made. They belong to a sect, which originally started in Russia, that for some extraordinary reason has a great many followers. After they have had one child they castrate themselves. . . . Their profession is cab driving.

I saw more eunuchs in Bukarest and Galatz than I have ever seen in Egypt or Turkey. They are queer lads, overgrown, as if something was wrong with their thyroid. Contrary to general supposition they are not tenors. Their upper lips seem to have become longer and withered – their jaws heavier – and their dispositions are charming. Perhaps, in this sect, we might see the solution of the modern taxicab driver.

Otherwise, there is not much of moment in Galatz. The British Consul's bath-room was to us the most delightful spot in it. When we turned up at his office, weather-beaten and worn, and asked for our mail, he handed us a whole pile of letters, took us into his sitting-room and stirred up the fire. After many months of life in a small boat, where we could not even stand up, we basked in this comfort. We soaked in every second of it because this would be our last contact with even semi-civilization. (We did not know then that there was a British Consul equally kind and hospitable at Sulina.)

A few miles below Galatz the Danube suddenly spreads out like a fan. These are the three channels in the great Danube delta – St. George's, Ismail, and Sulina. Only the last is navigable, the others having sand-bars at their mouths. The northern, Ismail, forms the frontier of mysterious Bessarabia. And a great many interesting things can happen to you in this life – depending upon which channel you take. Our eventual destination was Sulina, as that way only lay the Black Sea, but meanwhile a lot of strange things overtook us.

Some forty miles below Galatz, the wreck of an old Greek church, standing upon what seems the only solid land in the desolate marshes, marks the cross-roads. If you leave that church on the left you are bound for Sulina; if on the right you are headed for Bessarabia – and trouble.

CHAPTER FIFTY-ONE

Into Forbidden Land

*

THE name of the steamer was *Basil the Wolf*. That was the beginning. The chief of the secret police would not *visé* my passport. But that was before the beginning. So we omitted that formality and walked off *Basil the Wolf* on to the black pontoon of Ismail and were in the forbidden land of old Bessarabia.

Bessarabia, be it noted, is that strip of fertile grain land between the Dneister and the Pruth which, in 1878, Roumania lost to Russia, and which, as a reward for her Homeric part in the great war, she has taken back. But as – in spite of statistics – Bessarabia is essentially Russian, and as it is also a frontier against Russia, and as Russian agitators are always filtering across its frontier, it is an unhappy land, thoroughly pegged down by soldiers.

Last year Russian Bolsheviks came down from Odessa and landed in the lonely swamps of Bessarabia's coast. Before the Roumanians discovered them they had a revolution well under way. The frantic cruelty with which the Roumanians crushed that uprising has been kept a dark secret. Bessarabia, last year, was in a state of siege, so to speak. It is said a reign of terror took place inside. Sickening tales filtered out – tales of torture and mutilation too terrible to repeat – but tales of hearsay, nevertheless. Ghastly pictures as of the Inquisition, glimpsed through a smoke-screen of secrecy, a smoke-screen which for some significant reason the Roumanians do not wish brushed away.

I am told that a committee went in there to investigate and found, on the exhumed corpses, marks of instruments more frightful than sabre and bayonet; hamstrung muscles,

265

splintered bones. Who made up this committee I have not been able to learn – at any rate they held their tongues. When Stephen Graham went in there he was given a 'guide' – a Roumanian officer who was loath to permit him to go even to the bath-room alone. I did not wish to go into Bessarabia with the idea of 'finding out things.' I know how futile it is to try to get information from a terrified peasantry – peasants can lie as well as anyone else – and the flesh has rotted away from all the corpses.

I wanted to get into Bessarabia because it has been one of the taunts of my life. I wanted to go with the sturgeon-fishers – down to the sea – to see them drag long-nosed monsters from the depths with nets made of bare hooks. I wanted to see the wild swans off the great Danube bars. So, when the secret police refused to *visé* my passport – well, it was an invitation, so to speak.

I put forth the plan of driving up along the Black Sea coast in a peasant-cart over the marshes; then I made a quick detour around the Danube delta on *Basil the Wolf*. Beginning thus in the middle of the game I got a lead of two days over the avenging telegrams which, I am told, pursued me from Bukarest.

Ismail is as Russian as any tale of Chekov. Prodigiously wide, cobbled streets; flat-roofed, one-storied houses; a Byzantine pile of whitewashed Greek church – gold crosses on the tips of green, radish-shaped domes – tattered, bearded *isvostchiks* flogging skeleton horses to a gallop. Little *traktars*, from behind whose steam-drenched windows came the sounds of music and dancing. Drunken dancing. A flat horizon under a great dome of grey sky. Naked, shivering trees. Inexpressively dreary. It seemed as if, beyond Ismail, there was nothing.

The Hotel du Nord was an hotel only because it said it was. As there was no office, the proprietor was summoned by shouting. He slid in – a sad-faced Greek – gave us room No. 7 and told the maid to put some more rushes into the *petchka* – the stove built into the wall between rooms 7 and 8. Our request for tea drew a nod, and, an hour later, two glasses of boiling, straw-coloured tea. There was a big blotch of dried blood on the wardrobe of room No. 7.

Valparaiso Politkin, a Roumanian naturalized Argentine, told us that we might find Ismail somewhat crude. Speaking French with a strong Spanish lisp – '*n'ech pas?*' – he assured us, however, that the *haut société* at the tea-dance would be all one could wish. *Très haut* – and *très, très distinguée!* Exiled Russian aristocrats!

He was a grain buyer, Valparaiso – a 'cerealist,' he called himself – and while we waited for him to complete a toilet with plentiful rice powder on the face, much perfume and an astounding shirt of crossed hunting-horns in yellow and orange, I examined the mysteries of bowls of corn, millet, rape and wheat – the growing gold of rich Bessarabia. Then we walked through the stunted trees in the dark square to the tea-dance.

The dance was interesting because the women there – except the few rarely beautiful Russian *émigrées* – were all wives and daughters of the Roumanian officers stationed in Ismail. They were interesting – because there were so many of them. And sitting there, eating cake and cold goose, I had almost the feeling of being in a mess, a military station, garrisoned in some foreign land.

Otherwise this tea-dance in Ismail was almost comically like an affair given by the Century Club in the old home town. There was the same dragon-like dowager *couchant* behind the trays of cold food; there was the same young girl who seemed to know everybody and was always keeping things going. And there was an entertainer, brought down from Bukarest, who told interminable stories and barked like a dog. In him I detected a strange vein of brilliance. His wildly yapping impersonation of the fox-terrier orating before the house of his master, the *advocat*, would have made even a Boston audience laugh.

Here I was, without benefit of secret police, drinking white wine with the Roumanian overlords of Bessarabia. The room sparkled with officers – the chorus of *The Chocolate Soldier* would have appeared grooms by comparison – and my eyes smarted under the glare of so much gold lace. These were the men who 'held down' Bessarabia. The ex-Governor – the man who reigned in the 'time of the terror' – sat behind me with his wife. He was a heavy-faced man with an enormous curling black moustache – exactly like the small-town sheriff who loves to beat up the tramps. I realized that all this was disarming, that this scented gathering was but one side of the coin. To learn the other I would have to be dragged before the Governor – when the Governor was 'on duty.' I had no wish for that.

I asked Valparaiso if the peasants were happy.

'Oh, no,' said he; 'they are frightfully poor. I have never seen so much suffering. But then, you see, last year we had a bad crop. *N'ech pas?*'

I nodded, and in the course of a rambling conversation in which Valparaiso was extolling the virtues of the 'very civilized' Argentine, I dropped the name Tatar Bunar – the vaunted scene of an atrocity, some thirty miles from Ismail.

Valparaiso shut up like a clam.

INTO FORBIDDEN LAND

In the morning I heard weeping outside the Hotel du Nord. I saw a group in the street – ragged peasants. On their shoulders they held a coffin, blue, with a white-painted cross on each end. A priest, gorgeous in the panoply of the Church, stood, with one foot in his droshky, and moved his hand up and down. In an abysmal bass he chanted the solace of the dead. Then he stepped into the droshky. A loud wail broke from the peasants; and with the coffin joggling about on their shoulders they followed the priest in his droshky, plodding across the deep mud, down the long road of bare trees, wailing, crying out under the emptiness of grey skies, where – beyond Ismail – there is nothing.

CHAPTER FIFTY-TWO

In the House of the Lipovanes

★

WILKOWO is a sturgeon-village. Its men go down to the sea. And the sea comes to the village – wandering in willow-covered passages between the thatched houses – or running in a swift band past the black sheds where they cut up the huge fish and Kostia Bitcheff still builds his fine *lodkas* – fine skiffs, solid, with high prows – to stand the steep seas. Old Kostia Ivanovitch, who was here in 1878 when the land went to the Russians, and who was here forty years later when the Roumanians got it again and who wishes – But Kostia keeps his thoughts to himself.

The streets of Wilkowo are either water – or almost water. The pavements are board walks. Carts, even in the best summer's heat, sometimes sink to their hubs. But we arrived there the night before winter, in a hurricane of sharp rain; and we slithered about on the duck-boards, groped through the darkness and wind, over canals with the dark ghosts of canoes, past a white ghost of a church that seemed to rise from the moisture, and stood in the alcoves of a row of white buildings, where black figures about us mumbled in Russian, and we heard the crackling and munching accompanying the eating of sunflower seeds.

A hooded figure plopped through the slush, and was introduced as the Chief of Police. A soldier followed him about like his shadow. The pontoon engineer talked at length with him, in Roumanian – in whispers. In French, he said to us:

'Follow the soldier.'

'To the hotel?'

For some reason the pontoon engineer suddenly roared

with laughter. 'There are no hotels in Wilkowo – you wait!'

We went back along the slippery duck-boards. Where the road merged to a bridge to cross a canal the soldier flung open a gate. I saw the low, rounded and thick outlines of a thatched peasant cottage. The soldier flung open the door. A frightened *babushka*, her head wrapped in a black shawl, sat there beside a small lamp. We lowered our heads, passed under the dripping thatch, followed the old woman into the door at our left – and were the characters in a very real *Chauve-Souris*.

Twittering, twinkling, dim glimmering lights from silver, tinsel and gold! Turquoise-blue paint! Candles before stupendous, solemn-faced ikons! Out of the night into fairy-land.

That room was unbelievable. The ikon, a huge, wolfish-looking saint, with gaunt cheeks, seemed to dare one to speak. He was Hush! He posed there like a great ogre in the corner, and the thumb of his upraised right hand was pressed against the tips of the last two fingers.

The old woman put the tips of her last two fingers against her thumb and bowed. She bowed to the ikon every time she entered the room. A furry peasant who came to help her with something also bowed, crossing the floor without even so much as a look at us, ignoring our presence until he had made his peace with the saint. And they did not bow over their hands, as do most other Russians; they looked their saint in the eye, as if on a footing of friendship. In fact, their relationship to those grim painted ikons was the closest approach to flesh-to-flesh contact I have witnessed in religion. Animate, almost, in the flickers of candlelight the saint appeared to answer their bows.

271

'Lipovanes,' said the Roumanian 'engineer,' who seemed highly amused by all this; 'the strictest of Orthodox Greeks. The old woman doesn't even want us to smoke before her old ikon.' Saying which, he lighted a fresh cigarette from his old one and threw the glowing butt on the floor.

The peasant-woman, trained in the school of oppression, did not seem to notice. But something seemed suddenly to require her in the next room, and as she passed out I saw a huge foot angrily stamp out the butt.

The rooms under their thick hat of thatch were low, and everything seemed in miniature. Some great windfall of wealth – perhaps a 500-pound sturgeon – had given them enough cash to buy wall-paper. (The only peasant house with wall-paper that I have seen in the Balkans.) An astonishingly beautiful design of old red and gold! But the tiny bed in the corner was hand-made, almost a century old, and had a straw mattress that bunched up like a haycock. The old lady leaned over this, thrust her arms in its depths, and kneaded it like dough.

'I will make two places,' she said.

But the two places soon merged into one, and the Crew and I, struggling to keep clear of each other – and still stay in the bed – fell into a troubled reverie of rivers and islands and forests and glittering cupolas. From this I awoke when I fell to the floor and met the upraised, warning hand of the wolfish-faced ikon – 'Hush!'

The tiny room glowed with a strange cerulean light in the morning. At first I thought it must come from the carved woodwork. That was blue! Strangely blue – seemed to have more blue in it than blues ever have. But no, there was something else, a 'lightness' in the air. I felt unaccountably happy. I knew – I brushed the steam from the small window and looked out – there it was! The village of Wilkowo was deep in white snow.

We dressed, and, rubbing our hands, went into the other room for breakfast. This room was whitewashed, had a bench on one side, and a huge *petchka* – clay stove – filled one corner. Steps leading to this showed how the old lady and her daughter ascended to sleep there at nights. The daughter, her golden head cloaked in a shawl, was mending a fishing-net. The old lady took down a stupendous round loaf of bread from the wall, held it against her chest and hewed off two slabs. She turned the tap of the samovar and let the boiling water fill up our glasses with a straw coloured tea. Then she addressed her ikon – another saint in this room – and breakfast was on.

That was all there was to these breakfasts. And they grew daily less nourishing, as she never added more tea leaves to the pot – just put in more water. But she cut up a quince and dropped that in too – so perhaps that equalized matters. Bread, and a very occasional potato, was all these people ever ate. The husband sold all the fish. And to offset this Spartan diet the Crew and I gorged on caviare.

It was extraordinary, the emptiness of life in that simple cottage. Laboriously, generation after generation, they had collected their utensils and trinkets. From under the bed in our room they pulled out some of the finery of grandma – long dead. Our room, in fact, was their museum. Flower-pots at the windows, artificial flowers like great candelabra! Photographs on a white, unused table – and a blue shrine for the almost life-size ikons. In another corner they had a blue closet in which were six ancient plates – priceless! But they never went into this room. A spoon, a knife, a glass, and plenty of glowing reeds in the samovar. That was their life. That and sleeping on the top of the stove.

The old lady touched her ragged, quilt-like shirt: 'These are the only clothes I have.' One foot had on a slipper; the other was wrapped in cloth, from which three toes projected.

'We had a son – once,' she said, handing me a tiny photo and then suddenly beginning to cry. It was the face of a curly-haired, laughing sailor – killed in the war.

As she put it back on its honoured place on the shelf she turned and bowed to the ikon.

'And you?' I asked the young girl; 'in the spring don't you dress up and stand outside the church on Sundays?'

Her face burned a bright scarlet.

'She has cavaliers, yes,' said her mother; 'but I had another one much more beautiful. She is married.'

'Oh, yes,' said this daughter, without resentment; 'she was very, very beautiful. Here!'

She exhumed the bride's wedding coronet – little wax flowers and beads such as the French use for funerals.

And as she fingered the pathetic finery she looked out of the window. Perhaps, next spring, she, like Harsha, might be lucky enough to be taken to some alien home where she would sleep with her husband, his father and mother and the unmarried daughters on the top of the stove.

CHAPTER FIFTY-THREE

I Sleep on the Stove

★

THERE were six of us in the black fishing *lodka* – Feodor
Tshahinka, his brothers Simeon and Kostia, Matve, a partner,
Feodor's mother and myself. As we pushed off from the
Wilkowo slip Feodor summoned another *lodka* to put back.
He pulled a cloth from off something that lay in its bottom,
and I saw a huge ikon about as big as a window-pane.

'All gold,' said Feodor.

It was not all gold; it was gilded, but the fact that a boy
and girl were rowing this ikon home in dead winter weather –
the very fact that they had saved enough to buy such an ikon,
or even wanted to buy it – was surprising enough. I raised
my hands – it was a magnificent ikon!

Satisfied, Feodor gave the order to row. Feodor stood up
in the stern of the skiff – steering. He had a goatskin *shuba*
tied round his middle. Its hood hung down his back. A
peaked fur cap clung to the side of his head. And, under this,
sharp shoots of black hair shot down over his eyes – slant eyes,
very brown and quite wild. His high cheek-bones were burnt
black by the sun. His moustache drooped like that of a
Chinese, and a savage black beard dripped from his jaws.
Take a brush and paint me out of that skiff and you have
Ghenghis Khan's Mongol horde.

Simeon was red. Flaming hair shot away from his massive
jaws and red face. The top of his head was burnt bronze – a
smear of red hair cutting it like a gash. Kostia was comparatively hairless, thin featured, always smiling at something.
Matve's brows were fuzzy and black and quite hid his wind-
shaded eyes. '*Ras – dva – tree . . . !*' they leaped against the
crude wooden sweeps. And as they had also hoisted the sail

the *lodka* shot like a black arrow across the fast-freezing waters.

The green domes of Wilkowo dropped into the sunset – suddenly reared up in fantastic black silhouette. An island of the Danube delta appeared to rush toward us.

'How's that?' demanded Feodor, as he held the skiff down to a puff. 'We can go all day like this without stopping.'

The snow-clad, flat shores fell away from us. We entered that maze of desolate islands where live the Russian fishermen of Bessarabia – islands that stood barely a foot above water in an empty world of dead reeds. On the tip of one island stood a Roumanian outpost.

'*Pescar!*' cried out Feodor. 'Fishermen. The man with us goes out to fish – he has a pass.'

'Where?'

'To the sea.'

All this was howled as the skiff raced down on the land. The soldier saw Feodor, recognized him, and waved for us to go on. Feodor held the *lodka* down till her lee rail went under.

'There are soldiers everywhere,' grunted Feodor, 'and if you don't stop they shoot.'

We raced into the darkness until I, head tucked in my *shuba*, saw the hard silhouette of the mainland disappear in the night, and almost drowsed to the even beat of the sweeps. What men these fishermen were – mile after mile, without stopping. Suddenly I heard the old *baba* speaking.

'Marusha! *Daragoyia mia* – Marusha!' Sugar tones of endearment. Then I heard a child cry out from the bank, and the barking of dogs. 'Home,' said Feodor. The *lodka* was shot into a willow-plaited ditch cut in the low island bank. I stepped out on ice-crackling land. I stood among the cold mounds of hay, saw that I was in an apple orchard from whose trees hung thousands of hooks; I smelt fresh tar and the smell of burnt reeds; and a bent, little man, like a gnome, led me to the hut.

This was one room, with an enclosed entrance, half of which was taken up by a clay stove and bed. The other half held a table, and a bench that filled up one corner. Its floor was pressed mud. A bare-legged woman, with very sad eyes, pressed her hand timidly against mine.

Seven men, besides the old gnome – the Tshahinka father – entered that room. They stripped off their fur-lined jackets, unwound their neck-scarfs and rolled down their hip-high leather boots. The women put a great bowl of red *bortch* on the table. Each man took a huge wooden spoon, after giving me one, and we started eating forthwith. We dipped into the communal bowl, hauling out great chunks of cabbage and fish. It was the famous fisherman's *bortch* – red-hot. It filled a man up – warmed his very ribs.

I produced a big bottle and held it toward Feodor.

'Will you have some vodka?' I asked.

'How much does it cost?'

My start brought a howl of dismay from the others. '*Kak vam ne steadna!* Aren't you ashamed of yourself – as if the baren sold vodka!'

A dull red glow surged through the hairy mask covering Feodor; he took the bottle suddenly, thrusting the neck toward his mouth. 'Health!' he almost shouted. He pushed it, like a weapon at me. 'Health!' I swallowed deep.

That was when Feodor and I exchanged first names.

'A lot of work and a lot of vodka,' announced Simeon the Red, 'that is a fisherman's life.'

That hut was about twelve feet by sixteen. Its ceiling

almost touched one's head. Two women, the girl, and Old Tshahinka sat on the edge of the stove bed. The seven members of the Tshahinka fishing company, and I, sat round the board. There was a howling blue winter outside; the only window was shut and the stove was going full blast. The old man brought out a blue teapot filled with red wine. He did this three times, and we emptied it.

Suddenly Feodor threw back his head, opened his lips like a wolf preparing to snap, and uttered a sharp, piercing cry. '*Ya-a-iii!*' the Tshahinka company cried out in song. There is no way of describing that song. It was like the cries of charging horsemen. And, at intervals, the Tshahinka company all banged the table. Then it was like the burst of great seas.

Kostia, who had been smiling there silently, suddenly jumped to his feet. He seemed to fall backward and spin as he fell. I saw boots, waving arms and the smiling eyes of Kostia all mixed together. But the thud of his boots on the earth beat an exasperatingly fantastic tattoo.

When we went to bed the old man and his wife went to the far end of the room and climbed on the stove. Kostia and his wife lay down at this end – their child between them – then Feodor, stripped to his undies, lay down beside them, and I brought up the flank. The others lay in lines on the floor. The child cried, whispered, fell silent. In the dark the winter's snow outside showed blue through the panes. A high moon!

About three I awoke, saw Kostia's wife, with the lamp lighted, bowing toward their ikon. Then she climbed back on the bed and began to knead some bread which was on the raised part of the stove. Grunting slightly, she plunged her arms deep in the warm-scented dough Then she patted it, covering the wooden trough with a rag, bowed to the ikon and blew out the light. Feodor flung out a brown, hairy arm. I grunted, gave him a shove, and we all rolled over in unison.

I got a poke about five. Feodor was sitting up on the stove, rubbing his head: 'It's time to go fishing,' he said.

The men got up, each hacked off a big slab of bread, wrapped it in a rag and began to pull on his fur shirt. We kicked the snow from the seats of the skiff – I slumped down on a pile of reeds at its bottom – and, for breakfast, rolled a thick cigarette.

The moon was still high in the sky. The reeds were strips of pale ochre. The water was mauve. And as we poled over the bar a string of white swans rose with sharp cries – 'Wowk! Wowk!' – and the rising sun poured out its flame across a green scudding sea.

CHAPTER FIFTY-FOUR

Fishing Under Difficulties

*

'SOMETIMES,' said Feodor, 'we catch a sturgeon as big as this skiff.'

This, I felt – although I knew it to be true – was said to me to console me for the usual fisherman's luck. We had caught no fish, and we were very hungry – and very wet. The lines were a terrible tangle. A hurricane on the Black Sea had twisted the gear every which way, and we had rowed about for miles in a plunging sea before we even located the float. This was a bundle of reeds lashed together.

Feodor, as the captain of the fishing company, leaned over the stern of the skiff. Three men rowed along the length of the lines, and the fifth man stood amidships, ready to handle gaff, axe, or put on more corks as Feodor ordered.

The sturgeon lines are a most ingenious contraption. They are literally an almost endless fence, or barricade, or net of bare, very sharp-pointed hooks that just skim the bottom of about a sixty-foot depth of sea. They stretch for miles, with a huge hook every foot.

In structure they are long lines of plaited and tarred rope, about as thick as a young girl's little finger, from which dangle other lines about a yard long, on the end of which are sharp needle-like hooks. Cork floats every twelve feet are of such a size that this sinks, leaving the hooks to lie like a comb near the sea floor.

Does the sturgeon bite at these hooks? No, he does not. And I do not think that he even plays with them as he does with the cork floats when he climbs up the swift Danube. He merely swims through this comb of sharp steel and gets stuck. We got two this day – both caught by the tail.

FISHING UNDER DIFFICULTIES

The sturgeon is a bottom feeder. His mouth is in the first quarter of a very white, soft stomach. The rest of the sturgeon is almost armour-plated. His head is like steel; he has a line of scale shields on his back, another line on his sides and another one on each side of his stomach like bilge keels. But his ugly mouth pulls down like the lips of a purse; and he pushes his steel nose through the submarine world with this mouth hard at work. Mooching about, getting his breakfast, what with one thing and another, he suddenly comes to this line of bare hooks. He noses it – gives a flip with his tail – and is hooked. Then we pull him up.

'*Hai!*' cried Kostia, as a strange black and white monster thrashed the water alongside. He gave a flip with his gaff, and a long-snouted marine devil beat the floor of the skiff. His eyes were cold as moonstones. Bang! Bang! Bang! His head hit the floor-boards like a hammer.

It was so cold that the salt water froze on the bailer. Feodor, his hands wrapped in white wool, leaned over the stern and pulled in what seemed mile after mile of black line. Drenched to the skin, he untangled the snarls and shook clear the hooks. With curious, primitive knots they bound on new corks. Watching them, I nearly froze out of sympathy. I was wrapped to the ears in an enormous fur *shuba*. I had a pile of rushes to squat on, yet I felt that my backbone was a long stick of ice.

'Here,' I beckoned, holding out my last drop of vodka, 'you must take some of this.'

Feodor smiled, took half and gave me the rest. Smiled! 'For the first hour,' he said, 'it is bad; it hurts, but after that you don't feel anything.'

'*Chort!*' I swore, 'you talk like the man who said the first seven years of the war were the worst.'

Feodor suddenly pulled up his sleeve, showed me a mangled muscle and white scar. 'I got that in the Carpaths. Kostia here was stabbed in the wrist. We were fighting for Russia.'

'Russia!' suddenly boomed out Simeon the Red, who had rowed all day without speaking. 'Then we had a fine life!'

And there, on the Black Sea, with the spray freezing on us, these fishers spoke of old Russia. They are under Roumania now – with a soldier at each elbow – and, in Roumania, the fish belong to the state. Fishing is a Government monopoly. They must sell their fish to the Friguel, the sales company of the state. If they wish to keep fish for themselves they have to do it in secret, hide them, cut them up and walk off with them in their boots! But Feodor laughed.

'We are not fools – we eat up to here.' He drew his finger across his throat.

This Friguel – the spelling is phonetic – buys all the catch and sells it at a fixed price. Caviare, for example, is supposed to be put on the market at three dollars a kilo. But I know of no one – except a Government official – who ever got any caviare at that price. The rest of us pay five dollars.

This, explained our 'engineer' friend – the man the Crew caught going through our bags in our supposed absence – is due to a very clever sales trick. There is another company, he said, and the Friguel sells to this. It sells at three dollars and splits the difference – in market price. Both, he said, were the Government. Very clever – what!

So clever, in fact, that the sturgeon fishery of Orsova is a thing of the past. If you want to buy caviare there now you have to row across the river to Serbia. Many of the best sturgeon fishermen, I am told, have cleared out of Bessarabia, some even going as far as Siberia. And those who remain ameliorate conditions with bribery.

'Give a piece of fish to the soldier,' said Feodor, 'a piece like that, say' — he spaced off a good chunk near the tail — 'and then you can keep the rest for yourselves.'

The soldiers posted among the reeds or patrolling the desolate shore stop the fishermen and ask for their passes. Each man has a pass. His boat is numbered and also needs a pass. I had to get permission from the police and a written pass before I could go out with them. The Black Sea coast of Roumania is a region where soldiers sometimes shoot first — and ask questions afterwards.

Two friends of mine went for a walk in Sulina. They saw a fishing-skiff by the shore. A man lay in its stern, his mouth open. A wild-eyed boy sobbed in the bow. My friends thought the old fisherman must be asleep; then they thought he was drunk — then they saw that he had been shot through the head. The boy had been shot in the leg. A Roumanian naval officer out *pour le sport* had shot them. It had occurred to him to ask for the fisherman's pass. When he called, the fisherman nodded and then slowly moved away in his skiff. He was taking in his nets so as to row across to the officer. The officer thought he was trying to escape. It is said that he fired fifteen shots before he hit anything. Then one hit the boy's leg, another shattered the skull of the fisherman. The fisherman's papers were on him and all in good order. It was a mistake, and the officer was eventually transferred to another appointment farther up river and has since received his promotion. *Vive le sport!*

CHAPTER FIFTY-FIVE

Salt Water Again

*

ALL adventures or great hopes, as they near their consumma-
tion, begin to make one superstitious. You begin to talk
softly – to walk in fear of the gods. The Greeks never
embarked on a voyage unless the fates looked propitious. And
they flattered and bribed the gods for their favour. Crew and
I used to rap wood three times whenever we mentioned the
sea. When the Dutchmen laughed at us when we said we
meant to reach the Black Sea, I told Crew to say that we
were only going as far as Vienna. That seemed within
probability – also it was talking softly. But as the miles rolled
behind us, as city after city dropped over our wake and
countries lay behind countries, we began to say 'When we
reach the Black Sea.'

I used to console myself with the thought that if everything
went wrong – we could float down. Then –

'Because of low water this year it is feared the Danube
will freeze over early. The steamers loading at Galatz . . .'

The British Consul at Galatz read this out from his paper.
We were having tea in his warm, cosy home. And, although
the *petch* was going full blast, I felt a chill race down my
spine.

'But – but the river just can't freeze over – like that!'

He smiled, the somewhat sarcastic smile of the well-born
Englishman: 'The Danube,' he said, 'has been known to
freeze in a night. It was in 1923, I think, that we had forty
ships locked in the river.'

He was a nice consul, who had provided us baths, and he
added sympathetically: 'But that was exceptional. Usually it

is the "jam" ice, floating down from the tributaries, that clogs the river. Nevertheless, I should hurry.'

The 'jam' ice was already floating down from my brain cells to my heart. I couldn't hurry! The engine of *Flame* was broken. A new propeller shaft was being installed. She was high on the beach. Each morning had found a new set of promises and delays.

'Oh, yes!' said another Englishman; 'why, we've had 'em frozen in as they were leaving Galatz. Right out in the middle of the river — couldn't get ashore!'

I dropped into a black mood of doubt, forgot all about the talkative young thing who sat on my left — and must have left that tea with the reputation that, socially, I was a boor.

Galatz, the big grain port from the Pruth, is ninety-two miles from the sea. And the Danube, capricious as ever, widens and deepens there, so that one feels it would be like trying to freeze over the ocean. Then, where the ruins of an old Greek church rise from the rushes, it suddenly begins to fray out. One leaves the broad river, enters a narrow little branch to the right, swings past the town of Tulcea, in Dobrudja, and enters what looks like a creek cloaked with willows. That is the Sulina Canal — the only open outlet of the Danube — in thousands and thousands of miles of flat marsh. This is the famous — or infamous — Danube Delta, and it looked like the grave of my hopes.

I sat on the beach and watched the ice forming in pools. I put on more sweaters, I walked about nervously, came back — to push here, haul there, lend a hand with the wrenches and bolts. And at two-thirty one Saturday afternoon *Flame* was slid in the water, given a try-out, and the Crew and I slung our duffle on board. Without waiting to stow things we pushed off down the river. . . .

That night, after butting into a head, biting sea, we ran on till late in the moonlight, and as the early crescent dropped behind the black willows we dropped anchor above the island off Isaccea. I heard drums and flutes and saw lights through the tracery of trees. The peasants were dancing on shore. Their crops were all in, they had money to spend on white wine, and the long winter, when they would sleep long on the top of their stoves, was about to descend. The Crew and I turned in with nearly all our clothes on, dodged the dripping sweat from the damp cabin – congealed by our feeble little cooking-stoves. But –

'When we reach the Black Sea,' said the Crew, 'we simply must get some kind of stove.'

She had said 'when' and not 'if' – because *Flame* was cruising again. We were racing the winter.

Dawn, a gold-clear, cutting day, and I was glad that I had drained the water from my cylinder jacket the previous night. Our drinking water had a surface of ice. A momentous, stupendous day – a day of adventure. A fast, scudding run, when we simply bowled along in our race, and our first objective was reached – the old Greek church, pushing its radish dome over a silver spray of gnarled willows. We swung sharp to the right. We coursed down a rippling mud flood, past fishermen's little rush huts and by one old black fishing *lodka* with a veritable Tolstoy in its stern. A freak of cone-shaped black hills, a broken white fort, bulging green church domes and a minaret rising like a spear over a sea of low roofs – Tulcea stared at our wake.

A steamer had pounded past us in this narrow cut – *Albanian*, Italian mail – and suddenly we saw her white boat decks and black funnels charging into some puff balls of willows! 'Holy smoke!' I thought her steering-gear had gone wrong!

She was in the Sulina Canal! The Sulina Canal – home-stretch to the Black Sea! I started to laugh and to yell, both at once. It was a clean race from now on. Come on winter!

A man on the stone-faced, tree-lined bank came out of the white house bearing the red-white-and-blue flag of the European Danube Commission, stared at me surprisingly, put his binoculars on our flag and suddenly took off his hat.

I lifted mine in return. I looked ahead and saw a flat, yellow strip and a world of grey sky. A very thin strip and an unbelievable sky. The great Danube marshes.

At sunset we saw gaily dressed peasants walking along the bank road, a line of queer and very beautiful huts, where in this abundance of rushes the thatching was two feet in thickness and the sides were covered with rushes like fans, and where, in this wind-swept empty world, each house stood in its own wind-proof fence, made of plaited rushes like a mat.

'Please, mister,' said a Jugoslav employed by the Commission, 'you stop by here the night?'

We said we would, and anchored aft the float of the E.D.C. sounding-boat. He insisted that we come into his house and have jam 'and some cognac.' We came out in a flamingo-coloured sunset to hear fishers singing as they swept past, and walk down along the river-road, the only street of the village, to gaze over a rush-plaited fence at a bride and bridegroom dancing under the apple trees, three fiddlers stamping time with their feet and a tom-tom player giving queer shrieks as he thumped the skin heads.

What queer dreams that night – of the countries that lay in our wake.

Morning, a steamer's whistle; a great hull towering past, and a white-bearded captain calling down through a mega-phone. Leupkovic, the Slav, stood up at the oars of his boat –

SAILING ACROSS EUROPE

'*Commandi!*' From the port wing of the liner's bridge they threw overboard a bucket of lemons for Leupkovic.

A world, a world of sky over a featureless marsh. And here, suddenly, we felt the sea – a 'lift' in our senses. There was nothing to mark it – just the 'feel.' We knew it was there. Then like a dream, a foreign port in a reverie of adventure, appeared the gold-crossed, fantastic red Russian towers, the lighthouses, the slant sailing rigs and the black hulls of ocean tramps in Sulina! We ran down past a medley of foreign shipping, saw the snow-swept English lawns of the Danube Commission, faced the red and green lighthouses – and there, coffee-coloured, pounding and white, raced the everlasting waves of the barbaric Black Sea.

We had sailed across Europe.